Lean in a High-Variability Business

Lean in a High-Variability Business

A Graphic Novel about Lean and People at Zingerman's Mail Order

Eduardo Lander

Jeffrey K. Liker

Tom Root

Illustrations by

Jazmín Morales and Gabriela Morales

Routledge
Taylor & Francis Group
A PRODUCTIVITY PRESS BOOK

First Edition published 2022
by Routledge
600 Broken Sound Parkway #300, Boca Raton FL, 33487

and by Routledge
2 Park Square, Milton Park, Abingdon, Oxon, OX14 4RN

Routledge is an imprint of the Taylor & Francis Group, an informa business

ISBN: 978-1-138-38785-0 (hbk)
ISBN: 978-1-138-38776-8 (pbk)
ISBN: 978-0-429-42602-5 (ebk)

Typeset in Comic Sans
by codeMantra

Preface

None of us can remember having so much fun creating a document. As authors, a graphic novel makes us think differently. How can we help readers visualize an unfolding story and feel like they were there? How can we make our ideas conversational in small text bubbles? How can we effectively use the power of graphics to help tell the story? You may ask why did we want to do this and what we hoped to accomplish?

This is a story about one organization's Lean journey with inspiration from the Toyota Way. Over the years, we have been frustrated by a number of common misunderstandings about what Lean is, what the journey is like, and how to advance. Often these misunderstandings come from the way people simplistically talk and think about Lean. It is as if it is some concrete thing that you insert into an organization and step back to watch the results. If there are problems, it means you are doing it wrong or maybe your consultants are not very good at it. You get deluged with new terminology, maybe feeling a bit overwhelmed. However, senior management wants results, and they want them fast, so you madly deploy this Lean stuff across the enterprise, as quickly as possible. It is like a race. Some things stick and most do not. To make matters worse, it is difficult to apply all the Toyota's Lean concepts exactly as they do because, unlike Toyota, you do not make vehicles on an assembly line with one-minute cycle time repetitive jobs. What was management thinking when they suggested this Lean stuff? We refer to this as a mechanistic approach to Lean deployment. You are viewing the organization as a machine that needs some new parts or a turbocharger. Toyota is presumably the model to copy for the new parts and tools.

Another perspective views the organization as a living system with interacting parts and constant exposure to the environment. Since it is dynamic, it's hard to predict what obstacles you will face next. Just when you think you have it solved, new challenges arise from the market, competitors, government regulations, and every direction you turn to. When you look at your organization in this way, you see Lean through a different lens. The goal is to make your processes and people into a more adaptive system so you can navigate through all the complexity and uncertainty to continually achieve your goals. This is how Toyota views things and they summarize the Toyota Way as continuous improvement and respect for people. Each person becomes a partner in the struggle to learn and adapt, and specific tools are used in different ways across the organization to accomplish their goals.

To most people, this all makes sense, but few have experienced it. The story presented here focuses on a small company called Zingerman's Mail Order (ZMO). Tom Root was one of the founders of this spin-off of the Zingerman's delicatessen. The deli was founded to bring high-quality artisanal food to Ann Arbor, Michigan. Much of the food was hand-picked from visits around the world and creatively put together into sandwiches and many of the kinds of items you would find in a New York City deli. Employees started several Zingerman's businesses—a bakery, a creamery, a coffee roaster, a candy producer, and more. Ann Arborites, with the University of Michigan at the center, are a highly mobile group, and many faculty, students, and residents who move away wish they could take Zingerman's with them. ZMO was formed to serve that need by shipping high-quality artisanal food throughout the U.S. It consists of a call center and a warehouse as well as a large number of enthusiastic members who want to provide customers the best possible experience.

The Zingerman's community of businesses share a common culture that is centered around people providing excellent service. Servant Leadership is practiced throughout the organization. All employees share in the profits and finances are transparent. They are obsessive about training. What they had not experienced until Eduardo and Jeffrey got involved was Lean management. ZMO partners agreed they needed something to get out of a serious jam, a pleasant problem. Sales were growing so fast they kept needing to move to a bigger building every few years, at a high cost. Inventory was everywhere and fulfilling orders was a bit chaotic, particularly in December when they shipped half of the year's sales. They searched for help, and Eduardo was looking for a case study for his dissertation—an opportunity to introduce Lean in a high-variety operation that was very different from Toyota and study what happened. Jeffrey was Eduardo's advisor.

The journey continues today, over sixteen years from the start. It was not linear and from the beginning Eduardo explained that the tools of Toyota could not be copied. This was going to be a learning journey with ups and downs, successes and frustrations. We wish to share with you that journey. The book is divided into three parts:

1. **Discovering Lean Management**—This part provides some background on ZMO and Lean concepts and then takes a tour through the operation as it was in 2019. It follows one of Tom Root's famous tours and you will join a group to see the entire operation and all the cool Lean stuff.
2. **Management Learns to Think Lean**—Here we go back in time to when Eduardo was first engaged and ZMO was introduced to Lean. We follow management over a decade as they learned, tested ideas, and deepened their understanding of Lean while business grew—with huge improvements in operations and no more moving to larger facilities. The one thing they did not succeed at was engaging the rest of the associates in continuous improvement.
3. **The Power of Scientific Thinking**—The leadership team worked with Eduardo to learn problem solving with a number of failed attempts until they discovered Toyota Kata. They worked with Jeff's graduate class practicing the kata approach and finally associate engagement took off. They learned a whole different view of Lean—adapting to change through scientific thinking and becoming a true learning organization.

Our purpose is not to provide a 'recipe for implementation'—quite the opposite. We want you to get a feeling for the struggle, for the learning process. We explain and demonstrate many Lean tools within the context of the journey and how they were adapted for this particular business. And you get a ringside seat to the human drama of transformation and learning. We hope you will share this with a broad cross section of leaders and associates, and that it will lead to great discussions. It is written so that it can provide insights to experienced Lean practitioners and be read pleasurably by executives, managers, associates, and even some of your family members. Enjoy, learn, and then do. It is your learning journey and hopefully we have provided some inspiration and ideas you can use.

Eduardo Lander
Jeffrey Liker
Tom Root

Acknowledgements

This is the story of a remarkable company and a remarkable group of people that have embraced Lean and Toyota Kata to improve their processes and develop their people to provide better service to each other and to their customers. In 2004, when Jeff and Eduardo got involved with Zingerman's Mail Order (ZMO), there was an ongoing debate about how Lean management applies outside repetitive high-volume production environments as in Toyota. "We do not make cars," was a common refrain. Eduardo decided to experiment with this in a real high-variety company for his dissertation and ZMO took the leap as a learning partner. As a mail-order company with thousands of end items ordered and shipped and demand changing by the minute, they were an ideal partner for this joint research. They had to deal with food that could spoil and meet their bold promise of getting each order delivered on time with 100% customer satisfaction. For sixteen years and counting, ZMO has diligently tested ideas and run experiments with the aim of adapting Lean principles, concepts, and tools for their situation. It has been a unique learning partnership that continues today.

Our co-author Tom Root and his co-managing partners Toni Morell, Mo Frechette, and Jude Walton deserve the credit for allowing us to 'play' in their business and for being active participants in the process. But it has been the rest of the team at ZMO that has made it all happen. We want to thank them all and in particular the warehouse managers Betty Gratopp, Lisa Roberts, and J Atlee, for being the boots on the ground driving improvement and keeping the ball rolling even after multiple failed attempts. This is truly a joint effort and the idea of a graphic-based book was inspired by the funky cartoonish drawings that are part of the human-centered culture of the Zingerman's family of businesses. We appreciate you all!

Being a comic book based on real events, we have used representations of real people to convey our ideas by putting words in their mouths. Many thanks to everyone who lent us their personae. We hope your avatars are not too far off and that we have done some modicum of justice to your contributions.

Along the way, we partnered with Mike Rother when it became clear his Toyota Kata was a missing piece of the puzzle. The management team did a marvelous job in embracing Lean concepts and leading the transformation, but we were still too focused on the tools and not enough on engaging people in improvement. The turning point was introducing the Kata as we describe in the third part of the book. We are grateful to Mike Rother who has been coaching ZMO and provided editorial advice on this book.

When writing, you put words to paper thinking they convey your ideas clearly. Then someone else reads it, and all of a sudden those 'cleverly' crafted sentences and paragraphs don't make as much sense as you thought. The book was professionally edited by Emma Liker, who showed us the joy of clear writing without the clutter of extra words. If there is such a thing as 'lean editing', this was it. We are also grateful to Deb Liker who went through the whole book with her keen eye for errors of grammar, syntax, and punctuation (hopefully we caught all the Oxford commas!).

Given that drawings seem to be an important part of a graphic novel, early on, we set out to find an illustrator. Francisco Ocejo supported us by lending us one and later a second illustrator from his team at Alfra Lean advisors. Gabriela Morales started the book, joined later by Jazmín Morales, who took over the project and pushed it through to completion. Your drawings are what brings the book to life.

From Eduardo:

Writing this book has been a remarkable experience filled with learning about how to structure a book, about writing, and about what to do and not do in a comic book. More interestingly, it was also filled with learning about Lean and Kata. This I did not expect since we're telling a story I'm intimately familiar with. In retrospect though, I should have known better. Jeff agreed to be my advisor somewhere in the year 2000. Since then, I've been learning from every conversation we've had. Working closely on this book took that to a new level, particularly on how to think about and explain key ideas of Lean and Kata. Thank you, Jeff for continuing to teach and challenge me, but also for giving me room to run with my ideas.

It was Tom's idea to make this a graphic novel. This brought many challenges and delays as we struggled to get the images and the text right. In the end though, it was fun and it made the story more interesting and easier to follow. Good call Tom!

I'm especially grateful to my family for the never-ending support and patience that allows me to continue doing what I like to do.

From Jeff:

Originally, I was encouraging Tom to write a book based on his famous folksy plant tours (used in part I) and Tom was interested but wanted a graphic novel to fit with the Zingerman's culture. None of us knew how to write what is in essence a long non-fiction comic book, but it was Eduardo who emerged as the leader. Perhaps his Toyota training helped in bringing out the desire to communicate clearly through pictures. I appreciate how Eduardo grew over the course of this project learning to write in bubbles instead of paragraphs, creatively imagining graphics, and working through the details of corrective feedback on drawings and text. In the process we had to figure out what we thought happened and it was a growing experience for us all.

I also appreciate the involvement of my wife Deb and daughter Emma who waded through the entire book editing and rewriting. Deb was the workhorse on details like spelling and punctuation, and little evades her discerning eye. I asked Emma one day for fun to read part of it and she just naturally started editing pretty heavily. She quickly saw that we were being too wordy. Going from dissertations and business books to a comic book is a big change and Eduardo and I felt pretty good about making the transition… until we saw how Emma slashed sentences, eliminated extraneous words, and brought out the key points we had hoped for. It was a graphic novel. This was how we were supposed to write! If you read this book and it flows well and is a pleasure to read, thank Emma.

From Tom:

I would like to thank Dr. Liker for his years of support, encouragement and enthusiasm for all things Lean and how they apply to Zingerman's Mail Order.

I would also like to thank Dr. Lander. Your commitment to Zingerman's Mail Order, the staff here and our collective improvement have been valuable beyond measure.

Beyond being outstanding mentors, teachers, and practitioners of Lean, I feel very fortunate to call you friends.

Eduardo Lander is Founder of Custom Lean Systems and Founding Partner of Dobilo. He has been studying Lean since 1995. As a plant manager, learning from books and through trial and error; as a Doctor of Engineering student under Jeff Liker at the University of Michigan; from inside Toyota, working in the Chief Engineer function at Toyota Motor Europe; and as a consultant, working mostly with companies dealing with high variability. He now supports Lean transformations by helping organizations improve their processes and develop their people using Lean principles and Toyota Kata.

Jeffrey K. Liker is Professor Emeritus, Industrial and Operations Engineering at The University of Michigan and President of Liker Lean Advisors, LLC. He is author of the best-selling book, The Toyota Way, Second Edition, and has coauthored nine other books about Toyota including The Toyota Way to Service Excellence, Designing the Future, and The Toyota Way to Lean Leadership. His articles and books have won thirteen Shingo Prizes for Research Excellence. He was inducted into the Association of Manufacturing Excellence Hall of Fame and the Shingo Academy.

Tom Root is Managing Partner of Zingerman's Mail Order and Co-Founder of Maker Works in Ann Arbor MI. He has taught and practiced Lean principles for 15 years as Partner/Owner at Zingerman's Mail Order, in the Zingerman's Community of Businesses as Chief Operating Officer, and as a lecturer at the University of Michigan.

Part I

Discovering Lean Management

LEAN IN A HIGH-VARIABILITY BUSINESS

THE JOURNEY OF ZINGERMAN'S MAIL ORDER

Our story begins during peak production in December 2003. As founders, our vision for ZMO was to bring the quality, artisanal food of Zingerman's to our clients across the United States. Our success exceeded our expectations, growing every year, often by double digits. And yet, serious problems were surfacing that could threaten sustainable, profitable growth.

But wait... I get ahead of myself.

If you're a foodie or have been to Ann Arbor in Michigan (in the US), you have probably heard about Zingerman's.

Zingerman's Mail Order... or ZMO for short, is one of ten sister companies dedicated to providing guests with amazing artisanal foods while regaling them with unparalleled service!

ZMO is the one in charge of distributing this incredible food throughout the US. If you're craving that coffee cake, or those sinful brownies you used to have while in college at U of M, we've got you covered. We can even send you the fixings for your favorite Zingerman's sandwich.

A real problem and a fortunate discovery
Now, where was I? Oh yes... for ZMO, and for me personally, Christmas 2003 was a turning point. Let's listen in on one of our management meetings that holiday...
TOM
Tom Partner
I realize we are all very busy in the Christmas season, but we have been thinking about where we are headed as a company.
Mo Partner
Betty Manager
Toni Partner
We have been very successful and the partners owe every team member a personal debt for their energy and commitment. That's the good news.
BAD NEWS
COST
PROFIT
The bad news is that our costs are going up and profit margins are going down. Since we all share in the profits, it even hurts our wallets. As you know, our goal is sustainable growth so we can keep our loyal, hungry customers happy and provide employees a stable and fulfilling job.
Fast Movers
Don't go too far
we won't stay here long
Fast Movers
Our biggest problem is we're constantly moving to bigger spaces just to serve the Christmas demand.
MO
We've been doing it every two years... Heck, we just moved here and it's already tight!
It may not be obvious, but it costs a small fortune to move. And bigger places cost more money for rent and utilities... which we have to pay year-round even though we need the space only for Christmas.
Good point, Mo! So... does growth necessarily mean more space? Or can we make better use of what we have? I even wonder if we're doing our customers justice with the way we get our great food through the warehouse and to them.
How about we go to the line as a team and see what's going on? Perhaps we'll find some opportunities.

This is CHAOS!!
Yes, everyone's running around putting out fires!
Or at least, let's hope that's what they are doing.
And let's hope it's enough to get all the orders out the door.
Did you see they ran out of space for gift boxes? Last night they had to stack them in the office... and this is only our second Christmas here!

You think that's bad, the other night they were stacking gift boxes in the break room. We are going to have to put some tables outside... That's going to be one cold lunch!
Betty
TOM
But we need all that space only three weeks in the year.
Honestly, we don't know how much space or people we really need.
MO

THERE HAS TO BE A BETTER WAY...

The Lean Journey Begins
So, do you think we have some opportunities for improvement?
I sure hope so!
If we are trying to be the best in our business at satisfying our customers, we have to be better than what we just saw.
I agree completely, Mo. Let's get through this Christmas season and take a fresh look in January. I believe we have enough energy and creativity in our team to do something great.
At the same time, at nearby UM, Eduardo Lander has a key meeting for his doctoral thesis with his advisor, Professor Jeffrey Liker...
University of Michigan
Have you decided on a research topic?
I want to learn how to lead a Lean transformation in an organization.
Ok. I think I've heard that before. What is different about your interest?
People seem to think Lean does not work when there's a lot of variability, like demand changing day to day and having lots of different items. Is this true?
It's true people think so. I think it's because their image of Lean is what they see when they visit Toyota. And mostly they see only the assembly line where a few different types of vehicles are racing through the factory, jobs are very routine, and they are done in one-minute cycles.
Dr. Liker

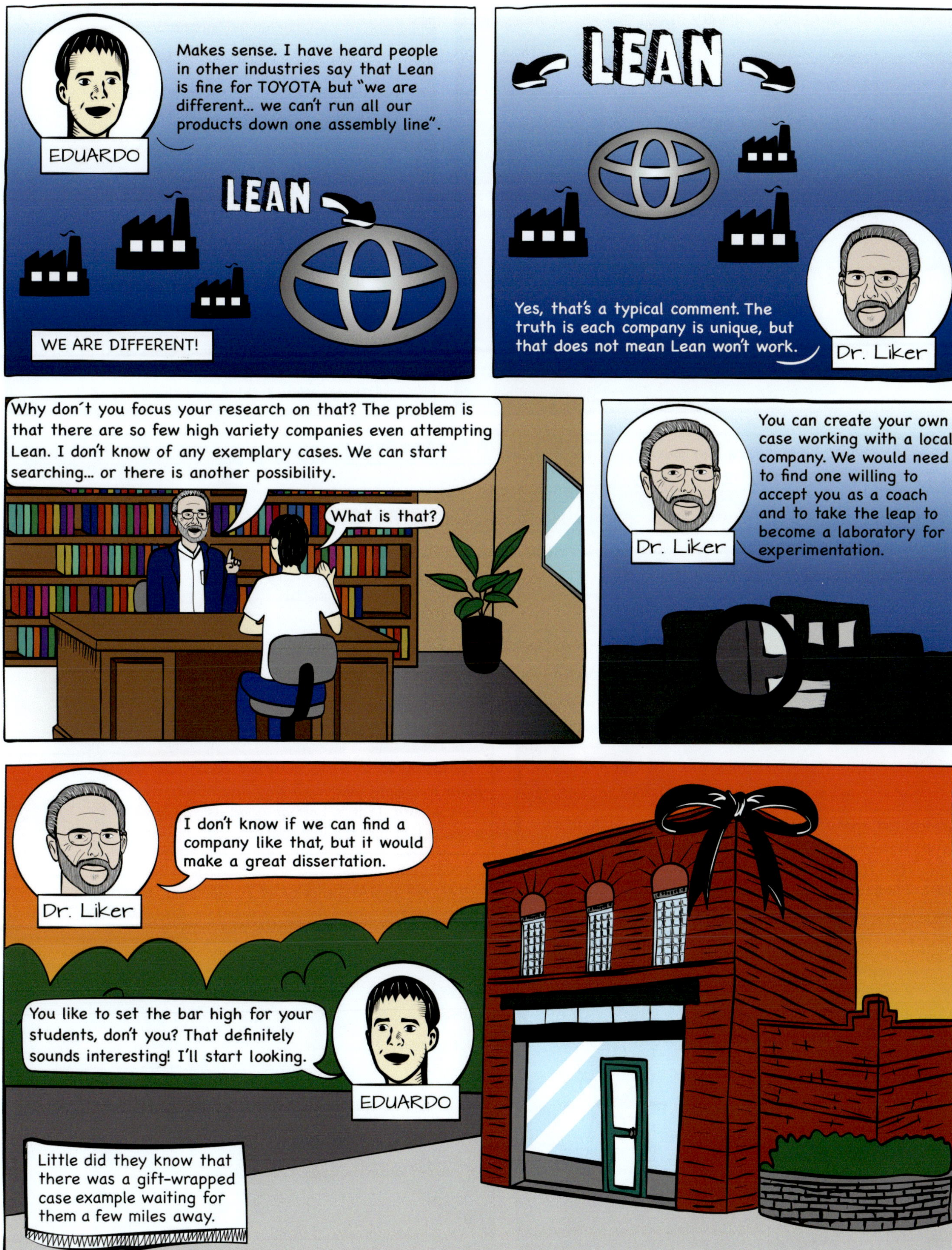
Makes sense. I have heard people in other industries say that Lean is fine for TOYOTA but "we are different... we can't run all our products down one assembly line".
EDUARDO
LEAN
WE ARE DIFFERENT!
LEAN
Yes, that's a typical comment. The truth is each company is unique, but that does not mean Lean won't work.
Dr. Liker
Why don´t you focus your research on that? The problem is that there are so few high variety companies even attempting Lean. I don't know of any exemplary cases. We can start searching... or there is another possibility.
What is that?
You can create your own case working with a local company. We would need to find one willing to accept you as a coach and to take the leap to become a laboratory for experimentation.
Dr. Liker
I don't know if we can find a company like that, but it would make a great dissertation.
Dr. Liker
You like to set the bar high for your students, don't you? That definitely sounds interesting! I'll start looking.
EDUARDO
Little did they know that there was a gift-wrapped case example waiting for them a few miles away.

Back to ZMO sometime in January
Hey Tom, there may be a better way after all!
Tell me more...
THE TOYOTA WAY
14 MANAGEMENT PRINCIPLES FROM THE WORLD'S GREATEST MANUFACTURER
JEFFREY K. LIKER
I'm taking an operations class at U of M, and they are making us read this book called The Toyota Way. I think you should read it.
What's it about? I'm not sure how much learning about Toyota is going to help us.
It's about operational excellence and how to do more with less, including less space. Toyota is the benchmark for 'Lean Management'. I can try explaining it to you, but it might be easier if you just read some of it.
A few days later
I'm convinced...
About what?
The Toyota Way! I like the part about how you have to create your own way and not try to copy Toyota. If it is half as good as the book says, it will make a huge difference.
And the best part is that the culture bit we mostly have already. Which is what the author, Liker, says is the toughest nut to crack. It fits very well with our philosophy about people and with ZMO in general.
TOM
ZMO mission: We share the Zingerman's experience, selling food that makes you happy, giving service that makes you smile.

By a happy coincidence, Mo was in a business class with Eduardo and learned he was a student of Dr. Liker. Eduardo was excited to learn about our interest. It turns out he was looking for a research site for his dissertation.

In May 2004, Eduardo came for a visit...

EDUARDO
Lean comes from the Toyota Production System... or TPS for short... and is a way of doing more with less for the benefit of all stakeholders.
Maximize Value to Customers
A thinking system for continuous improvement
STABILITY
TOYOTA PRODUCTION SYSTEM
Typically when people refer to Lean, they are looking for the quick fix tool kit. There are a set of tools for removing waste and making processes more efficient. But there's a lot more to Lean than that. It has been described as a set of tools, because that's what people easily see when they visit a Toyota plant.

Yes, I've heard they use many visuals. Like cards to manage inventory?
That's true. Visuals help them reach a shared understanding of the situation.
KANBAN
The cards are called kanban. You attach them to containers of items, like your brownies, and only print enough cards for the number of containers you want circulating in the shop.

But they also promote continuous improvement by helping you see problems. For example, if containers are moving without kanban, you probably have too much inventory.
That sounds interesting... keep going.
KANBAN
EDUARDO
What kanban does is provide a visual standard. Let's say we will only have three containers of brownies to pick from when we fill orders. When one container is empty, we send the card back to the warehouse, like an order form, to bring out another one.
MILK
MILK
MILK
It's similar to how a supermarket replenishes milk. If customers take away 10 gallons of milk, they replenish the shelf with 10 new gallons. Pretty simple, really.
The expectation here is that three containers should be just enough brownies to keep the pickers well supplied. If someone brings out four containers, one will be missing a kanban. There's too much inventory... we just highlighted a problem!!
BROWNIES
BROWNIES
BROWNIES
KANBAN
NO KANBAN
So, if we take this opportunity to investigate and make changes, we may be able to make improvements?
You got it! By showing you discrepancies to the standard, kanban highlights opportunities to strengthen your operation.

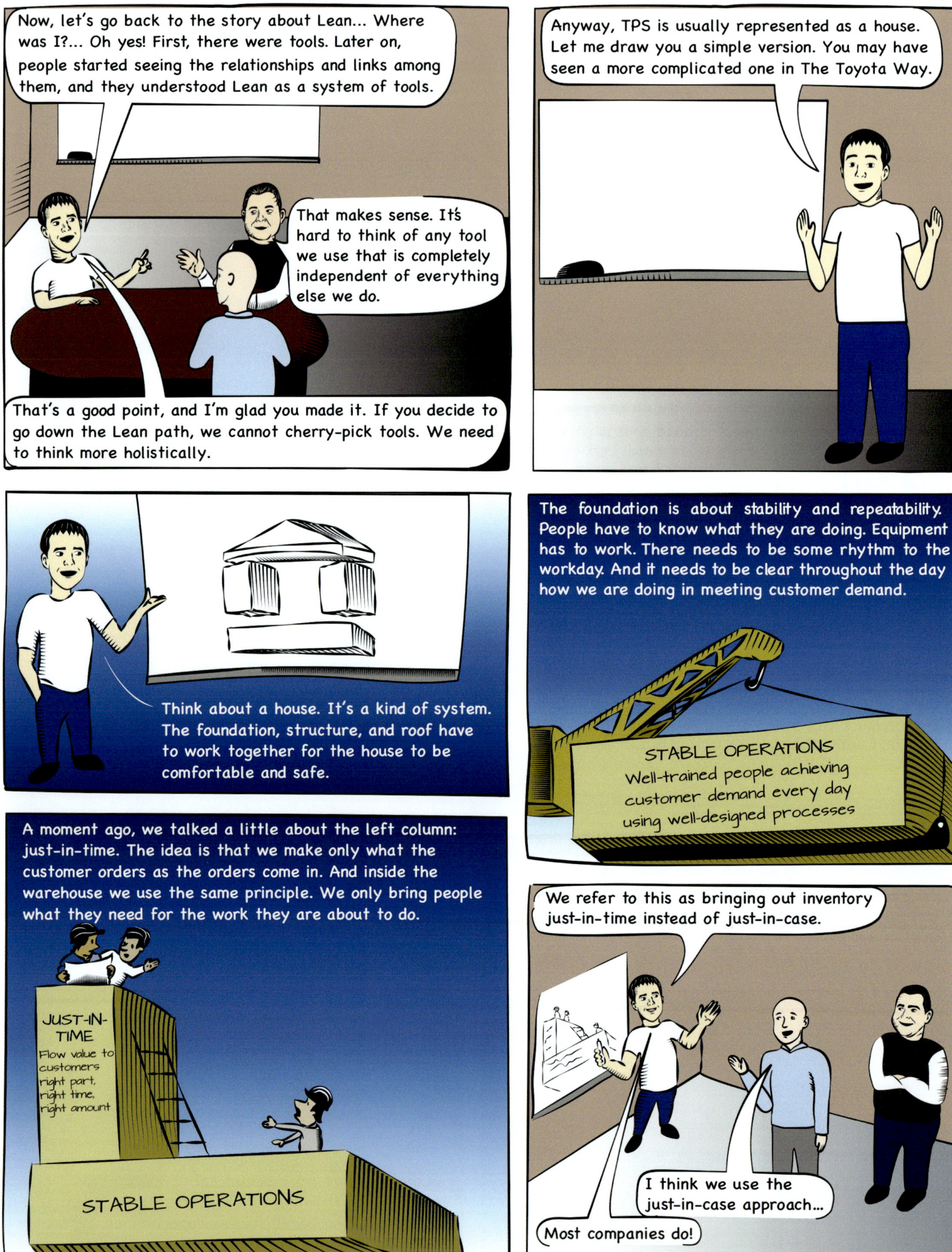

Now, let's go back to the story about Lean... Where was I?... Oh yes! First, there were tools. Later on, people started seeing the relationships and links among them, and they understood Lean as a system of tools.
That makes sense. It's hard to think of any tool we use that is completely independent of everything else we do.
That's a good point, and I'm glad you made it. If you decide to go down the Lean path, we cannot cherry-pick tools. We need to think more holistically.
Anyway, TPS is usually represented as a house. Let me draw you a simple version. You may have seen a more complicated one in The Toyota Way.
Think about a house. It's a kind of system. The foundation, structure, and roof have to work together for the house to be comfortable and safe.
The foundation is about stability and repeatability. People have to know what they are doing. Equipment has to work. There needs to be some rhythm to the workday. And it needs to be clear throughout the day how we are doing in meeting customer demand.
STABLE OPERATIONS
Well-trained people achieving customer demand every day using well-designed processes
A moment ago, we talked a little about the left column: just-in-time. The idea is that we make only what the customer orders as the orders come in. And inside the warehouse we use the same principle. We only bring people what they need for the work they are about to do.
JUST-IN-TIME
Flow value to customers right part, right time, right amount
STABLE OPERATIONS
We refer to this as bringing out inventory just-in-time instead of just-in-case.
I think we use the just-in-case approach...
Most companies do!

JUST-IN-TIME
BUILT-IN-QUALITY
Stop and fix problems
STABLE OPERATIONS
The right column is about building in quality in every step of the process instead of waiting to find errors through inspection or customer complaints.
EDUARDO

Maximize Value to Customers
Best safety, quality, cost, delivery, morale
JUST-IN-TIME
Flow value to customers right part, right time, right amount
PEOPLE CONTINUOSLY IMPROVING
BUILT-IN-QUALITY
Stop and fix problems
STABLE OPERATIONS
Well-trained people achieving customer demand every day using well-designed processes
The roof shows what Lean is trying to achieve: maximizing value to customers by providing products and services with the highest quality, lowest cost, and shortest lead time... all at the same time. And doing that in a way that is safe for employees and keeps them motivated.
EDUARDO
In the center is the reason you want motivated employees. You do not want people checking their brains at the door when they come to work. You want them engaged in thinking about how to improve their work so they can provide more value to customers.

We do not always think of workers as innovators, but in TPS they are.
Hmm, interesting, but a lot of what I've heard or read about Lean has to do with increasing efficiency...
It can certainly help with efficiency, but it's not only about that.

A breakthrough in the Lean movement came with a book by Womack and Jones called Lean Thinking. They said Lean is a way of thinking about maximizing value to the customer while minimizing waste. This shifts the focus from the tools to the people in the organization.
Hmmm... I think I get what you're saying. The people doing the work know the work the best. They feel the daily problems firsthand and know when something is broken. We need their help to improve, so we can more efficiently provide better service to our customers.
LEAN THINKING
BANISH WASTE AND CREATE WEALTH IN YOUR CORPORATION
JAMES P. WOMACK
DANIEL T. JONES
That's very exciting! It is the core of our philosophy at Zingerman's. We believe in a kind of workplace democracy. We want everyone involved in improving so we can provide a better service to our customers every day.
Absolutely! We even share with them all the financial numbers... something called open-book finance. And, we also have a gain-sharing program that rewards everyone for the overall performance of the company.
Now you are getting me excited! You seem to have the kind of culture that would fit very well with Lean.
That's great! What else do we need to know?
Let me see... let's go back to the evolution of Lean... You may remember the 4P model from Dr. Liker's book. Let me try drawing that one as well.
This is Dr. Liker's redesigned version of a model Toyota developed to explain their more general management philosophy – The Toyota Way. TPS is part of this. The starting point is the philosophy, and it seems that is what excites the TPS experts in Toyota. What is your philosophy? What is your purpose as an organization? What would the ideal state look like if all parts of the system worked together to satisfy your customers?
I think the Zingerman's philosophy fits well in the base.
PHILOSOPHY
Long-term systems thinking
Based on what you say and what I've seen, I agree. It seems to be well-articulated and employees buy into it. You seem to have a great foundation!

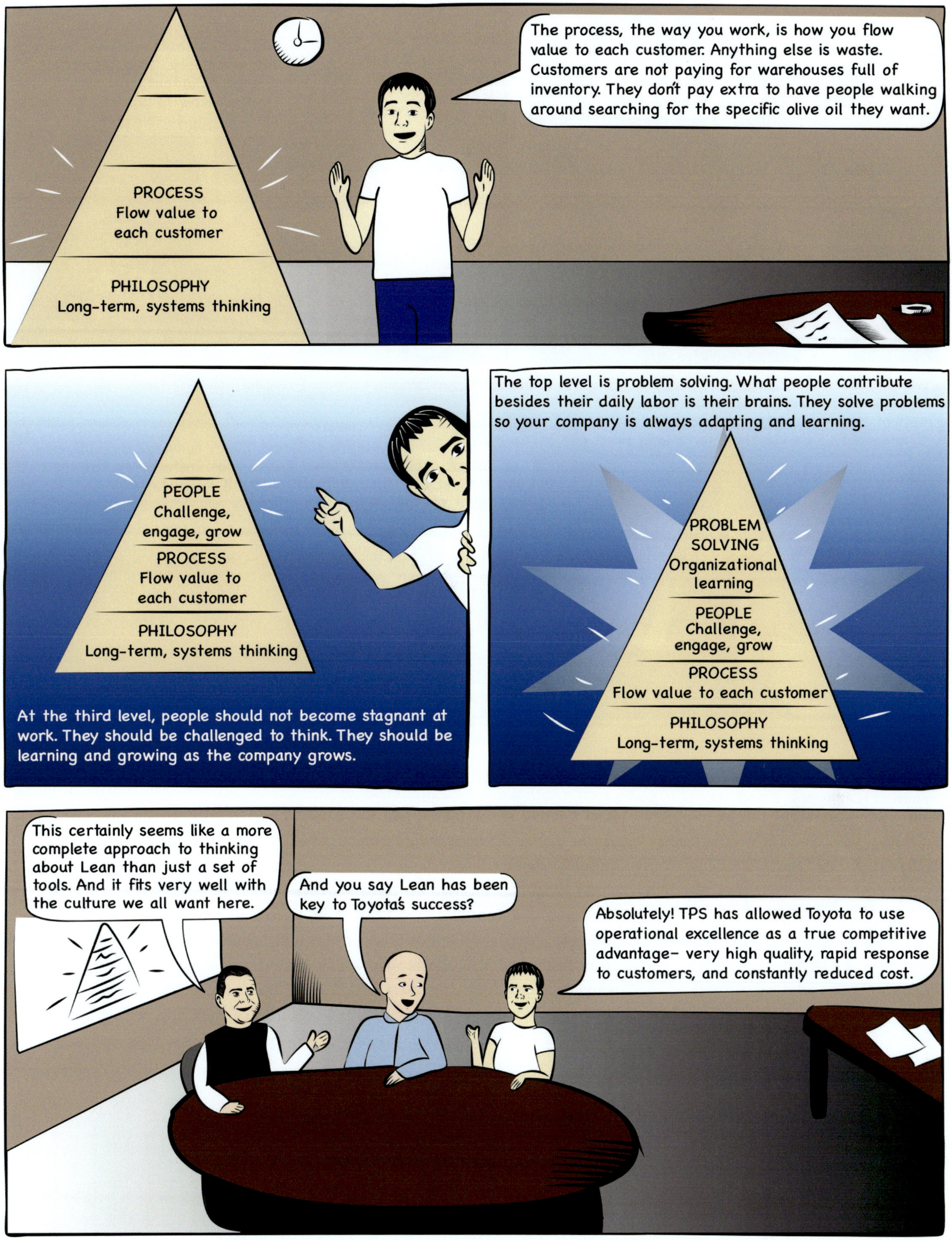
PROCESS
Flow value to
each customer
PHILOSOPHY
Long-term, systems thinking
The process, the way you work, is how you flow value to each customer. Anything else is waste. Customers are not paying for warehouses full of inventory. They don't pay extra to have people walking around searching for the specific olive oil they want.
PEOPLE
Challenge,
engage, grow
PROCESS
Flow value to
each customer
PHILOSOPHY
Long-term, systems thinking
At the third level, people should not become stagnant at work. They should be challenged to think. They should be learning and growing as the company grows.
The top level is problem solving. What people contribute besides their daily labor is their brains. They solve problems so your company is always adapting and learning.
PROBLEM
SOLVING
Organizational
learning
PEOPLE
Challenge,
engage, grow
PROCESS
Flow value to each customer
PHILOSOPHY
Long-term, systems thinking
This certainly seems like a more complete approach to thinking about Lean than just a set of tools. And it fits very well with the culture we all want here.
And you say Lean has been key to Toyota's success?
Absolutely! TPS has allowed Toyota to use operational excellence as a true competitive advantage- very high quality, rapid response to customers, and constantly reduced cost.

Let's leave the past behind for a while and travel to the present so I can show off how we do things now. I'll be giving you one of our world-renowned tours!
Just kidding... but we do have visitors almost every week that want to come and see what we have done with Lean. Our managers, floor leaders, and front liners guide them and provide explanations of our processes and the challenges we're facing. Let's listen in on one I'm guiding right now. It's July 2018, past the intense Christmas season but right in the middle of summer sale. Since January, we've been planning and making improvements for the next Christmas Season.

Welcome to ZMO! We're very glad to have you all here. I like to begin tours with our mission statement.
mission statement
we share the zingerman's experience
selling food that makes you happy
giving service that makes you smile
in passionate pursuit of our mission
showing love and care in all our actions
to enrich as many lives as we possibly can
Please take a look and tell me what words you find unusual.
Hmm... experience... smile
Love...
Love? Wow.
Love and care.
I don't see anything about money.
Right! And, for a customer service-oriented organization, you'll notice that the word customer doesn't exist either.
That's right...
And this was absolutely intentional!

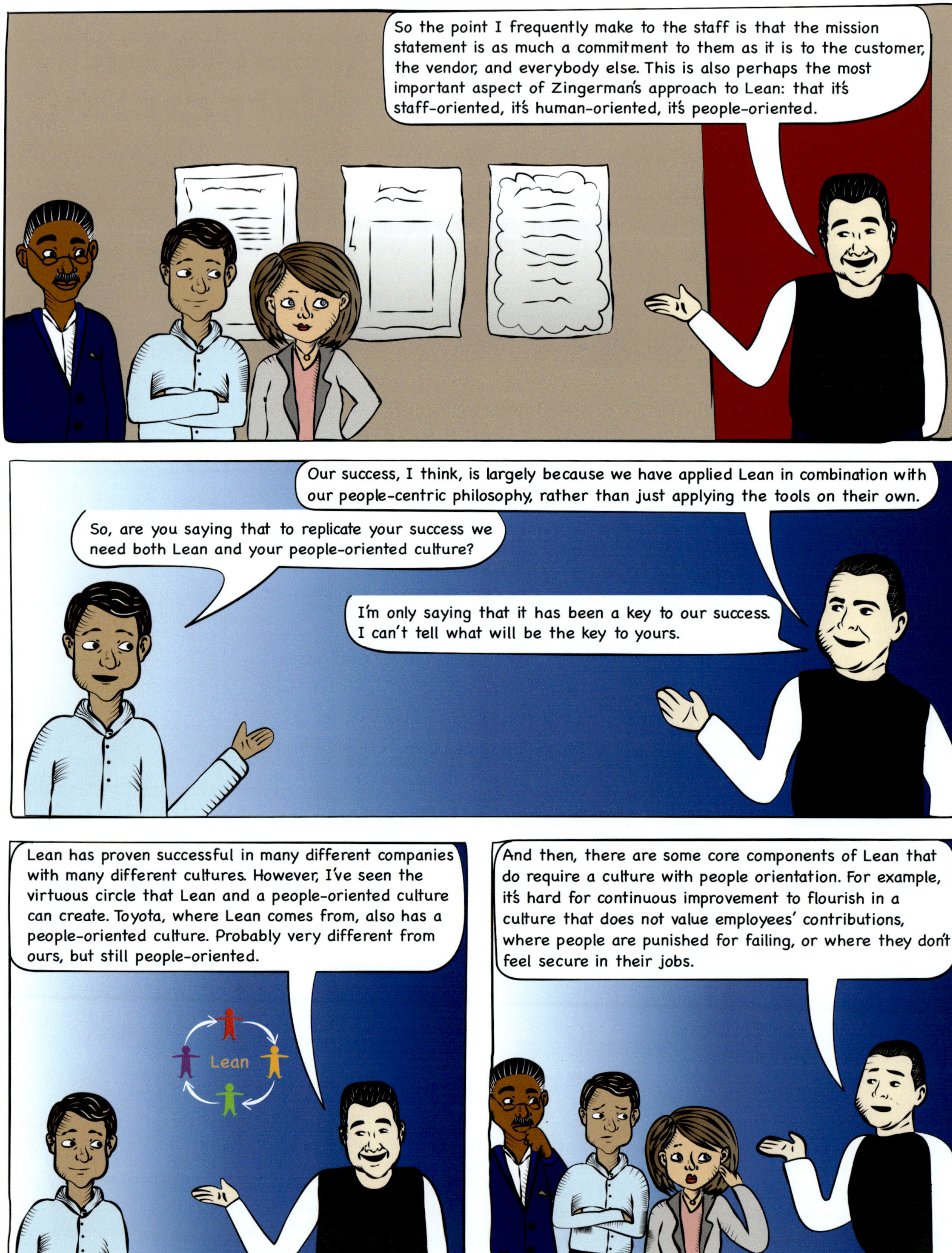

So the point I frequently make to the staff is that the mission statement is as much a commitment to them as it is to the customer, the vendor, and everybody else. This is also perhaps the most important aspect of Zingerman's approach to Lean: that it's staff-oriented, it's human-oriented, it's people-oriented.
Our success, I think, is largely because we have applied Lean in combination with our people-centric philosophy, rather than just applying the tools on their own.
So, are you saying that to replicate your success we need both Lean and your people-oriented culture?
I'm only saying that it has been a key to our success. I can't tell what will be the key to yours.
Lean has proven successful in many different companies with many different cultures. However, I've seen the virtuous circle that Lean and a people-oriented culture can create. Toyota, where Lean comes from, also has a people-oriented culture. Probably very different from ours, but still people-oriented.
Lean
And then, there are some core components of Lean that do require a culture with people orientation. For example, it's hard for continuous improvement to flourish in a culture that does not value employees' contributions, where people are punished for failing, or where they don't feel secure in their jobs.

You make a good point. It just seems like a very tall order... to change both at once, I mean.
I never said it would be easy. Well, I thought it would when we started, but that's another story...

If you're serious about Lean, implementing it will change your processes, your people, and your culture. I don't think there's an option where one of those doesn't change. In my opinion, the people orientation at the core of our philosophy has been an enabler of the people and cultural changes that came as we implemented Lean.

If you have a people-oriented culture, reinforce it and take advantage of it in your Lean journey. If you don't, perhaps our experience will help convince you to shift in that direction. Our people-oriented culture, which is based on Servant Leadership, has enabled Lean. But the best part is that Lean has also enabled our culture.
That's very interesting... Can you tell us more?
Well, Lean makes processes and standards visible. This allows the people closest to the work to evaluate performance, identify problems, and take the right action at the right time... precisely the culture we want.

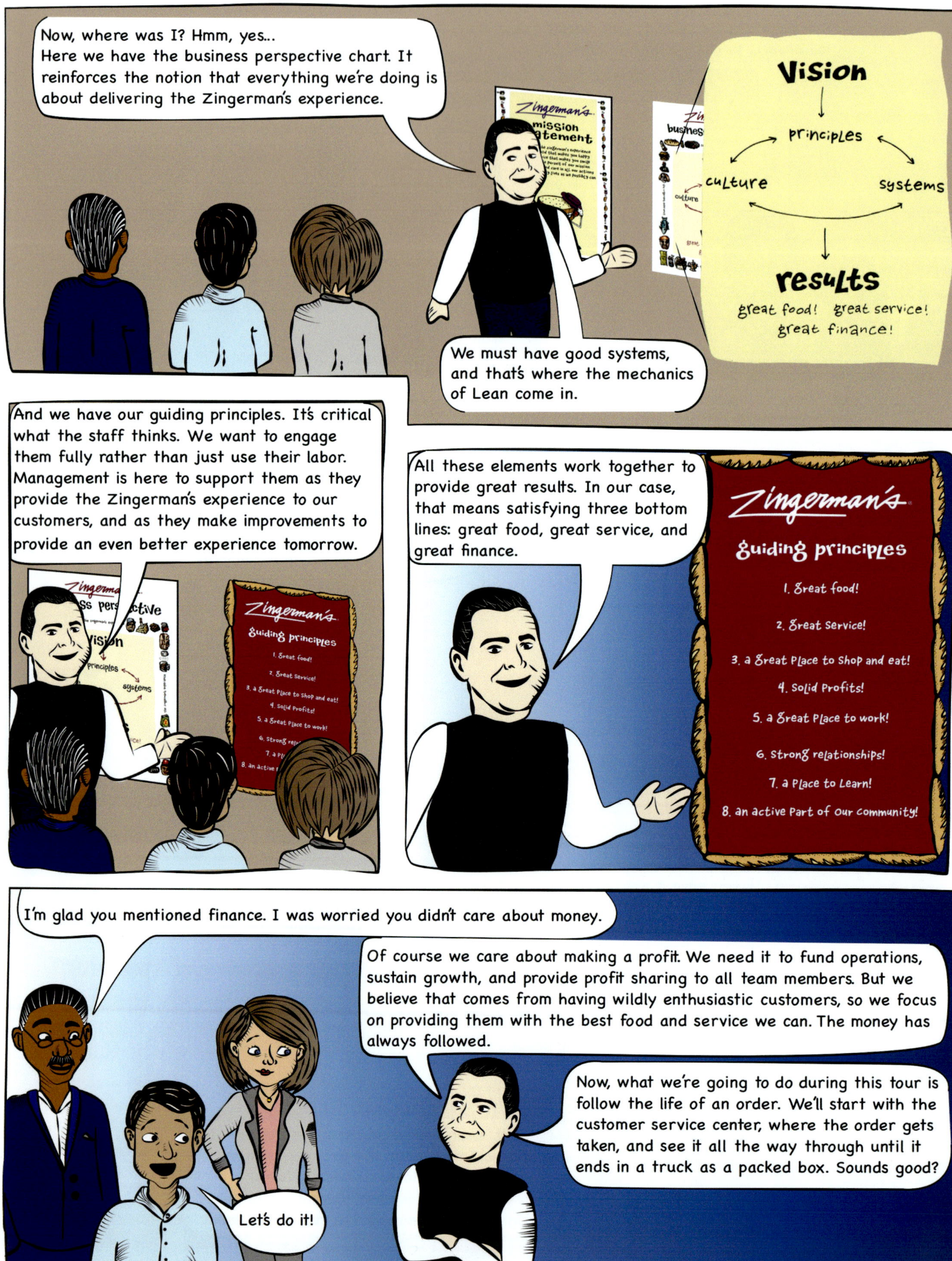

Now, where was I? Hmm, yes... Here we have the business perspective chart. It reinforces the notion that everything we're doing is about delivering the Zingerman's experience.
Vision
principles
culture
systems
results
great food! great service! great finance!
We must have good systems, and that's where the mechanics of Lean come in.
And we have our guiding principles. It's critical what the staff thinks. We want to engage them fully rather than just use their labor. Management is here to support them as they provide the Zingerman's experience to our customers, and as they make improvements to provide an even better experience tomorrow.
All these elements work together to provide great results. In our case, that means satisfying three bottom lines: great food, great service, and great finance.
Zingerman's
guiding principles
1. Great food!
2. Great Service!
3. a Great Place to Shop and eat!
4. Solid Profits!
5. a Great Place to work!
6. Strong relationships!
7. a Place to Learn!
8. an active Part of our community!
I'm glad you mentioned finance. I was worried you didn't care about money.
Of course we care about making a profit. We need it to fund operations, sustain growth, and provide profit sharing to all team members. But we believe that comes from having wildly enthusiastic customers, so we focus on providing them with the best food and service we can. The money has always followed.
Now, what we're going to do during this tour is follow the life of an order. We'll start with the customer service center, where the order gets taken, and see it all the way through until it ends in a truck as a packed box. Sounds good?
Let's do it!

The group goes to the service center
We call the people here Service Stars. They take orders on the phone.
Before we get into the details, please keep in mind that ZMO has a lot of variability, including a huge seasonal variation. 50% of our sales happen in December.

Wow! Half your sales in one month?
How do you handle that?
Weekly Sales
Well, there are many things we do. For one, we spend all year planning and improving to ensure those few weeks go smoothly. We also bring in a lot of people. We end up with about 10 times more team members than usual.
Ten times more people?? That's got to be complete chaos!

This level of seasonality sets a lot of limitations on the business. For example, there are things you cannot do when people are only here for a short period of time. You can't rely on training alone. I can't spend six months training for a job I will do only for four weeks.

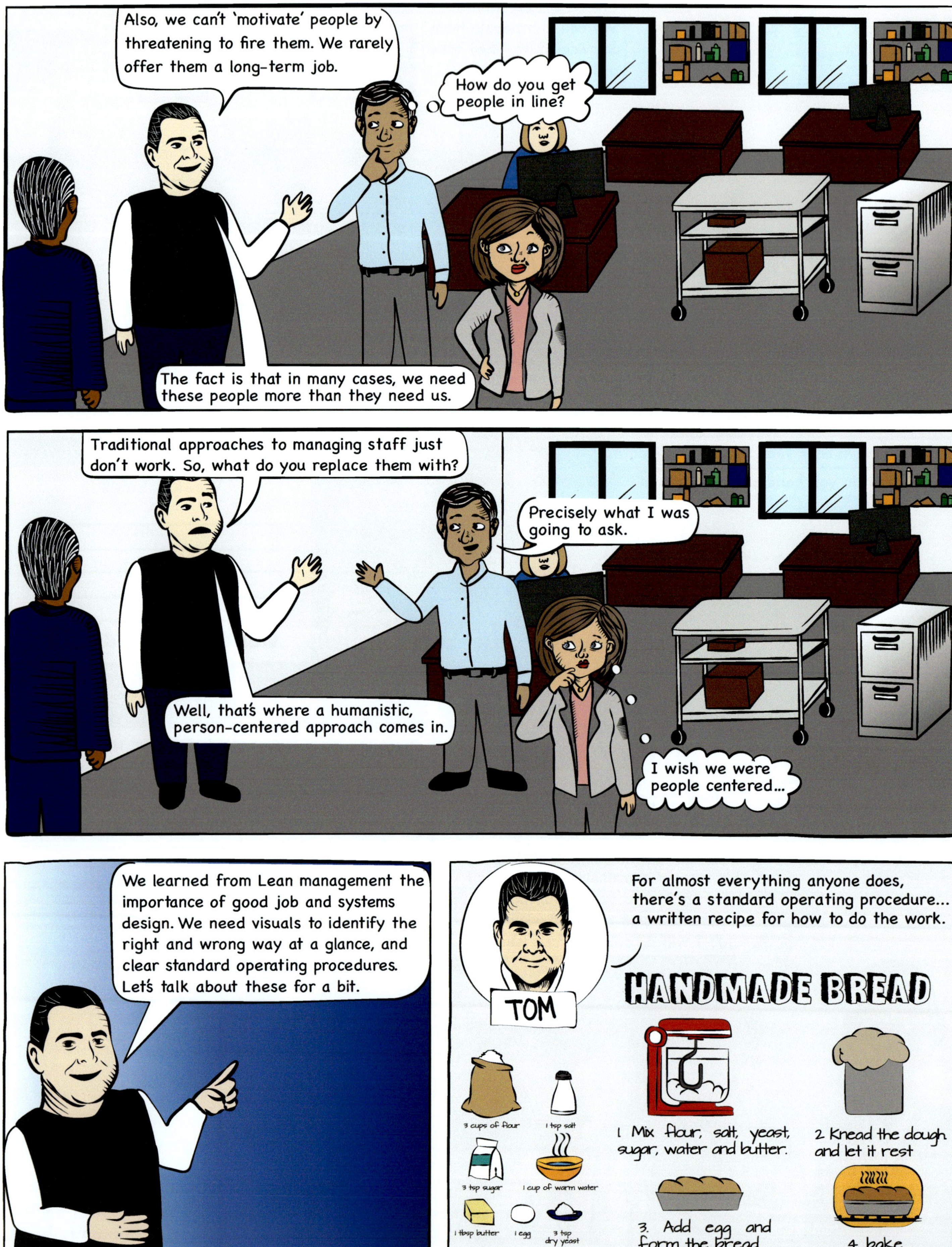

Also, we can't 'motivate' people by threatening to fire them. We rarely offer them a long-term job.
How do you get people in line?
The fact is that in many cases, we need these people more than they need us.
Traditional approaches to managing staff just don't work. So, what do you replace them with?
Precisely what I was going to ask.
Well, that's where a humanistic, person-centered approach comes in.
I wish we were people centered...
We learned from Lean management the importance of good job and systems design. We need visuals to identify the right and wrong way at a glance, and clear standard operating procedures. Let's talk about these for a bit.
TOM
For almost everything anyone does, there's a standard operating procedure... a written recipe for how to do the work.
HANDMADE BREAD
3 cups of flour
1 tsp salt
3 tsp sugar
1 cup of warm water
1 tbsp butter
1 egg
3 tsp dry yeast
1. Mix flour, salt, yeast, sugar, water and butter.
2 Knead the dough and let it rest
3. Add egg and form the bread
4. bake

This helps a lot with the holiday training because I can go over a document with you and say: Let's try it this way.
I can see that. But you need an SOP that is correct and simple. Otherwise the employees will get frustrated.
Absolutely! That's why we put so much time into improving our SOPs... and into learning from our temporary employees.
So SOPs are a big thing... hmmm... good work design is another one. Let's talk about that...
A few years, ago ZMO decided to build its own order management system. None of the off-the-shelf products met our needs.
What? There are plenty of systems out there...
That means two things. One is that we could not find a piece of software that would allow us to define the sequence of work in the way we wanted to do it.
We've had the same experience. Off-the-shelf products dictate their work sequence and are hard to adapt.
But building and maintaining your own system is hard... and expensive. Isn't it?

Yes. As small as we are, we now have 3 dedicated programmers, plus IT support from the Zingerman's office... and I am a closet IT guy myself.
TOM
But the benefits of having a tailored system that supports the process we want and the flexibility to change it as conditions shift or we make improvements far outweigh the costs.
Our IT system drives us nuts!
Interesting...
The second reason for building our own system, is that we couldn't find anything that matched our approach to service. We want unrivaled personalized service. For example, most order management systems are designed to limit what the Service Stars can do. They assume there are geniuses in marketing that come up with perfect gift boxes, so Service Stars should not change them.
Makes sense...
Our approach is exactly the opposite. The Service Stars are very intelligent individuals capable of making good choices... let's empower them to make up the gift box the client really wants.
TOM
Full customization?!
Zingerman's
TOM
Of course, we still have standard kits, gift boxes, and gift baskets designed by marketing. But if the customer wants to change something in them, or create a completely different one, they should be able to. We could not find software that allowed this, so we built our own around our standard procedure for taking orders from guests.

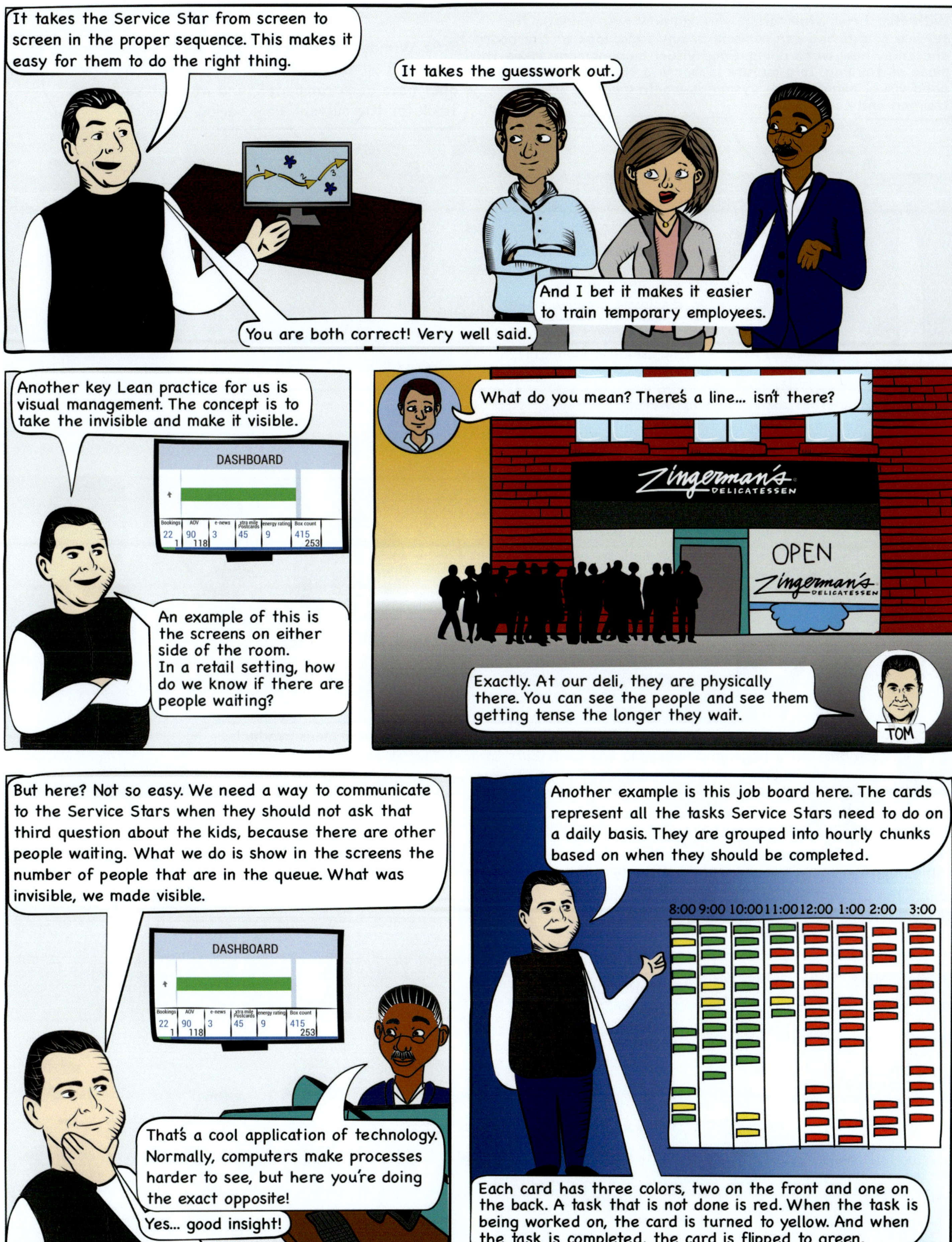

It takes the Service Star from screen to screen in the proper sequence. This makes it easy for them to do the right thing.
It takes the guesswork out.
And I bet it makes it easier to train temporary employees.
You are both correct! Very well said.
Another key Lean practice for us is visual management. The concept is to take the invisible and make it visible.
DASHBOARD
Bookings AOV e-news xtra mile Postcards energy rating Box count
22 1 90 118 3 45 9 415 253
An example of this is the screens on either side of the room. In a retail setting, how do we know if there are people waiting?
What do you mean? There's a line... isn't there?
Zingerman's DELICATESSEN
OPEN
Zingerman's DELICATESSEN
Exactly. At our deli, they are physically there. You can see the people and see them getting tense the longer they wait.
TOM
But here? Not so easy. We need a way to communicate to the Service Stars when they should not ask that third question about the kids, because there are other people waiting. What we do is show in the screens the number of people that are in the queue. What was invisible, we made visible.
DASHBOARD
Bookings AOV e-news xtra mile Postcards energy rating Box count
22 1 90 118 3 45 9 415 253
That's a cool application of technology. Normally, computers make processes harder to see, but here you're doing the exact opposite!
Yes... good insight!
Another example is this job board here. The cards represent all the tasks Service Stars need to do on a daily basis. They are grouped into hourly chunks based on when they should be completed.
8:00 9:00 10:00 11:00 12:00 1:00 2:00 3:00
Each card has three colors, two on the front and one on the back. A task that is not done is red. When the task is being worked on, the card is turned to yellow. And when the task is completed, the card is flipped to green.

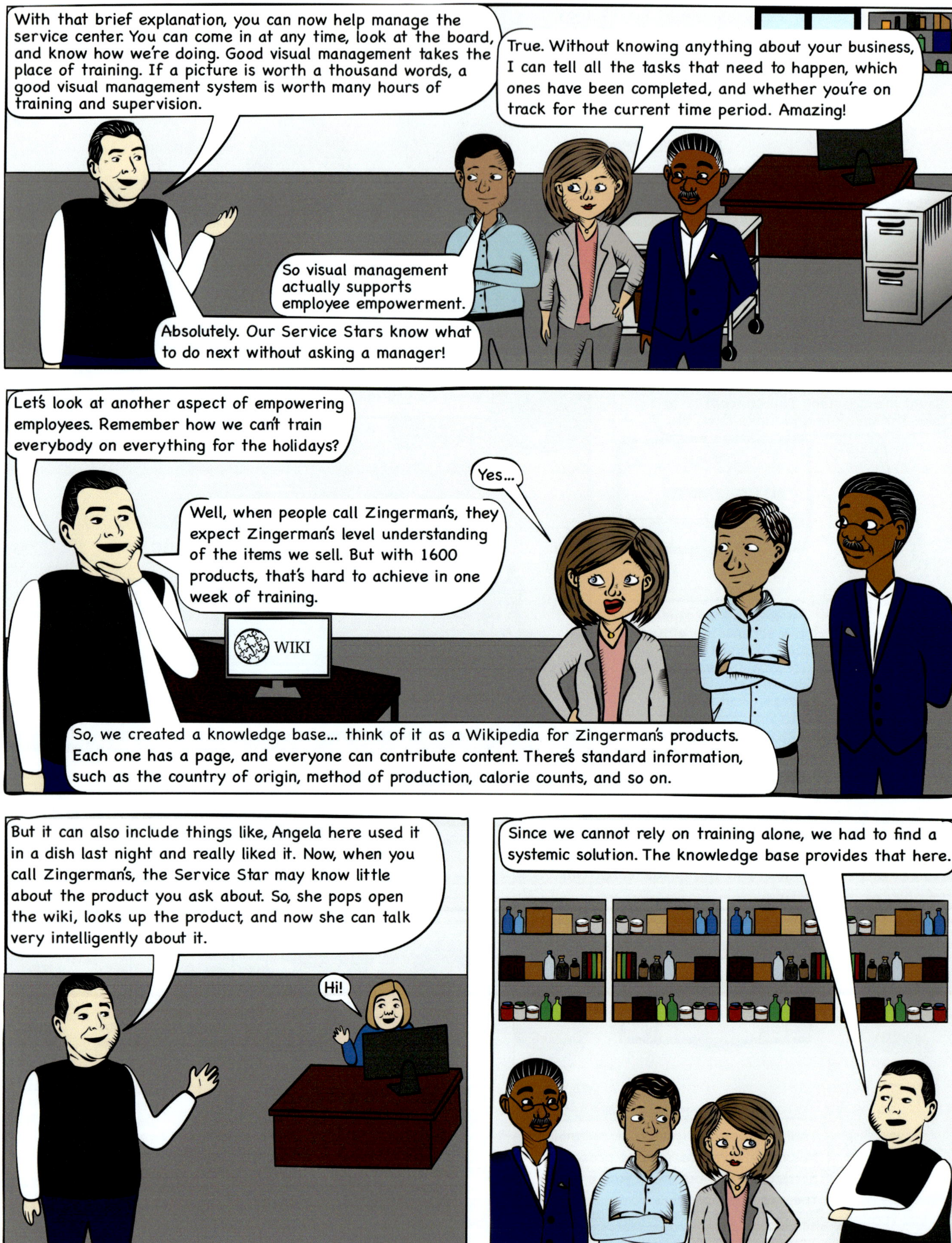

With that brief explanation, you can now help manage the service center. You can come in at any time, look at the board, and know how we're doing. Good visual management takes the place of training. If a picture is worth a thousand words, a good visual management system is worth many hours of training and supervision.
True. Without knowing anything about your business, I can tell all the tasks that need to happen, which ones have been completed, and whether you're on track for the current time period. Amazing!
So visual management actually supports employee empowerment.
Absolutely. Our Service Stars know what to do next without asking a manager!
Let's look at another aspect of empowering employees. Remember how we can't train everybody on everything for the holidays?
Yes...
Well, when people call Zingerman's, they expect Zingerman's level understanding of the items we sell. But with 1600 products, that's hard to achieve in one week of training.
WIKI
So, we created a knowledge base... think of it as a Wikipedia for Zingerman's products. Each one has a page, and everyone can contribute content. There's standard information, such as the country of origin, method of production, calorie counts, and so on.
But it can also include things like, Angela here used it in a dish last night and really liked it. Now, when you call Zingerman's, the Service Star may know little about the product you ask about. So, she pops open the wiki, looks up the product, and now she can talk very intelligently about it.
Hi!
Since we cannot rely on training alone, we had to find a systemic solution. The knowledge base provides that here.

Now, one of the wiki entries, if it's a shelf-stable product, is a number that refers to a location on this wall. So the Service Star can walk over and grab the bottle of vinegar she's discussing with the client, and now it's almost like a personal tasting.
Not knowing anything about the product before, she can now talk about the smell, the bottle, the fact that Angela loved it... the whole story if you will. And it's all right here.
Again, it's a systemic solution to empower the Service Star, who cannot memorize every one of our products.
This is very cool! You're giving everyone access to the collective knowledge you have accumulated.
What I like is that Service Stars can give it their own spin. By having the physical product they can interact with it and make comments that would otherwise not be possible or feel too scripted.
That's right. It combines an IT solution with physical cues to support the people doing the work. To help them do a better job of selling our products and serving the guests.
I love it! This one and the other visual systems you have here. They are simple, yet so powerful. We could use this in so many ways.
Thank you. So, this is where the order gets created - a person calls to place an order for themselves or to send a gift to someone else. As we move on, we're going to talk about different order-taking scenarios and their implications.

The group moves next door to the Corporate Gifts area
In the Service Center, we take individual orders. But we also do corporate gifts, and those orders are handled here.
This sale cycle is a little different. We have one point of contact into an organization... one customer, but that interaction can represent 50, 100, or maybe 200 individual orders. This represents a whole different problem for production.
Let's say you call today to order 50 sour cream coffee cakes for 50 different people.
Hey... That's not a bad idea!
If we release those orders to production in the sequence they were received, we will have one person picking sour cream coffee cakes for 50 orders, while everyone else stands around with no work.
I have to do 50!
We have no work

On the production floor, we do not want imbalances in workload or consumption. We don't want streaks or runs on a product. One, because it overworks the individual, and two, because it overworks the product. Right? We'll run out. The shelf gets over taxed and replenishment cannot keep up.
This is fascinating. First, you tell us you face huge variability throughout the year and have found ways to deal with that, and now you tell us you avoid having variability on the production floor. This seems a bit contradictory.
Well, whenever you have variability, you need a combination of inventory and extra capacity to cover the peaks. This adds cost to running the business and hides problems, so we constantly strive to reduce it by leveling out the schedule.
Seasonality is hard to deal with. It's hard to convince a customer that it's ok to receive their Christmas order in July. So we have to be flexible enough to deal with that. But there's a lot of variability that we can control and level out, especially within a day.
We have many issues with variability. How do you get rid of it?
What we do is level the orders. This is a common Lean concept Toyota calls Heijunka. In fact, it is the foundation of the Toyota Production System. It creates the stability needed to support Just-in-Time and Built-in-Quality.
I've heard about Heijunka... but it seems very complicated.

It can be. With all the different products and variability we have, we could not do it manually. So we enlisted IT to help. Remember the software we put orders into? We call her EVE, and we will find her many times as we go through the tour.
Hello!
TOM
Once regular and corporate gift orders have been entered, EVE takes them and sorts them into a sequence that's more convenient for production. We level the picking of products, but by spreading the workload there, we also do it for other areas down the line. In this way, we don't end up with one person working like crazy while everyone else stands around, and we don't run out of a product because too much of it has been pulled in a short period of time.
I cannot release the work I've completed... I'm blocked.
I can't keep up! And I'm almost out of product!
I have no work... I'm starved!
1
2
3
4
5
100%
Workload
1 2 3 4 5
1
2
3
4
5
100%
Workload
1 2 3 4 5

I've seen attempts at leveling before, but never in a high-variety business like yours. Do you level only corporate orders?
No, we level everything. You're right corporate orders are the most critical since they enter EVE in large batches and tend to contain similar products. But the leveling algorithm doesn't distinguish between order types. They all go into the same bucket and get leveled together.
Sorry, but wouldn't it be more efficient to prepare the 50 coffee cake orders one after the other in one big batch? I mean, the person picking is already at that spot. It's common sense, right?
The short answer is NO. It may seem more efficient if you look at one picker's productivity. When you look at the bigger picture of how we utilize all of our staff though, it is far more efficient to level.
In our case, we have problems every time we have runs on specific items. It will become clearer when we go out on the floor.
I guess we have a lot of rethinking to do at my company...
There is a lot about Lean thinking that seems like the opposite of common sense. Eduardo, our Lean consultant, certainly had to work hard to change the way we think. But don't let that get you down. That's actually part of the fun!
I think you and I have very different concepts of fun...

Before we go to the floor, there's one more thing I want to show you here. We talked about visual management in the Service Center. Well, another thing we do at Zingerman's is open book management.
That means everyone here understands the organization's financial health and wellbeing. And one of the tools of open book management is this board here.
On it, we have the metrics we choose to track, each one owned by a person. And we show the results, which are evaluated at a weekly meeting. I point this out because it's a great example of visual management. In most organizations, the financial information is known by the accountant, probably the owner, and maybe a few select managers. It's usually kept secret so employees don't know how much money you are making... or losing.
Sounds familiar...
Here, we take all this invisible information and publish it in a public space where every staff member can see it.
Wait. This board has all your financial information and you keep it where everyone can see it? Even visitors?
Yes, you can walk in here and see how we're doing... once you learn how to read the board.
We display every metric the group has decided is worth tracking and evaluating on a regular basis. In this particular board, most of the numbers are financial ones.
Don't your people get nervous when things are not going well?

Precisely the point! In this way we get to share the stress... and also celebrate success together. Everybody is responsible for the organization's health and wellbeing, and everybody is informed about it. And we all get bonuses based on profits, so everyone is very interested. Open book management brings a radical democratization of financial intelligence, while Lean promotes the radical democratization of operational intelligence.
Wow... that's deep!

Through visual management, we strive to provide the right information in the right place, so people can make the right decision at the right time. Metric boards do the same for financial and other key indicators.
So, can we see how you're doing?
Of course!

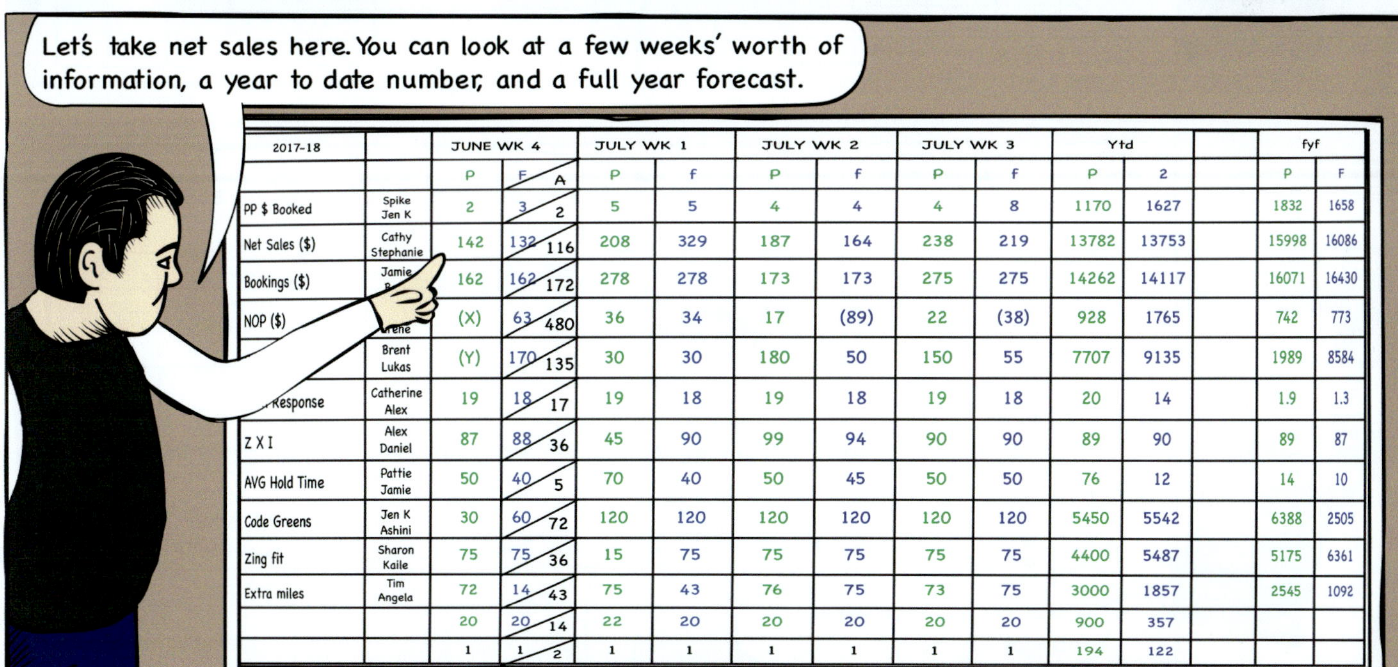
Let's take net sales here. You can look at a few weeks' worth of information, a year to date number, and a full year forecast.

2017-18		JUNE WK 4		JULY WK 1		JULY WK 2		JULY WK 3		Ytd			fyf	
		P	F / A	P	f	P	f	P	f	P	2		P	F
PP $ Booked	Spike Jen K	2	3 / 2	5	5	4	4	4	8	1170	1627		1832	1658
Net Sales ($)	Cathy Stephanie	142	132 / 116	208	329	187	164	238	219	13782	13753		15998	16086
Bookings ($)	Jamie	162	162 / 172	278	278	173	173	275	275	14262	14117		16071	16430
NOP ($)		(X)	63 / 480	36	34	17	(89)	22	(38)	928	1765		742	773
	Brent Lukas	(Y)	170 / 135	30	30	180	50	150	55	7707	9135		1989	8584
Response	Catherine Alex	19	18 / 17	19	18	19	18	19	18	20	14		1.9	1.3
Z X I	Alex Daniel	87	88 / 36	45	90	99	94	90	90	89	90		89	87
AVG Hold Time	Pattie Jamie	50	40 / 5	70	40	50	45	50	50	76	12		14	10
Code Greens	Jen K Ashini	30	60 / 72	120	120	120	120	120	120	5450	5542		6388	2505
Zing fit	Sharon Kaile	75	75 / 36	15	75	75	75	75	75	4400	5487		5175	6361
Extra miles	Tim Angela	72	14 / 43	75	43	76	75	73	75	3000	1857		2545	1092
		20	20 / 14	22	20	20	20	20	20	900	357			
		1	1 / 2	1	1	1	1	1	1	194	122			

Wow... and the colors mean something?
I wonder how my company is doing...
The green is a planned number based on the yearly budget. The blue is a revised forecast and is updated at the weekly meeting. The black number shows the actual result.
We have a week of history and three weeks of future, and we're always looking at that 4-week moving window.
So if I look at the booking numbers for last week... the plan called for 162... thousand, I assume.
Yes, that's correct.
The forecast was reiterated at 162, but the actual came in at 172.
That's it!
So that was a good week.
It was better than expected... You got it!

And there you go. The power of visual management. With very little instruction, you can now evaluate our performance on all the key metrics we track.
I've been here 15 minutes, and I can tell how they are doing. I've been at my company 15 years, and I have only a vague idea of how that's going...
So everyone can recognize that it was a good week for the company, even if it did not feel that way in their own work.
Correct. It provides feedback on overall performance.
Next, we're heading out to the production floor. Now that the order exists in EVE, it needs to become real, and that starts with it getting picked. So, that's where we're headed next.
I can't wait to see that!

The group goes out to the warehouse... to the end of the pick line.
Here we are on the production floor. The area around this yellow conveyor is the pick line. Here, pickers get the needed products from the markets and place them in an order tub on the conveyor.
But before that happens, we have to get the products ready. We have two types of items:
perishable and
shelf stable...
and they are treated differently.
One of the unique ideas we got from Lean, is perpetual replenishment using a pull system. We implement it, for the most part, using kanban.
I've seen that! That's where you have little pieces of paper running all over the place, no?
Well, they don't actually run all over the place. Kanban is a very defined and disciplined system. Let me show you how it works here.

By the side of the pick line, we have markets filled with products. Here we have one that is shelf stable... honey. And attached, we have this card called kanban.
N2
N1
The card says you can find this product in a location... 14E-3F. Since it begins with a number, it's a back stock location. This is the 'from' location... where it's stored before coming to the market.
Honey
From: 14E-3F
Quantity: 3
In Single Faced
width toward front
P-WHI
LS 4 OF 4
It indicates a quantity of 3, so each card will trigger a batch of 3 jars of honey to be brought to the market.
It also shows the product code... P-WHI. This is a unique identifier every product has.
It says this is a line side kanban – LS – and that this is card 4 of 4... so there are 4 of these cards in circulation.
And it shows a 'to' location on the line side market N1-B3, where I took the jar from.
So, this card tells me all I need to know to replenish the line.
Yes, it's that simple! It tells you to get 3 P-WHI from 14E-3F in back stock and bring it to N1-B3 at the line. So again, with minimal training, you could now step in and contribute to processing orders.
Again the power of visual management... I need to get some of these!

This replenishment process forms a kanban loop between back stock and the line side market. It provides the instruction to bring more product when the quantity it represents has been consumed. Let me draw it for you.
LS Kanban
Routes
Pick
Back stock market
Line side market
So this is the perpetual replenishment you mentioned? Consumption triggers replenishment...
Exactly! The kanban tells us both what to do and when to do it. The timing bit is as critical as any of the information on the card.
Now, let's do a little math. If we have 4 kanban and each one represents 3 jars, how many jars should we have on the shelf?
Kanban
Kanban
Kanban
Kanban
I'm going to go out on a limb and say 12, max.
That's correct! The number of jars in the market should never exceed 12. If it does, we have a problem and should investigate what happened. Perhaps someone is not following the process and needs further training.

Now, as pickers take jars from the shelf, we will end up with fewer than 12 in the market. But we should never run out. If we do, we have a different problem as the picker cannot fulfill the next order.
!
EMPTY
But how can you run out if you replenish every time a jar is picked? What am I missing?
Well, we do not replenish immediately... we use timed routes. Otherwise, we would need many more people just standing behind the markets, waiting for a kanban to be triggered and running to get more product from back stock.
That would not be very efficient...
We set the market size... the number of kanban and the quantity per kanban... and the route frequency in a way that minimizes the chances of running out. However, it does happen occasionally, and we have to investigate why.
A typical culprit is the streaks or runs on products we discussed before. If we get orders for more than 12 jars of this honey within one replenishment cycle, we will certainly run out.
So this is why leveling, instead of batching, is so important for you?
Yes! With a properly leveled sequence, even in a day when demand for honey is high, we should not see orders for 12 jars close together. You're starting to see how everything is interrelated...
Now Jason... we talked about this seasonality we face, where volume can go up 10 times or more in December. What do you think happens to the markets at that time?
Well... you need more product... the market has to get bigger.

What if I told you that for most products, the size for the line side market does not change? And what if I added that the size is right for both the high and low demand periods?
I would say you're smoking something. How can that be possible? Wait... you're changing the replenishment!
Yes...by replenishing more often, you provide the volume of product your pickers need during Christmas.
Correct! And correct! We adjust the replenishment frequency according to the speed at which the line is running... which is a direct result of the number of orders we need to process. During a slow demand day, we may replenish every two hours. During the Christmas rush, we do it every 15 minutes.
Someone brings product to the line every 15 minutes? I would like to see that!
Slow day: Every 2 hours
Pick
Routes
Backstock market
Line side market
Peak day: Every 15 min.
Come back in the first three weeks of December.
So these markets work just like a grocery store. Products are displayed on shelves, and when customers have taken enough items, more are brought out.
That's it!
Now, let's look at this from the perspective of the pickers. We like to say they are like surgeons.
N2
N1

Mike, if I was on the operating table, and the surgeon needed more gauze... would I want him to walk away to get it?
Certainly not! Someone else should do it.
Gauze.
This is exactly how we want pickers and everyone on the line to work. We don't want them to walk away from the line to go find what they need.
They have to focus on picking, so they need a reliable mechanism to signal that they need more. And that's the purpose of the kanban, which in Japanese just means signal or sign.
We attach the kanban to the product and put it in the market. As a picker, when I grab this jar from the shelf, I take the card off and place it in the nearest kanban chute... the collection points for kanban. This tells the route runner, 'hey, bring me some more honey next time you come around'.
N3
N2
That's great! And so simple...
Simple and visible to everyone, so people can understand and improve it.
Anyway, this ensures a perpetual supply of product. At the end of the day, when we're done picking, there will be close to 12 units of honey on the shelf. For a shelf stable product, that's great.
Yes, it will not go bad and you want it there to start picking orders the next day.
That's right. But for a perishable product like bread, the last thing we want is to end the day with a full market.
That does pose a different problem, doesn't it?
It does, so we can't use the kanban in its traditional sense to manage a perishable product. We need another technique for that. Shall we go take a look at how we handle bread?
I was going to say... That sounds even more interesting.

The group enters the bread prep area...
Here we are at bread prep. We get bread from the Zingerman's Bakehouse in town. We bag it, label it, and place it in a tote to go to the bread market. And we do that following a kanban signal from the line.
Wait a minute, I thought you said you used a different system for perishable products.
We do... we use a hybrid kanban system.
Ok... but what do you mean by that?
Let me explain... The kanban are exactly the same as the ones we saw before. However, here when the kanban comes back from the line... when the signal is thrown that more is needed... we're going to ask EVE, and she's going to tell us whether we should replenish it or not.
EVE is your IT system, right?
Yes. Now, the line is like a petulant child. It's always saying "give me more, give me more". Sometimes mom, played here by EVE, has to say "ahh... you've had enough".
It seems EVE is a stricter mom than I am.
You've had enough!
We want more!

When a kanban for paesano bread comes back saying "I need more", we ask EVE... "should we give the line more?" EVE sees we need 152 for today and have put only 30 out, so...
152>30
Yes, give the line another 10.
So, we keep the Kanban in rotation and give it to the baggers to process.
EVE keeps a running count of what has gone to the line compared to what's needed...
That's exactly right. When we're down to the last 2 and the kanban comes back asking for 10, EVE is going to say "no, that's too much".
Only two!
And we control it at this station where we print the labels that the baggers need. So, in this last iteration, where only two more loaves are needed, only two labels will come out.
I think I got it. The people working here need to go through EVE to print the labels and every time they print one, EVE deducts it from the total needed for the day, correct?
You got it, Mike! In this way, we ensure that only what is needed is produced, and we avoid over stocking.

So when the next kanban comes back...
...when the next one asks for 10 more, we go to EVE again... "should we give more paesano to the line?" EVE is going to see we already provided the 152 loaves needed for the day and say no. All we do is take the kanban out of circulation and hang it on the board here.
No, no, no... you've had enough!
In this way, you use kanban to ensure constant replenishment throughout the day to avoid running out, and you use EVE to end the day with empty markets... EVE prevents overproduction!
That's right!
I see that for the people working here, EVE makes it very easy. If the line asks for more, they ask EVE... if ten labels come out, they bag ten loaves. If only two come out, they do those. If none come out, they're done for the day. They don't even have to make decisions!
Yes! And this is a great example of the way in which EVE has been developed. Since we do it in-house, EVE grows with the needs of our people. We automate activities to support the process and the people... to make their jobs easier.

Now, this area is divided into several work stations. The one we were looking at is in charge of managing the kanban... getting them back from the line, asking EVE what should be done with them, and printing labels.
We then signal someone else to go get the bread... we call them taxi drivers. We give them the kanban and labels, and they take the needed bread to the bagging station.
In the bagging station, we have space for three bread racks. One the baggers work from, one incoming with the next bread to bag, and one outgoing with any loaves left over.
3
1
2
The second and third spaces serve as signals... visual kanban if you will... to tell the taxi drivers where more work is needed. This makes it easier for them to decide which bread to move next.
So the bagging station helps regulate the work of the taxi driver? That's clever.
Yes. It also prevents congestion at the bagging stations which cause delays. If the incoming tray for a station is full, we cannot give it more work.

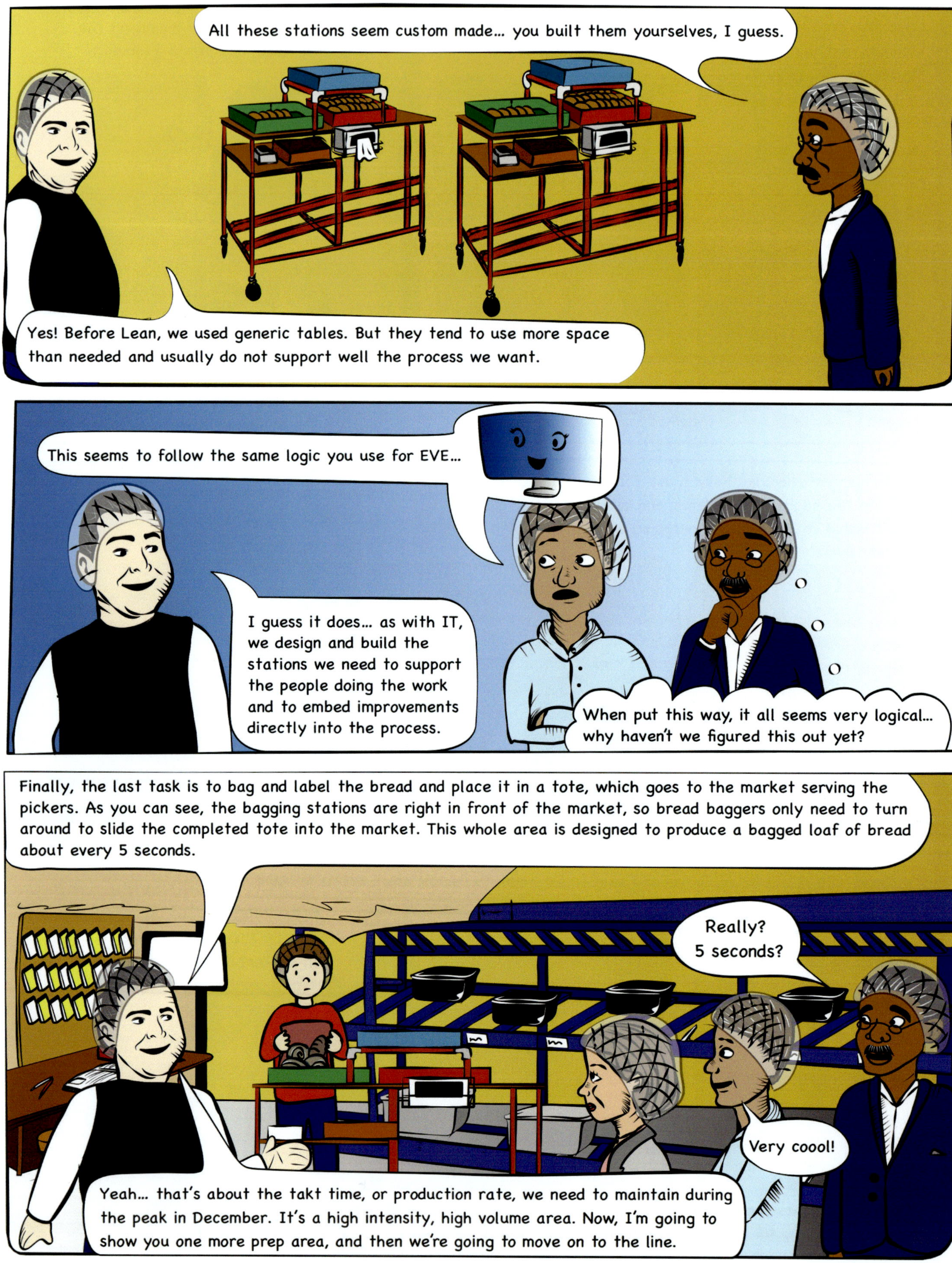
All these stations seem custom made... you built them yourselves, I guess.
Yes! Before Lean, we used generic tables. But they tend to use more space than needed and usually do not support well the process we want.
This seems to follow the same logic you use for EVE...
I guess it does... as with IT, we design and build the stations we need to support the people doing the work and to embed improvements directly into the process.
When put this way, it all seems very logical... why haven't we figured this out yet?
Finally, the last task is to bag and label the bread and place it in a tote, which goes to the market serving the pickers. As you can see, the bagging stations are right in front of the market, so bread baggers only need to turn around to slide the completed tote into the market. This whole area is designed to produce a bagged loaf of bread about every 5 seconds.
Really? 5 seconds?
Very coool!
Yeah... that's about the takt time, or production rate, we need to maintain during the peak in December. It's a high intensity, high volume area. Now, I'm going to show you one more prep area, and then we're going to move on to the line.

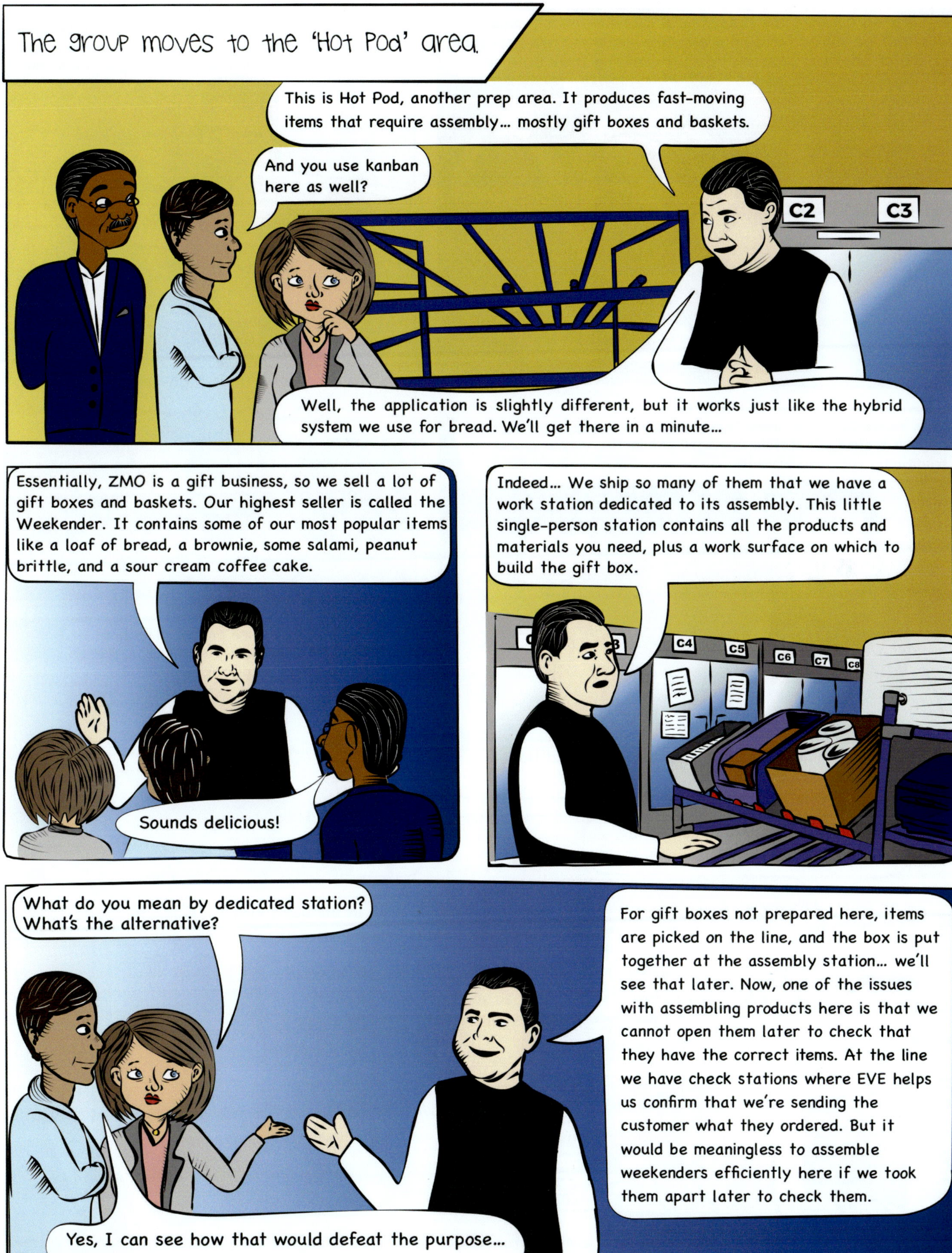
The group moves to the 'Hot Pod' area.
This is Hot Pod, another prep area. It produces fast-moving items that require assembly... mostly gift boxes and baskets.
And you use kanban here as well?
C2
C3
Well, the application is slightly different, but it works just like the hybrid system we use for bread. We'll get there in a minute...
Essentially, ZMO is a gift business, so we sell a lot of gift boxes and baskets. Our highest seller is called the Weekender. It contains some of our most popular items like a loaf of bread, a brownie, some salami, peanut brittle, and a sour cream coffee cake.
Sounds delicious!
Indeed... We ship so many of them that we have a work station dedicated to its assembly. This little single-person station contains all the products and materials you need, plus a work surface on which to build the gift box.
C4
C5
C6
C7
What do you mean by dedicated station? What's the alternative?
For gift boxes not prepared here, items are picked on the line, and the box is put together at the assembly station... we'll see that later. Now, one of the issues with assembling products here is that we cannot open them later to check that they have the correct items. At the line we have check stations where EVE helps us confirm that we're sending the customer what they ordered. But it would be meaningless to assemble weekenders efficiently here if we took them apart later to check them.
Yes, I can see how that would defeat the purpose...

So, here we followed the Lean idea of mistake proofing. Lean says that we should focus on preventing mistakes from happening instead of becoming good at finding and solving them later on.
LEAN
That seems like the logical thing to do.
It does, doesn't it?
Well, here at the Weekender station we have all the items we need, plus this very expensive, high-tech, card board template for making a Weekender.
G-WEE
SUMMER
B-FRM-LOF V6-D1
A-SCC-SN V6-B1
A-BRO V6-B4
A-BLN V6-B3
P-VDP V6-A1
M-DSG V6-A4
P-BRT-S V6-A3
BIG FLAVAH BOX
I love their high-tech solutions!
Now, remember how given the seasonality we face, we cannot rely on training or active management in the way a more traditional company would?
Yes, long training is not an option, and traditional control methods do not work...
Perfect, you were paying attention! Now, let's see how a systemic approach helps us get superior results here.
Mike, how do you think someone makes a Weekender at this station?
Well, I assume it's a fill in the blank kind of thing... if the product fits on the template, it goes in the box.
Right! And in case you have any doubt, the template also gives you the code and address for the items so you don't have to guess.
So I grab each product and place it on the template...

That's right. And when all the boxes are filled, you know you've got everything. It makes it easy to do the right thing and hard to do the wrong thing.
Yes, it does. Even the size and shape of the template images help prevent mistakes. It will be obviously wrong if I place a square item on top of a round shape or a small item where this B-FRM-LOF thing should go.
I don't even need to know what these things are...
Exactly! That's a huge help when trying to train seasonal workers quickly.
With this approach, I can walk you to the station and explain how things work. In 15 minutes you can be assembling weekenders and making a positive contribution to the business.
I can see that happening.
Yes... and as an employee, I would feel good about it. I would know I'm doing it right and that my work is providing a customer what they want.
EMPLOYEE
CUSTOMER
That's right! You feel in control and you get immediate feedback if you make a mistake.
Once again, the simplicity and effectiveness of your solutions blows me away.
Thank you... the people here will certainly appreciate that. This is another example of how the constraints of seasonality force us to creatively design the work so it's easy to learn and get right, using systemic solutions instead of relying on training and active management.

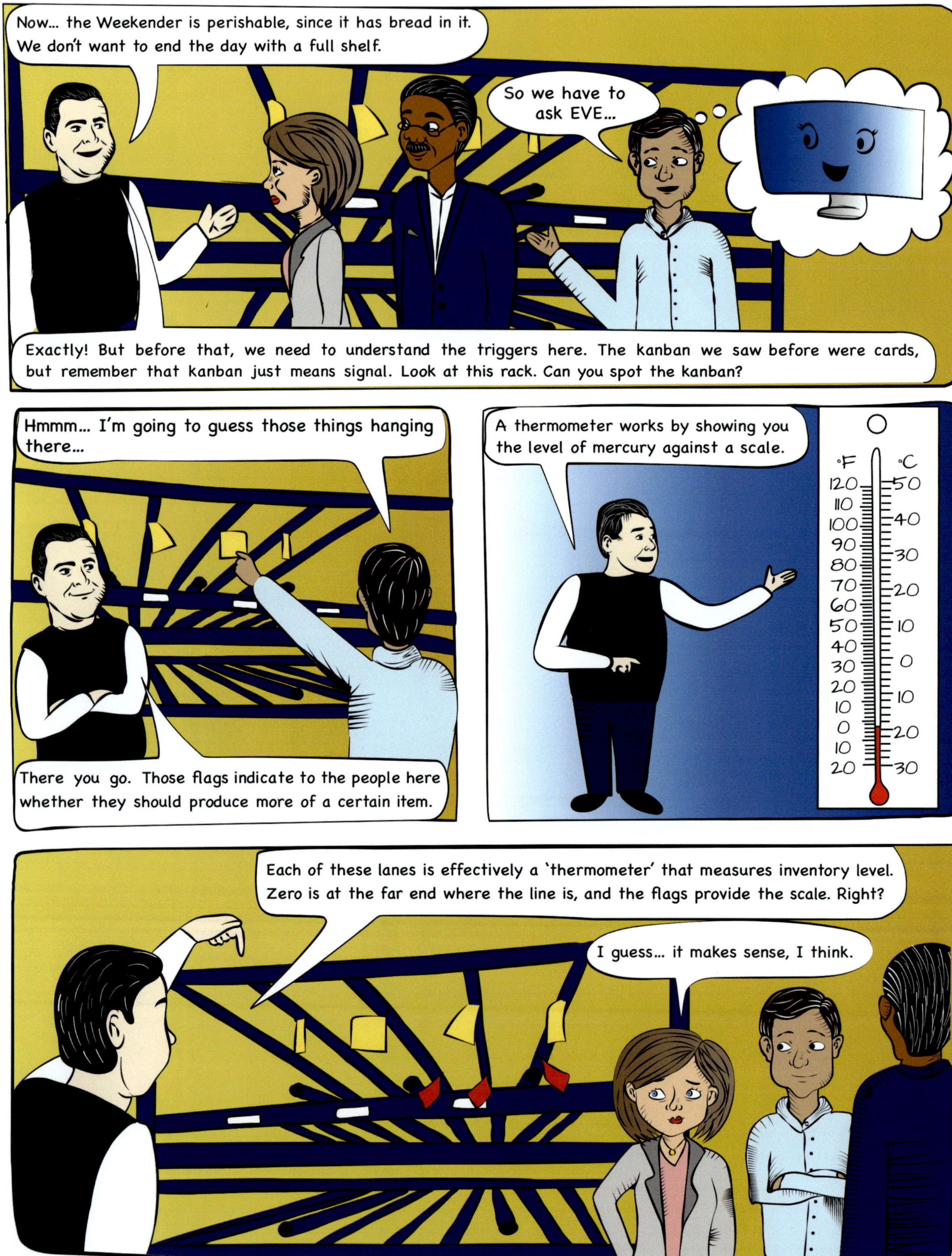

Now... the Weekender is perishable, since it has bread in it. We don't want to end the day with a full shelf.
So we have to ask EVE...
Exactly! But before that, we need to understand the triggers here. The kanban we saw before were cards, but remember that kanban just means signal. Look at this rack. Can you spot the kanban?
Hmmm... I'm going to guess those things hanging there...
There you go. Those flags indicate to the people here whether they should produce more of a certain item.
A thermometer works by showing you the level of mercury against a scale.
°F °C
120 110 100 90 80 70 60 50 40 30 20 10 0 10 20
50 40 30 20 10 0 10 20 30
Each of these lanes is effectively a 'thermometer' that measures inventory level. Zero is at the far end where the line is, and the flags provide the scale. Right?
I guess... it makes sense, I think.

Well, when we see one of these yellow flags hanging down, that's the line asking for more.
= MORE
It's like caution... we're getting low, no?
Right. The line is just saying "I used some, please start making more.".
Now, if we can see one of those red flags hanging down, we're running very low. The line is consuming a lot of this item, and it's telling us to focus on replenishing it or we will run out.
Red is emergency, then.
Yes! The flags tell us what's needed, and the colors help us prioritize. If I come to the market and see yellow flags and a red one, I should produce the item with the red flag.
So these flags are the kanban. But remember, the product is perishable, so we have to ask EVE. When the line says, "make me Weekenders", we come over here to EVE. This time we use the screen, as we do not have a physical kanban to scan. We find G-WEE and it says the total we need is 22 and the total left to prep is zero.
No more!
This means the 22 Weekenders we needed today have already been made and placed in the market.
No more work needed.
Exactly! And that's it for Hot Pod. Shall we head over to the line and see how we produce the orders?

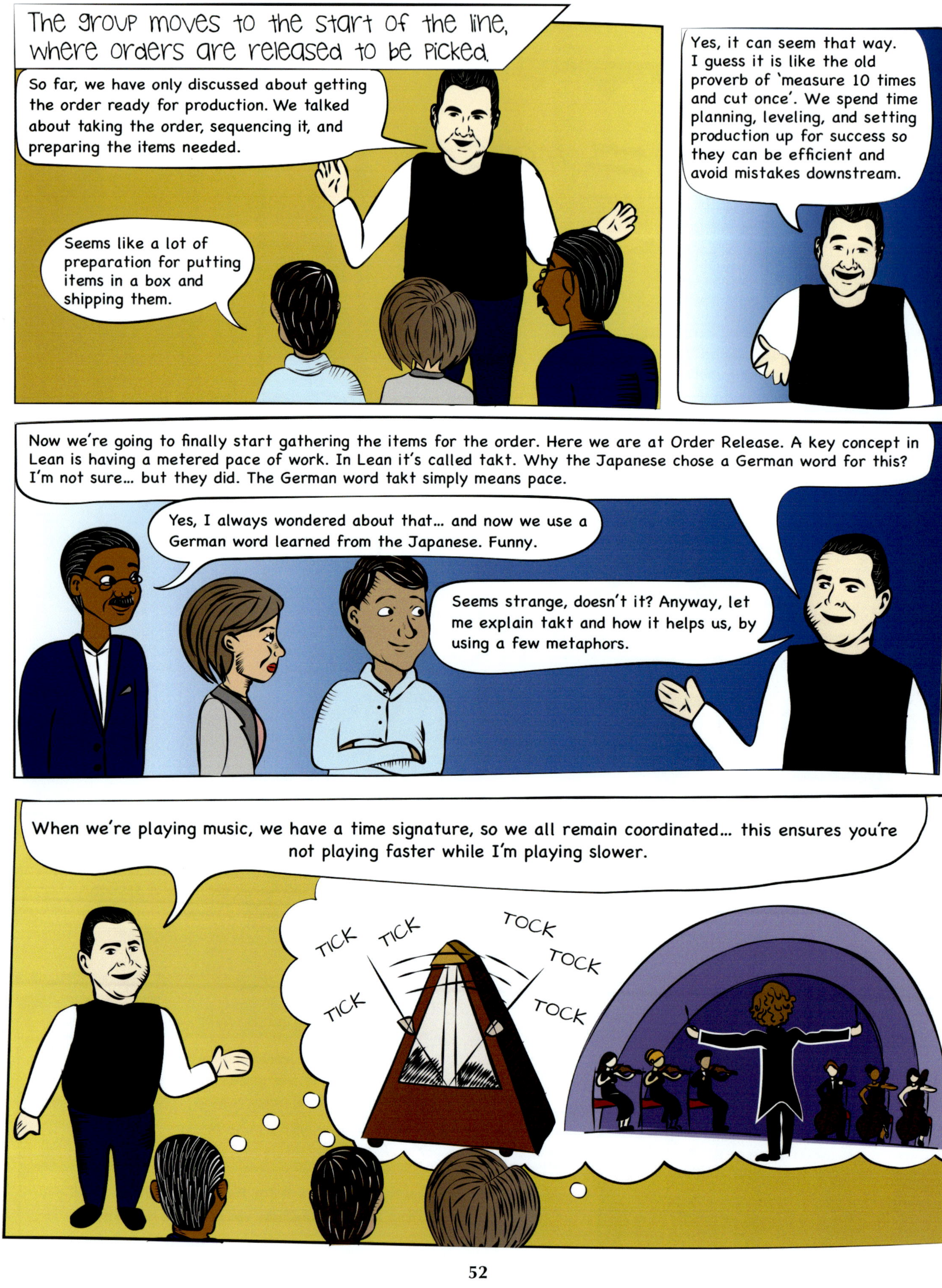
The group moves to the start of the line, where orders are released to be picked.
So far, we have only discussed about getting the order ready for production. We talked about taking the order, sequencing it, and preparing the items needed.
Seems like a lot of preparation for putting items in a box and shipping them.
Yes, it can seem that way. I guess it is like the old proverb of 'measure 10 times and cut once'. We spend time planning, leveling, and setting production up for success so they can be efficient and avoid mistakes downstream.
Now we're going to finally start gathering the items for the order. Here we are at Order Release. A key concept in Lean is having a metered pace of work. In Lean it's called takt. Why the Japanese chose a German word for this? I'm not sure... but they did. The German word takt simply means pace.
Yes, I always wondered about that... and now we use a German word learned from the Japanese. Funny.
Seems strange, doesn't it? Anyway, let me explain takt and how it helps us, by using a few metaphors.
When we're playing music, we have a time signature, so we all remain coordinated... this ensures you're not playing faster while I'm playing slower.
TICK TICK TICK
TOCK TOCK TOCK

If we're in a rowing team, there's the coxswain, who is shouting stroke, stroke, stroke… This keeps everybody pulling at the same rhythm. Because if we are not synchronized, what happens to the boat?
Stroke
Stroke
Stroke
We hit each other's oars… we go in circles… we go nowhere!
Exactly.
So takt is the guy in the Viking ship with a giant drum… boom, boom, boom… making sure we all pull at the same pace.
So where's your Viking?
Boom!
Boom!
Boom!
Well, we decided against hiring one… they get bored when not looting and pillaging… and they are too noisy!
I bet they are!
But we do need to create a heartbeat for the production line. So, who do you think we turn to?
I'm guessing EVE…
You got it!
I do that as well…
So, here at the order release computer, we tell EVE how many orders we want released in a given period of time. Right now, we're printing three orders every 96 seconds. So what takt would that be?
32 seconds
96 divided by 3 gives us… a 32 second takt.

That's right, Jason! This means we're putting an order on the line every 32 seconds. And by knowing this takt number... this pace, magic things can happen. For example, I know how long it takes to bag a loaf of bread. So, if I want to sync bread prep with the line's consumption, I can use takt to calculate the number of people I need bagging bread to support the speed at which the line is running.
So, by knowing the speed you will run at, you can figure out the number of people you will need?
Exactly! Since we know the time each job takes, we can figure out how many people we need and where they should go.
Tom, can you run us through an example of how this works?
Sure... if a job takes 64 seconds to complete and we're running a 32 second takt, how many people does that station need?
You would need... two people to keep up with the pace.
That's right! And by repeating that for every job on the floor, we can calculate how many people we need at each station... for both prep areas and on the line. But that's not all...
Takt also tells us when the day will end. If we have 100 orders left and we're doing one every 32 seconds, then 3200 seconds from now, we will be done.
It makes your day predictable...
Absolutely! And that's a big deal for us. Remember, we operate with a lot of variability and take orders for same-day shipping. The work we need to complete depends on the number of orders, so it's different every day.
TOM
Before we used takt, we could not predict when the day would end, or even if our pace was fast enough... and we couldn't tell if we should stop taking orders. Everyone was constantly anxious we would not ship to every customer on time.
Should we stop taking orders?
I don't know...

Just in time.
Anyway, accurately predicting when the day will end allows us to make better decisions earlier and with more certainty. For example, we know exactly how many more orders we can take and still be on time for when the truck leaves.
But there's more... takt also allows us to evaluate the performance of any station at any point in time. If we're putting an order on the line every 32 seconds, how often does pick need to complete an order? That is, how often should one order move from the pick area to the check area? On average, of course...
Every 32 seconds?
That's right!
And how often does an order need to leave the check area?
Every 32 seconds.
Right again!
32s
32s
32s
And this is the case for all stations down the line. Now, how often should an order come out at the end of the line?
Every 32 seconds as well.
Yes!
And what do you think happens when a station goes slower?
If other stations maintain the pace and one does not, you will see orders pile up, won't you?
Yeah! Orders will accumulate coming into that station, which can block stations upstream since they will not have space for the work they complete.
And what about downstream?
The line would empty out, wouldn't it?
Correct!
Downstream of the slow station, we have the opposite effect. People start running out of work... stations get starved. And by the way, the slow station is your bottleneck.

BOTTLENECK
I could go faster if I had more work.
WORK! WORK! WORK!
No space to move completed work... I'm blocked.
Nothing to do... I'm starved.
FLOW of ORDERS
We will talk a bit later about how we react to these effects. The important point here is that releasing at takt allows us to see how the line, prep areas, and even routes are performing against the planned speed. Setting a strict pace for releasing orders defines the standard against which we can measure the performance of most processes. And we can do this at any time through simple observation.
That's an interesting point...
So takt is a magic number... it allows us to calculate the labor needed, makes the day predictable, helps us evaluate performance, and ensures everyone is pulling on the oars at the same pace.
Magic indeed!
It is... and it's EVE again that is enforcing this takt for us.
Which again makes it easy. No one has to think about it... no one has to check their watch... just wait for the next order to come out of the printer. So elegant!
And we don't have disagreements over the appropriate pace. "You're working too fast." "No, you're working too slow". None of that... it's all defined and planned. We all work at the right pace.
You're going too slow!
No! You're going too fast!

Seems so reasonable when you put it that way... So, how are the orders picked?
Let's move right into that. The work order comes out of the printer and is placed in one of these tubs.
Orders then move down the line... along the grocery store. And what we do is a little personal shopping for our customers.
ERIC
So Eric here is going to take an order and start gathering the items needed by taking them from the market and placing them in the corresponding tub. This is what we call picking.
I see he moves multiple tubs at the same time...
Yes, that's to reduce walking. Three tubs at a time seems to work best, so that's our standard batch.
TOM
Now, we actually pick in a fashion much like a relay race. Eric does not pick everything by himself. He starts the order and picks the items from the first zone. Then he hands it over to someone else a little bit down the line, just like passing the baton.
This approach sets us up for this interesting thing we do called Help Your Neighbor. If you look down the pick line, you see flags standing out from the conveyor, yes?
Yes! They are hard to miss.
They indicate where a picker should hand over the order tubs to the next person. It's the drop-off zone. Once I'm done picking in my area, I leave the tubs there for the next picker.
Got it... I think.

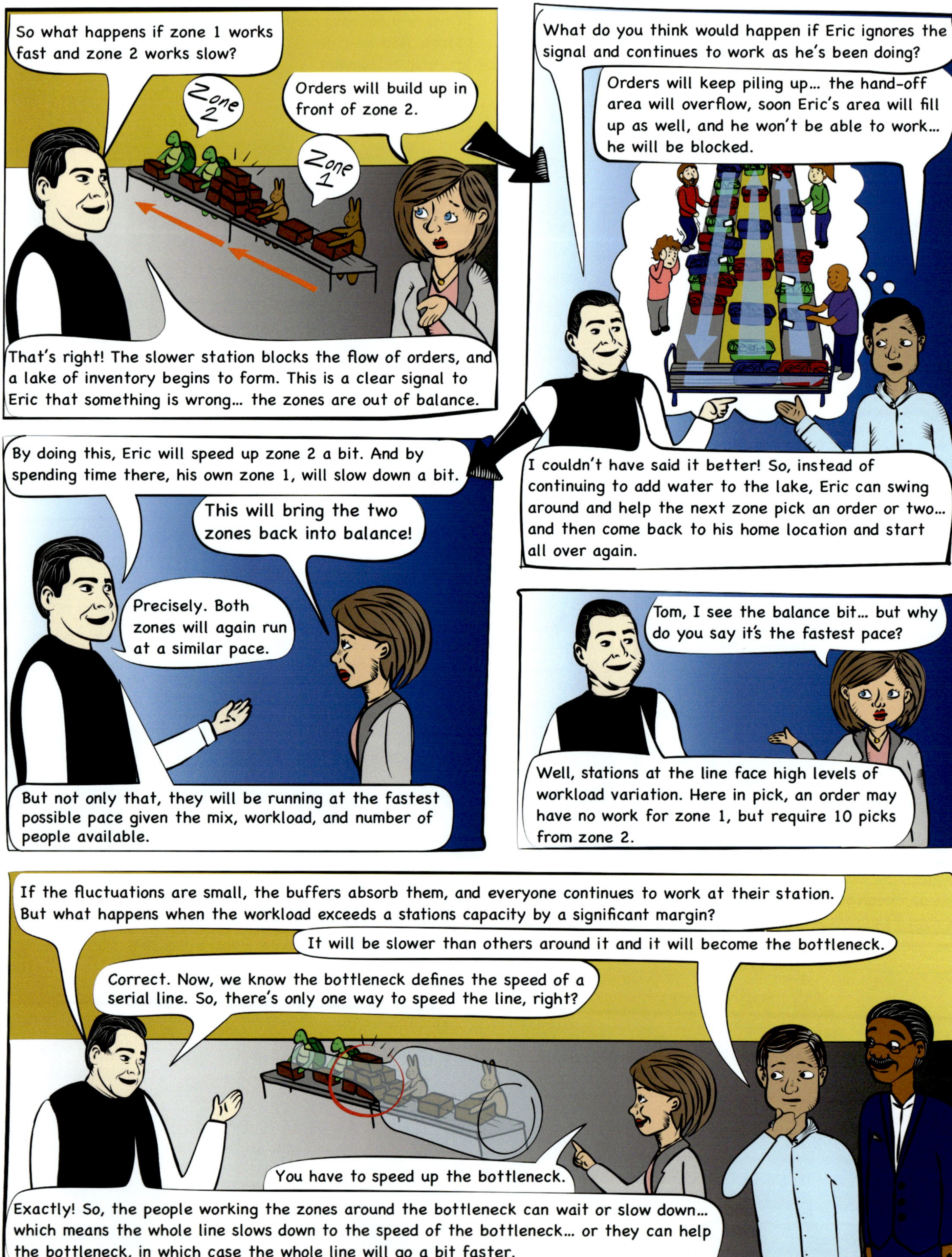

So what happens if zone 1 works fast and zone 2 works slow?
Zone 2
Orders will build up in front of zone 2.
Zone 1
That's right! The slower station blocks the flow of orders, and a lake of inventory begins to form. This is a clear signal to Eric that something is wrong... the zones are out of balance.
What do you think would happen if Eric ignores the signal and continues to work as he's been doing?
Orders will keep piling up... the hand-off area will overflow, soon Eric's area will fill up as well, and he won't be able to work... he will be blocked.
I couldn't have said it better! So, instead of continuing to add water to the lake, Eric can swing around and help the next zone pick an order or two... and then come back to his home location and start all over again.
By doing this, Eric will speed up zone 2 a bit. And by spending time there, his own zone 1, will slow down a bit.
This will bring the two zones back into balance!
Precisely. Both zones will again run at a similar pace.
But not only that, they will be running at the fastest possible pace given the mix, workload, and number of people available.
Tom, I see the balance bit... but why do you say it's the fastest pace?
Well, stations at the line face high levels of workload variation. Here in pick, an order may have no work for zone 1, but require 10 picks from zone 2.
If the fluctuations are small, the buffers absorb them, and everyone continues to work at their station. But what happens when the workload exceeds a stations capacity by a significant margin?
It will be slower than others around it and it will become the bottleneck.
Correct. Now, we know the bottleneck defines the speed of a serial line. So, there's only one way to speed the line, right?
You have to speed up the bottleneck.
Exactly! So, the people working the zones around the bottleneck can wait or slow down... which means the whole line slows down to the speed of the bottleneck... or they can help the bottleneck, in which case the whole line will go a bit faster.

And Help Your Neighbor makes it easier for people to choose to help the bottleneck. Got it!
Yeah. Help Your Neighbor balances the workload between stations while maximizing the speed of the line... and best of all, it does it autonomously.
What do you mean?
In the old days, we could only handle imbalances by having someone actively manage the line. "Hey, you, go over there! You, come here!".
Maybe those are old days for you...
Right. The problem is the reaction time is too slow. It takes a while for the manager to notice the problem, figure out what to do, and communicate the change, and even longer for people to rotate to new positions.
It does seem awfully slow...
And that's not all. Since the problem is now big, it takes a while to solve, and more time to be sure it's gone. And then the manager has to think about taking action again, and communicate it to the people... and they have to move back to their old locations... Too much time! Think about it. Now we're running at a 32s takt, but during Christmas, the line can reach a 6s takt. Say we take 15 minutes to identify and react to a problem. What would happen?
That's... 150 orders, if my math is correct. They will pile up quickly!
That's right! If we don't react immediately, the line will soon be blocked.
Or you need bigger buffers... a longer line.
Yes, but we don't have space. Besides, someone would need to watch the line all the time. Both add cost... and are unnecessary. These are smart people at the line. If we give them a way to see the problem —it's flooding here... it's drying up there- they will step in and do the right thing at the right time.
Hmm... I guess you're right.

So we set up visual cues, we teach people what to look for—tubs piling up there or the line emptying out here—and we teach them what to do... go help the neighbor station and then come back and start again. And they do this dance every time there's an imbalance.
And this works with your holiday crew? It seems complicated for the short training they get, no?
The Rules
Blocked
No Work
Well, the rules are simple. When you run out of work, go help the station upstream to make some more work for yourself. When you're blocked, go help the station downstream to open space on the line for the work you complete at your station.
Hmm... you make it sound so obvious and easy.
Don't get me wrong, we still struggle with it in some areas, but it's usually because the signals are less obvious, or there's some hurdle for people to provide help easily.
It's good to hear there are things you have not figured out yet.
Believe me, there's plenty. The more you improve, the more you find things that need improving.
One last point... relying on a manager to move people around means we only tackle imbalances when they get big. As a result, orders move through the line in large waves, creating workload imbalances all over the place. Not at all what we want!
People are smart. Let them contribute. They don't need to be actively managed if we give them a systemic way of identifying and reacting to the issues they face.
This is such a different view on people... how can I bring this to my company?
Help Your Neighbor systemically solves the problem of autonomously assigning labor to where it is needed the most at any point in time. It eliminates the need for active management of the line and ensures we tackle imbalances when they are small. In this way, we get small ripples instead of large waves in the flow of orders.

It seems to me this is similar to your kanban... it's a signal that some action is needed.
There you go. It's simply good visual control. Make clear and visible what the standard is, so it's obvious when you are not achieving it and action is needed. In this case, an empty or overflowing buffer signals that someone needs help.
Do you use Help Your Neighbor only in pick?
No, it's active between all stations on the line, and even with support stations in some cases.

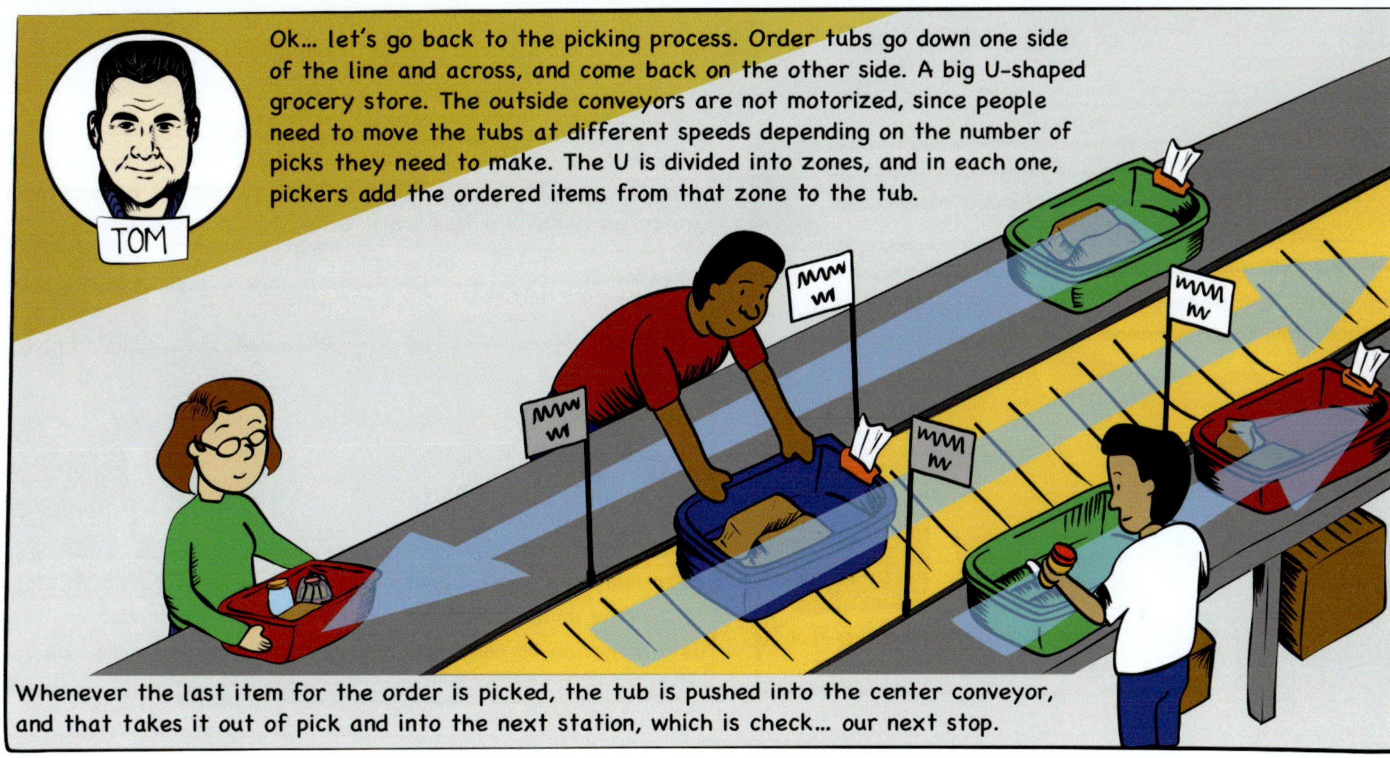
TOM
Ok... let's go back to the picking process. Order tubs go down one side of the line and across, and come back on the other side. A big U-shaped grocery store. The outside conveyors are not motorized, since people need to move the tubs at different speeds depending on the number of picks they need to make. The U is divided into zones, and in each one, pickers add the ordered items from that zone to the tub.
Whenever the last item for the order is picked, the tub is pushed into the center conveyor, and that takes it out of pick and into the next station, which is check... our next stop.

Stable Flow & Leveled Workload

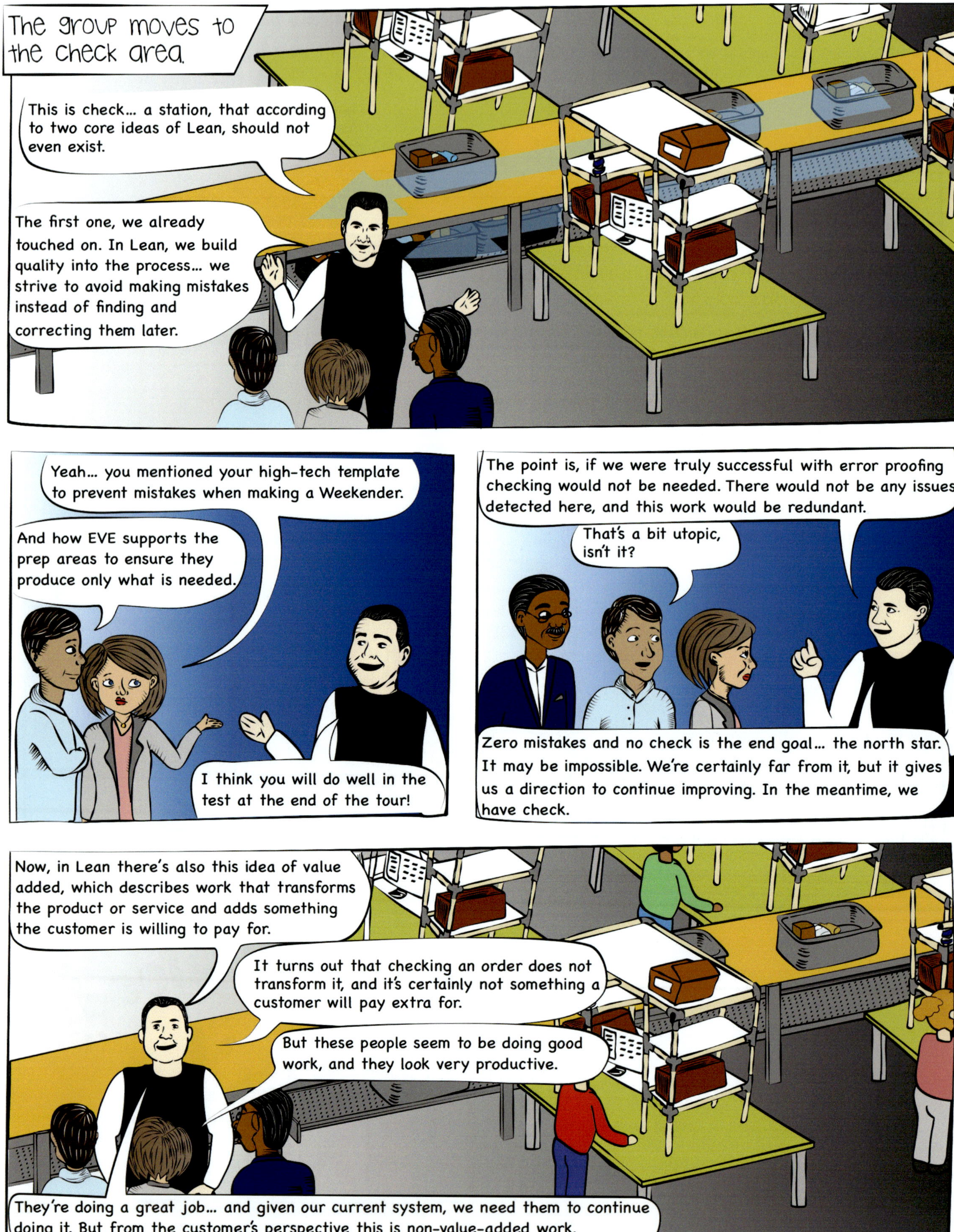
The group moves to the check area.
This is check... a station, that according to two core ideas of Lean, should not even exist.
The first one, we already touched on. In Lean, we build quality into the process... we strive to avoid making mistakes instead of finding and correcting them later.
Yeah... you mentioned your high-tech template to prevent mistakes when making a Weekender.
And how EVE supports the prep areas to ensure they produce only what is needed.
I think you will do well in the test at the end of the tour!
The point is, if we were truly successful with error proofing checking would not be needed. There would not be any issues detected here, and this work would be redundant.
That's a bit utopic, isn't it?
Zero mistakes and no check is the end goal... the north star. It may be impossible. We're certainly far from it, but it gives us a direction to continue improving. In the meantime, we have check.
Now, in Lean there's also this idea of value added, which describes work that transforms the product or service and adds something the customer is willing to pay for.
It turns out that checking an order does not transform it, and it's certainly not something a customer will pay extra for.
But these people seem to be doing good work, and they look very productive.
They're doing a great job... and given our current system, we need them to continue doing it. But from the customer's perspective this is non-value-added work.

Let's try this out... Mike, let's say you call us to place an order: "Hello, I'm interested in one of those Weekenders." And the person on the phone says "Sounds good. For $100, I'll ship it to you, but for $105, I'll make sure it has the right items in it." Which would you order?
I probably wouldn't! When I place an order, I expect it to have all the right items in it. Why should I pay more to ensure that happens?
Exactly! No one is willing to pay extra to get what they ordered.
So you're saying that checking is not a value-added activity, but it's necessary. Without it, you would ship wrong orders to customers.
A small percent yes, and in our world, that's much worse than doing some extra work.
So check is necessary but does not add any value. As with other activities, we try to minimize the effort needed to run it so we can operate as cheaply as possible.
That makes sense. Since it doesn't add any value, its whole cost is a direct hit on the bottom line.
That's right. So, we have optimized the station and process.
Let me demonstrate...
What we do is remove a tub from the line and place it here on the table. We then scan the bar code on the order, which will bring it up here on...
...EVE, of course!
Paesano Bread; Sour Cream Coffee Cake; 2 Ortiz Tuna tins; one pound of Parm; Magic Brownie
Where else? And EVE is going to look at the list of things that should be in that order.
Then, I'm going to scan each item as I move them to the empty tub I also have here on the table.
Looks easy...
Each time I scan an item, EVE will confirm if it should be in the order. If it should not, it will give me an error message.
Paesano Bread; Sour Cream Coffee Cake; 2 Ortiz Tuna tins; one pound of Parm; Magic Brownie
And if you have two or three units of the same item?
EVE will count each scan as one and keep a running total to compare it to the quantity requested.

Now, when the tub I took from the line is empty, I tell EVE I'm done. At this point, I don't know whether everything required by the order is there. So I press the 'Done' button to tell EVE I've scanned all the items. She then compares what was scanned against the order to see if anything is missing.
Paesano Bread: ✓
Sour Cream Coffee Cake: ✓
2 Ortiz Tuna tins: ✓✓
one pound of Parm: ✓
Magic Brownie: ??
You're missing the brownie!
Since the order is not correct, a screen pops up to give EVE more information about what's wrong. The brownie is broken, or the bar code did not scan, or it's missing.
The mistake condition will be recorded... and guess what we use that for.
To reduce future mistakes?
Right! So, check is a non-value-added station that is trying to work itself out of a job by giving us information we can use to reduce the need for its existence.
That's kind of cool...
It is, isn't it? Now, if everything is ok when I tell EVE I'm done, she's going to say, "good job, put that tub back on the line".
It's good to go!
Now, when we first started doing check with the bar code scanner, we were using colors on the screen. But when I'm checking, my focus is on the product and the scanner, not the screen.
So people would make mistakes in checking?
They could, if they got into a rhythm of passing correct products into the second tub... or they had to slow down to lift their gaze to the screen for every scan. Neither of those resulted in a good process or provided a good experience for our team members.
But you made a big investment and improvement by introducing scanners, no? That was not good enough?
Well, one of the central concepts of Lean is continuous improvement. There's always a better way, so you're constantly looking to build a better solution on top of the improvement you just made. Every improvement is just a steppingstone for the next one.
That's a nice way to put it.

So, when we realized our solution was not fool-proof and there were further opportunities in productivity, we started looking for ways to improve it.
If you believe there's always a better way, it's only natural to look for the next step as soon as you're done with the previous improvement... interesting!
We found a form of visual management that is not visual at all... audio. So, in every station, right above your head, there's a little speaker.
When you scan something that's supposed to be in the order, you hear a happy sound. When you scan an incorrect item, you hear a sad sound... ehh, ehh, ehh.
WRONG
This audio feedback tells the operator something's not right.
And then you look at the screen...
That's right... It draws my attention, and I look up and deal with the issue. But I don't have to do it for every item.
Furthermore, if I scan something in a glass container that needs to be corrugated in cardboard, I hear breaking glass... which reminds me to corrugate it.
You scan it, and the speaker gives you the signal because EVE knows this item requires corrugation.
Exactly... EVE again works in the background to support the process.
I'm everywhere!
So, I scan everything, and I hit the done button. If all is well, I hear applause... yeahhh... and I put the order back on the line.
Applause!!
Aawww!!
If there's something wrong, I hear 'awwww'. And that tells me to put this order in the mistakes area.
So you take orders with mistakes off-line?
Yes, a different area deals exclusively with correcting the order before putting it back on the line. There are many different types of mistakes, and some may take a long time to solve. We may even have to talk to the customer.

So, this is our check station... even though it's not value added, we have worked hard to make it as effective and efficient as possible.
Check Station #3
And similar to other stations, I don't need to know anything about the order or the products to do the job well. EVE gives me the feedback I need.
You're right. Only a small amount of training would be needed for you to be effective at check. However, posted right here is the standard operating procedure for working at this station.
In a few pages, it provides all the information you need. It even includes a sheet explaining how long it should take to do the work... what your cycle time should be.
Check Station
I can see how that could be useful.
So, even if you're new and unsure about the work, we've got you covered. We have the printed documentation right here. You can follow it step by step. After doing it a handful of times, you'll be proficient... and the workstation design reinforces doing the right thing.
Check Station #3
Tom, for a station that should not exist, check is awesome... even if it's not adding any value.
Check Station #3
Thanks! Let's move on to the next process.

The group proceeds to the Assembly area
Here we assemble the rest of the gift boxes and baskets. We have multiple assembly stations, so we can add people to match the speed of the line.
Earlier, you saw how we make a Weekender over at Hot Pod. If you order a standard recipe Weekender, it will get made there. If you customize your Weekender, or if you order a lower volume gift box, we will make it in this area.
Empty crates
Right! High volume efficiency there... low volume complexity here. Got it!
That's right. These work stations are designed to make any gift box or basket. Hot pod is built for efficiency... assembly is designed for flexibility.
So, here's an example... the items have been picked and checked, and they arrive at the station in a tub with their work order. Right?
Yes, plenty of products in the tub. But different from Hot Pod... they were doing their own picking there, no?
That's right. There, we assign high volume gift boxes that require only a few items. That allows us to have stations where everything needed is within easy reach.
If you followed Hot Pod's approach, each station here would have every item you sell...
Which is physically impossible. So instead, items arrive in a tub.
And the work here is to arrange them in a box or basket to make the gift the customer wants.
Makes sense so far...
Now, we have about 250 different gift boxes and baskets on sale at any given time. Each one has multiple variations. And on top of that, they can all be customized any way the client wants.
So, how do you train someone to make all these in a day or two?
Impossible!
Exactly... you don't! So again, we need a systemic solution.

Here we have...
...sweet EVE!
Right! So, when I scan the work order, EVE brings up pictures of how to assemble the required gift box.
It shows the bottom, middle, and top layers. It also tells me the container I need.
Done
Bottom
Middle
Top
So all I have to do is get the container, put a little filling material inside and add the bottom items. Follow that with more filling material and the brownies. A little more filling, and then the card on top. That's it.
When I hit done, the gift box label prints out.
Seems easy enough. I see this bar at the top of the screen has been filling since you scanned the work order... I assume it's a timer?
0:06
Correct... and it's the time for this specific gift box.
I was wondering that... if it was an average time it would not be very useful feedback, would it?
That's right.
EVE supports the team member by providing the whole standard operating procedure... how to make the gift box and an estimate of how long it should take.
I love how EVE is integrated into the process. If I'm working here, it gives me instant feedback on whether I'm doing a good job.
Well, people do better work when they can tell how they are doing, don't you think? The images help them judge the quality of their work, and the timer helps them judge their speed.

It's another example of empowering the workers.
Yes... remember we started by saying our commitment to enriching lives isn't just to the customer, it's also to staff members. And it's not just to permanent staff, it's also to the people who are only here during the holidays.

We designed all these systems to empower and support them. To make it easier to do the right thing, and harder to do the wrong thing.
Impressive!
So that's it for assembly... we have only a couple more stations to see.

Zingerman's

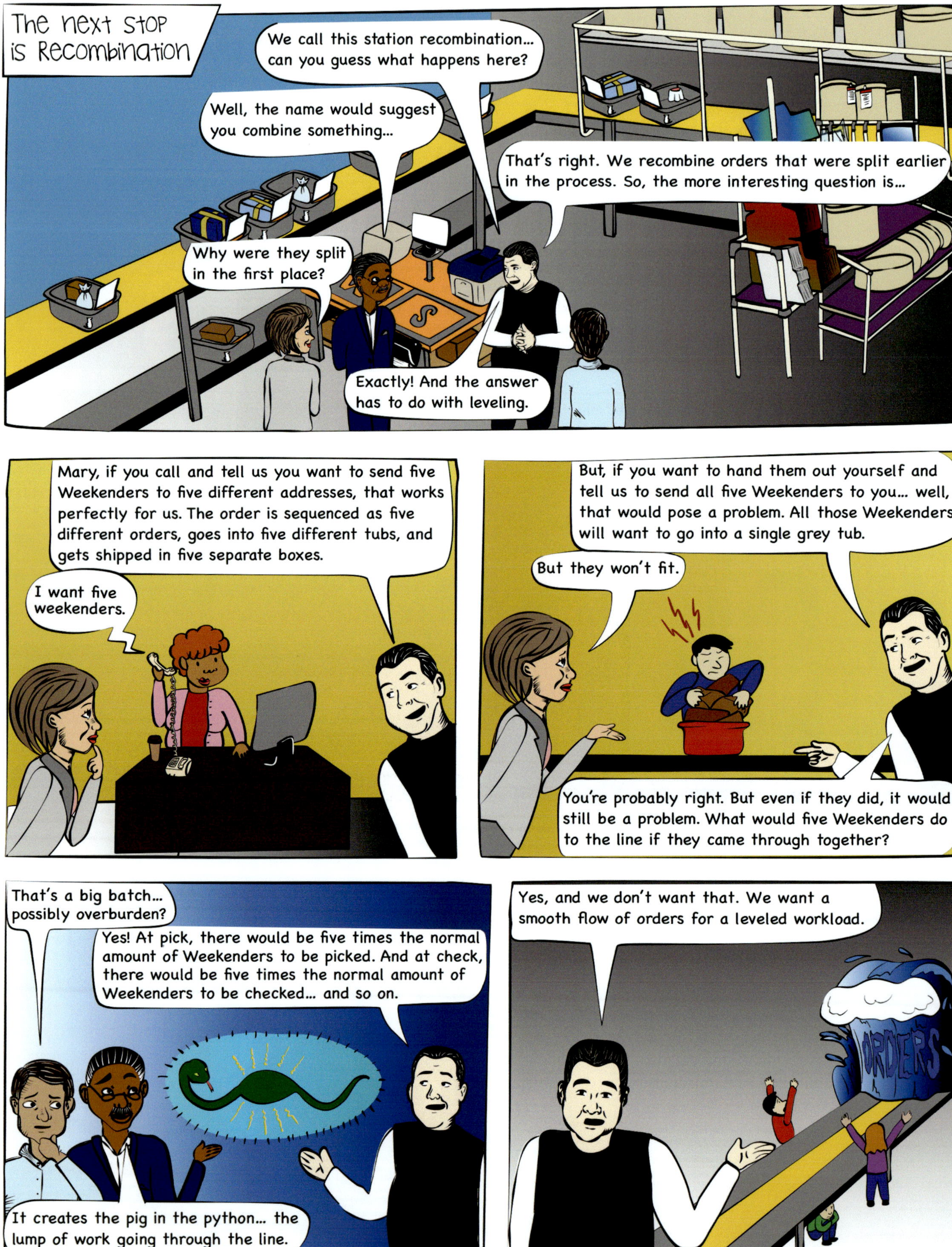
The next stop is Recombination
We call this station recombination... can you guess what happens here?
Well, the name would suggest you combine something...
That's right. We recombine orders that were split earlier in the process. So, the more interesting question is...
Why were they split in the first place?
Exactly! And the answer has to do with leveling.
Mary, if you call and tell us you want to send five Weekenders to five different addresses, that works perfectly for us. The order is sequenced as five different orders, goes into five different tubs, and gets shipped in five separate boxes.
I want five weekenders.
But, if you want to hand them out yourself and tell us to send all five Weekenders to you... well, that would pose a problem. All those Weekenders will want to go into a single grey tub.
But they won't fit.
You're probably right. But even if they did, it would still be a problem. What would five Weekenders do to the line if they came through together?
That's a big batch... possibly overburden?
Yes! At pick, there would be five times the normal amount of Weekenders to be picked. And at check, there would be five times the normal amount of Weekenders to be checked... and so on.
It creates the pig in the python... the lump of work going through the line.
Yes, and we don't want that. We want a smooth flow of orders for a leveled workload.
ORDERS

So when EVE is preparing the schedule, we tell her: "If you see multiple gift boxes in one order, break it up so they go around the line separately."
And if you break them apart... at some point, you have to recombine them to ship them together.
And that's precisely what happens here.
So how do you match the orders? I would assume EVE helps here as well.
If you need help... I'm there!
Of course! The process is very simple. We present the order to EVE, and she tells us what to do.
Don't worry, this is a one-part order... and here you go, replace the work order by the packing slip.
Zingerman's mail order
And of course, the packing slip is printed only as needed.
Of course! EVE gives us only the packing slip for the scanned order. When that's in the tub, we can send the order down the line.
Beep
Now, if it's a multi-part order, we scan it, and EVE checks again.
Wait... there's another part to this order. Go ahead and put it on the shelf.
So the staff member puts it on the shelf until the other parts show up.
EVE knows everything!
Yes, she's pretty smart.
As other parts of the order show up, they go onto the shelf as well. When the last of the five Weekenders comes around, EVE tells us to get them all, and it prints the packing slip... our signal that the order is ready to continue down the line.

So, recombination is pretty straight forward, but it gives me the chance to tell one of my favorite stories about our people focus. When we first designed the recombination area, we wanted to divide the workload equally between both sides of the line.
EVEN
ODD
Makes sense... you have two stations on either side.
Seems logical no? So, we came up with what we thought was a clever solution... this side will deal with odd numbers, and the other side with even ones.
Each one of these orders has a number, so this would guarantee an equal division of labor.
Simple and clean. Seems like a great solution indeed.
It does, doesn't it? We were very proud of ourselves.
TOM
Everything worked fine until the first day of peak holiday volume. We had all these people on the line and all these orders coming at us, but the line was failing. We came over to recombination... and it looked like it had exploded. There were tubs everywhere. So we asked the staff, "what happened? what's going on? You do the odd orders, and they do the even ones..." They looked at each other, and after some time, someone said: "we're not sure what odd and even are."
ODD??
EVEN??
Ok... not what I expected.
Neither did we. Now, there are three ways we can process this information. One is to say... "you can't hire good people anymore."
I know a few people who would say that...
It's not true, but it's one conclusion we can come to.
A second thing we can do is complain about the educational system... "it's not preparing the people we need!"
It's certainly a shame on our schools!
EDUCATIONAL SYSTEM
IN
OUT
Probably true. But complaining about it does not solve our problem.

The third option is to recognize that the process we chose did not serve the individuals doing the work. The people did not fail, they are not the problem... it was the process that failed them.
The people are not the problem, the process failed them! I wish I had recorded that for some people at my company.
Wait! Certainly, if you had better people... hmm... people better prepared by their schools, things would have gone well.
Maybe... but the point is that no matter how clever we think the solution is, if it does not allow the individual to succeed, it's not a good solution.
This, I would say is the difference between applying Lean as a set of tools without a philosophy behind it, and the way we try to apply it here. The individual comes first, and the process must help them succeed.
If the process does not serve the individual, it's not the right process. That blows me away!
It changes the perspective entirely! Can I ask how you solved the issue?
Well, we sort orders only on one side of the line. The other side deals with single tub orders. Simpler, and it helps with space as well.
There you go... also an elegant approach.
Yes! It turns out there were several clever solutions to feel proud of. Some simply serve the people better than others.
Which gets me to the other thing we learned... if we had involved people in the area in designing the process, we would not have proposed a solution that did not work for them. We just weren't at that level of engagement yet.
So, engage the people to design a process that helps them succeed. Sounds like a simple...hmm... recipe? That's the term you use, no?
Engage people
Design / improve
Successful Process
Easier said than done sometimes, but it has certainly worked for us. And the best thing is that it helps people develop and grow. So, that's it for recombination... next stop is pack and ship at the end of the line.

The group moves to the packing and shipping area
First, let's take a quick look at pack... anyone wants to guess what happens here?
This is a hard one... I'm going to say you pack orders.
Perceptive, Mary!
Packing is a game of 3D Tetris. We look at the items in the order tub and decide what's the best box size to deliver the items safely to the customer while minimizing shipping cost.
However, this is Tetris in expert mode. All kinds of combinations of products come down the line, and we have over 12 box types to choose from.
And choosing the wrong box costs you money.
Right. If it's bigger than we need, we pay more in shipping. If the items don't fit, the packer has to start again. This results in lost labor and may slow down the line.
I can't wait for the clever solution that helps packers make the right decision... you have one, right?
Well, we have one that supports packers in making the right decision some times. Do you see that wall at the end of the line?
The one where all the containers are hanging?
That's the one. About half the orders we ship include a gift box or basket assembled in a standard container. That wall has a sample of each one, color coded with the outer box it goes into.

So... as a packer, if I get a gift box or basket, the wall will tell me which box I need to use, right?
Yes! I think you're ready to jump in and help us get some orders out the door.
Anyway, this information is in the SOP as a matrix, but people hardly use it because it's complicated and time consuming.
Seems like another solution that did not serve well the individuals using it.
Indeed. So, we tried to make things more visible.
Interesting approach... for half your orders. What about the rest?
We're still working on that. For now, we rely on the individual's judgement. But at least for half of the orders, we reduced the time it takes to choose the right box. This has made the job better for the people working here and significantly increased productivity.
Another win-win situation.
Yes, it is!
Now, there's one more thing I want to show you here. Remember takt? The rhythm that defines the speed of the line.
Yes, the intended heartbeat based on customer orders...
Beep... Beep... Beep...
Exactly. In the human body, I can determine the pulse rate in different places. The same is true for the line. I can choose any point and count the number of orders passing by. If I then divide the time by the number of orders observed, I get the cycle time at that point and can compare it to the takt.
That's true on average...

Anyway, we will see in a bit that the last station before the orders go into the truck is shipping. One day we were running slower than expected, so we investigated and found that shipping was buried in work and could not keep up.
About 30 minutes later, they were standing around twiddling their thumbs. Some 30 minutes after that, they were buried again. And this pattern seemed to repeat.
Lots of variability… I guess from these waves of work you keep talking about.
Yes, so we took a few pulse readings at the corner between pack and ship and sure enough, the cycle times were oscillating. That meant the problem was not being created by the shipping station. We took another set of readings between recombination and pack and found a fairly stable flow.
So the problem was originating at pack.
That's right… we found the point of cause. Now, there's a concept in Lean called Genchi Genbutsu or Go See, which means you go and develop a personal relationship with the work.
Go to the Gemba and experience the work…
So I came here, took a position at a station, and tried to pack some boxes. Now, I'm an owner here, so I'm supposed to know how things work…
You don't want to look foolish.
Especially in front of the holiday staff that have been here for only a few days and are already doing a much better job than I can.

So, on the bottom line here, I can choose from a number of orders. At any given time, there's about three tubs I can reach.
So, being the guy that's supposed to know how things work, which order do you think I choose?
Easy
Easy
Hard
The easiest one... that's what I would choose.
If I see one that I know how to pack, you better believe I'm going to take that one.
I bring it up to the table, pack it, and put it on the top conveyor to go to shipping. I'm feeling pretty good.
I look down again and still have three to choose from. What do I grab next?
Another easy one...
Easy
Hard
Hard
Of course. And this went on for about 30 minutes. After that, there were no easy ones left. That's when it occurred to me that everyone working here was doing the same thing.
Everyone was cherry picking the easy orders.
That's right! The problem was that we were letting people choose... and most of us, if given the choice, will do what's easiest. Not because we're bad people, just because it's easier. But at some point, the harder orders had to be processed.
Take Me
And that was causing the periods of slow cycle time...
Exactly. So, to eliminate the variability, we had to remove the choice. What we did was Velcro to the side of the line a little label saying: 'Take Me'.
So now people take whatever tote is sitting on top of the label? No need to decide, so no cherry picking.
Yes. The good news is that sometimes the order is an easy one. The bad news is that sometimes it's not. In the end, we all get about the same number of hard and easy orders, and it levels out. But the ultimate good news is we eliminated the variability causing the waves of flood or famine at shipping.

And all of that with a simple card...
Cheap and easy. Many times, the best solutions do not require money or sophistication. It's just about understanding the problem well enough to know what to do about it.
That's great!

Ok, so once the box is packed, it goes onto the top conveyor and on to shipping, where a destination label, with the information the carrier needs, is applied.
Looks like another one of your custom-built stations.
It is. We've designed it and the process to be as simple as possible... always keeping the user in mind.

Basically, you take the box off the line, set it on the scale, and scan the bar codes. Eve prints the right label. You apply it to the box and place it on the bottom conveyor... and off to the truck it goes.
Simple and straight forward. My kind of station.
Mine too. It's one of the few places they let me work during the holidays... but don't tell anyone... remember, I'm supposed to know how things work around here.
That's it for the line. There's just one more thing I want to show you.

OPEN IMMEDIATELY!
OPEN IMMEDIATELY!

The group goes to the backstock area, where the hiring stations are set up
The last stop in this tour is really the beginning—hiring.
I've been wondering how you bring so many people in. The number of interviews, checks, and paperwork must be a nightmare.
It was. Then we learned that Lean could be used in other areas beyond moving product and fulfilling orders. But before I explain, can you tell me how you hire people at your company?
We advertise for the positions, have an initial screening based on submitted documents, narrow down the pool, and then bring people in for interviews. Depending on the position, there may be multiple rounds of this before we select who we want and put out offers.
That's how we used to do it. We would issue an open casting call... "we're hiring", and 2000 people would line up outside in October in Michigan for six or eight hours. Worse than buying tickets for the UM vs Ohio State game.
But it would be fairly cold, no?
It could be... definitively not the best time to be outside, but unfortunately, our process imposed that experience on a lot of these folks.
After all the waiting, we would 'interview' them. Imagine spending six hours meeting a person every five minutes. How good do you think the conversation and resulting notes would be?
Not good... that would be one hard day.
Yes, it was hard to remain engaged. In the best of cases, the notes were pretty cryptic. But after a few hours, they settled into a set of five or six observations... 'Seemed nice' or 'Smiled'.
Vague impressions are not a good way to hire.
Did I get the job?
76 down... 20 more to go.
Not at all. Besides, after all that pain and suffering, the individuals would leave not knowing if they had a job. And we were left with 2000 applications with cryptic notes written in the margins, and we were expected to make hiring decisions... because that's how we always did it.

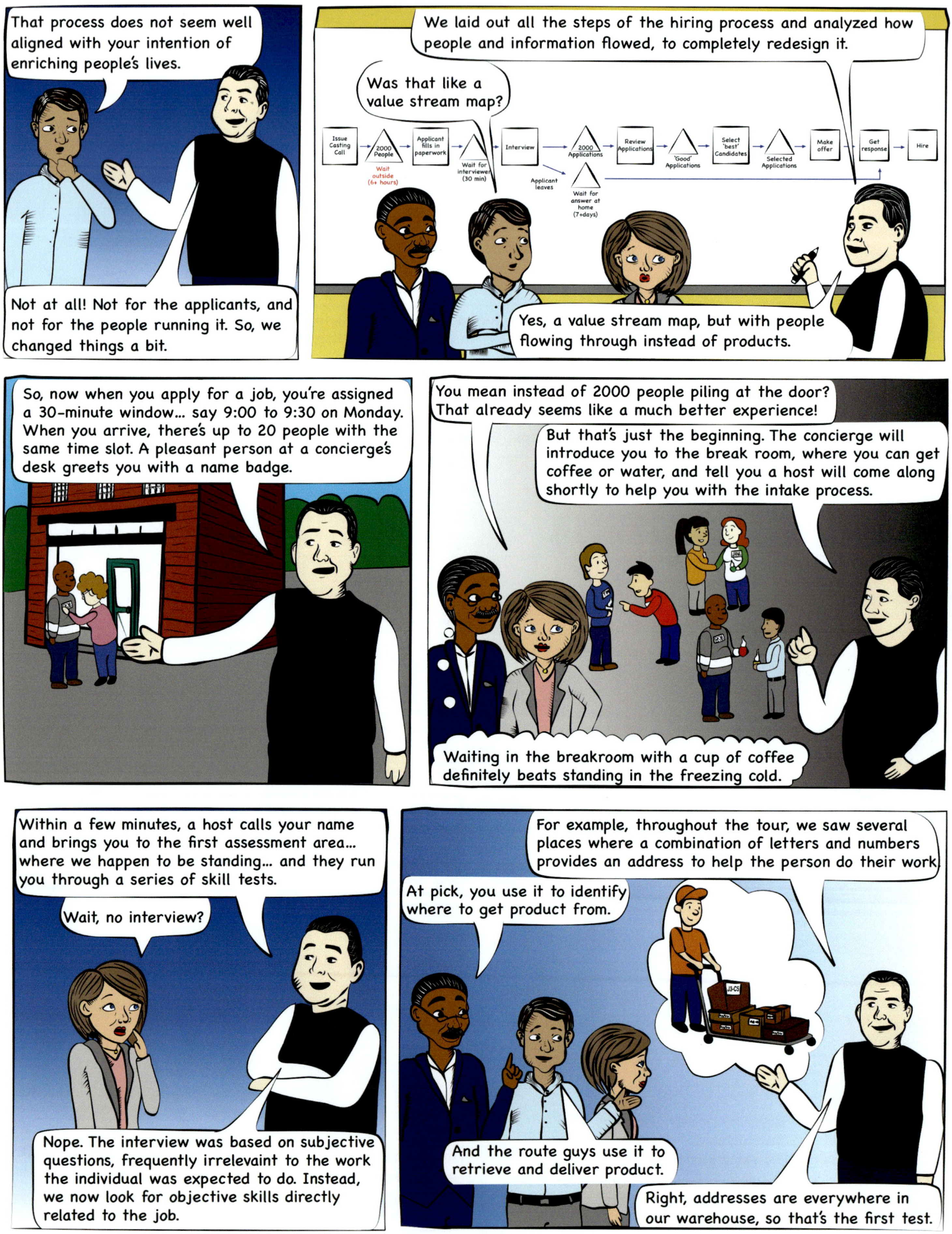

That process does not seem well aligned with your intention of enriching people's lives.
Not at all! Not for the applicants, and not for the people running it. So, we changed things a bit.
We laid out all the steps of the hiring process and analyzed how people and information flowed, to completely redesign it.
Was that like a value stream map?
Issue Casting Call
2000 People
Wait outside (6+ hours)
Applicant fills in paperwork
Wait for interviewer (30 min)
Interview
2000 Applications
Applicant leaves
Wait for answer at home (7+days)
Review Applications
'Good' Applications
Select 'best' Candidates
Selected Applications
Make offer
Get response
Hire
Yes, a value stream map, but with people flowing through instead of products.
So, now when you apply for a job, you're assigned a 30-minute window... say 9:00 to 9:30 on Monday. When you arrive, there's up to 20 people with the same time slot. A pleasant person at a concierge's desk greets you with a name badge.
You mean instead of 2000 people piling at the door? That already seems like a much better experience!
But that's just the beginning. The concierge will introduce you to the break room, where you can get coffee or water, and tell you a host will come along shortly to help you with the intake process.
Waiting in the breakroom with a cup of coffee definitely beats standing in the freezing cold.
Within a few minutes, a host calls your name and brings you to the first assessment area... where we happen to be standing... and they run you through a series of skill tests.
Wait, no interview?
Nope. The interview was based on subjective questions, frequently irrelevaint to the work the individual was expected to do. Instead, we now look for objective skills directly related to the job.
For example, throughout the tour, we saw several places where a combination of letters and numbers provides an address to help the person do their work.
At pick, you use it to identify where to get product from.
And the route guys use it to retrieve and deliver product.
Right, addresses are everywhere in our warehouse, so that's the first test.

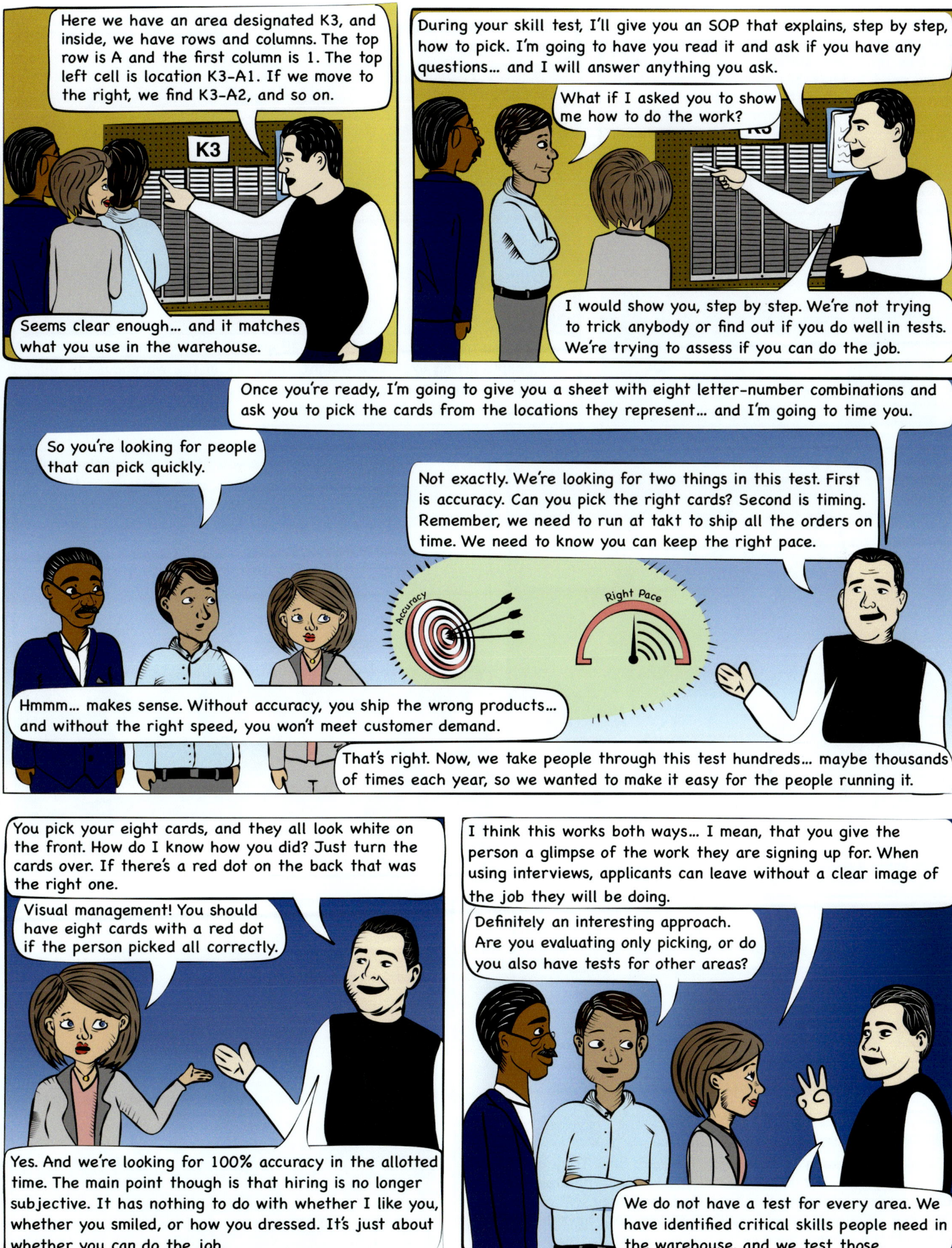
Here we have an area designated K3, and inside, we have rows and columns. The top row is A and the first column is 1. The top left cell is location K3-A1. If we move to the right, we find K3-A2, and so on.
K3
Seems clear enough... and it matches what you use in the warehouse.
During your skill test, I'll give you an SOP that explains, step by step, how to pick. I'm going to have you read it and ask if you have any questions... and I will answer anything you ask.
What if I asked you to show me how to do the work?
I would show you, step by step. We're not trying to trick anybody or find out if you do well in tests. We're trying to assess if you can do the job.
Once you're ready, I'm going to give you a sheet with eight letter-number combinations and ask you to pick the cards from the locations they represent... and I'm going to time you.
So you're looking for people that can pick quickly.
Not exactly. We're looking for two things in this test. First is accuracy. Can you pick the right cards? Second is timing. Remember, we need to run at takt to ship all the orders on time. We need to know you can keep the right pace.
Accuracy
Right Pace
Hmmm... makes sense. Without accuracy, you ship the wrong products... and without the right speed, you won't meet customer demand.
That's right. Now, we take people through this test hundreds... maybe thousands of times each year, so we wanted to make it easy for the people running it.
You pick your eight cards, and they all look white on the front. How do I know how you did? Just turn the cards over. If there's a red dot on the back that was the right one.
Visual management! You should have eight cards with a red dot if the person picked all correctly.
Yes. And we're looking for 100% accuracy in the allotted time. The main point though is that hiring is no longer subjective. It has nothing to do with whether I like you, whether you smiled, or how you dressed. It's just about whether you can do the job.
I think this works both ways... I mean, that you give the person a glimpse of the work they are signing up for. When using interviews, applicants can leave without a clear image of the job they will be doing.
Definitely an interesting approach. Are you evaluating only picking, or do you also have tests for other areas?
We do not have a test for every area. We have identified critical skills people need in the warehouse, and we test those.

Besides this one, we have two other assessments. One is for basic computer skills. You saw that most stations have a computer, so we need to know the person is comfortable enough with them to be effective.
Are you comfortable with computers?
I can see how that's important. You can't do much around here if you cannot talk to EVE.
20 lbs.
True! The last test involves lifting a 20-pound tote. Although we do not want people lifting excessive weight, the work in the warehouse is fairly physical. We need to know that the person can do it… and to Mary's point, that they want to do it as well.
So what happens after the three tests?
If you did well in all three, at the last 'station' they applaud you… because you have been hired! Simply passing these skills assessments means you got the job.
Only then, we have you fill out the employment paperwork. Not before… why waste your time and ours with paperwork that will not be needed if you don't get the job?
I have a job!
Seems so logical when put like that…
Now, if you struggle with any of the assessments, we're going to send you through the 'No Door'. Behind closed doors, there's a person that knows you were not successful at one or more test.
The person is going to thank you for your time. They are going to be very nice, but they will tell you we unfortunately cannot offer you a position at this time. And then they will allow you to leave through a secondary door so you don't have to parade through the public space.
Yet another example of putting the individual's well-being at the center of the process design.

Even if we do not hire you, you're still part of the community whose lives we want to enrich. We don't want you to feel embarrassed.
Anyway, this is how we do intake now. We run this process as often as we need to. If we get into the second week of Christmas and still need a few people, we run an intake round.
A much improved process indeed.
So that's it for the tour... unless you have any questions?
Tom, you have been using Lean management for several years. You showed us many improvements, and you obviously have an engaged workforce. But from a business perspective, can you share some results?
There have been many wins, like lower inventories, improved service quality, and reduced labor costs. For example, over a 10-year period demand has more than doubled, and yet the number of people we need in December has remained about the same. And, every holiday season has been smoother than the last, providing a better experience for everyone involved.
But perhaps most significantly, while doubling sales, we managed to remain in the same space... saving millions of dollars.
K3
Sales
Service Quality
Space
Inventory
Labor costs
While using Lean management
Let's leave my alter-ego to handle the visitors and go back to our story in 2004.
TOM

Part II
Management Learns to Think Lean

Begin with the big picture, then dive in

Ok! That should give you an idea of where ZMO is today. Now let's see how we got here. Remember Eduardo's first visit in 2004? We're going to pick up where we left it.

What happens when an area finishes its prep work?
People clean up and help another area. When all prep areas are done, they all go to the line.
Do you ever miscount?
Oh yeah, quite frequently.
What happens then?
Someone from the line steps away and prepares the missing items.
Steps away from the line... hmmm... and if you have too many of an item?
Depending on the product, we may leave it for the next day or take it apart.
Ok. And do gift boxes and baskets have some of these items you have to prep?
Some of them, yes.
So people do all the prep for say, bread, and then they go assemble gift boxes and baskets?
Basically yes, so we start with the bread needed for the boxes and baskets going out that day.
That way, people who finish in other areas can start with boxes and baskets as soon as possible.
Makes sense. So you prep a batch of bread and then use part of that to prep a batch of gift boxes. A double-cycle prep... hmmm... got it.

Throughout the visit, Eduardo was drawing and taking notes. At the time, we did not know what he was doing. In fact, he was drawing a rough current state value stream map... with just enough information to understand the process and identify main opportunities. Let's show you how his diagram is going. Rectangles represent processes and triangles inventory, and boy, did we have a boat load.

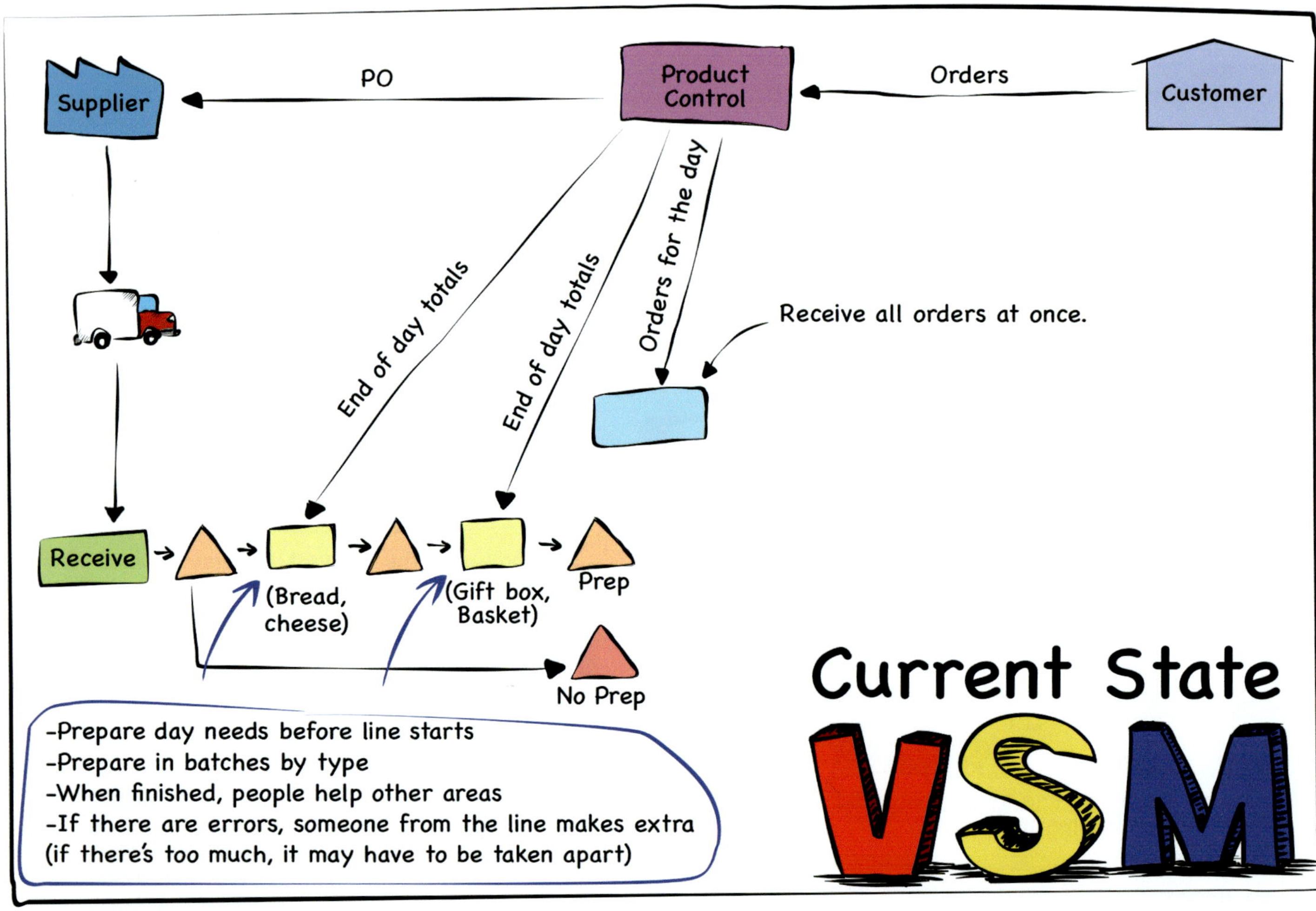

I imagine that on big days, the space can get tight. How many orders do you produce in a day?
Friday
X-mas
100
5000
Off season on a Friday, we can have fewer than 100 orders. On a peak day during Christmas we can have around 5000.
Wow! That's some variability. So you can have over 5000 prepped items in inventory?
Exactly! Can you imagine this place before line start during Christmas?
The night shift does all the prep work. By the end, they are struggling to find space.
TOM
That's an understatement! This past Christmas, we had to stock gift boxes in the office and the breakroom, and even then we could barely walk in the warehouse.
24
That happens about every two years, and then we move to a bigger location.
Yes, to a space that's too big for 50 weeks of the year.
We just took over the suites next door. That wall is coming down soon.
During those big days, is inventory in the way of people running the line? Do they struggle to find what they need?
Cheese Room
Yes! And Yes! Especially at the beginning of the day.
Particularly with gift boxes. The first ones go to racks by the line, but the rest go on any available flat surface! The day shift doesn't know where the night shift left them.
Any more questions on prep? The line is starting to run, so we can see the processes there.
Let's go.

Ok, so back to the Anchor... Work orders are printed in the office and come to the Anchor table. Here, they are placed in tubs and released to the line.
Are orders in any particular sequence?
Not really. They are usually printed in the order they were received, but sometimes they get mixed up.
Does it matter?
Probably, but don't worry about it for now.
Work Order
Pickers in each zone look at the work order and pick the products needed from their area.
Sorry... what information is on the order?
For the pickers, item code and quantity needed.
Just the code? How do they find the items?
Products are usually in the same location, and maps show where things go. You will see the boards when we get to dry goods. Plus, all products are labeled.
After being at a station for some time, it's not hard to find the items you need.
So, a combination of pickers knowing where things are, and labels and maps to help them. Got it!
Ok. Pickers on this side of the line pick bread, pastries, and gift boxes and baskets. Orders then continue to the outer conveyor on the other side of the line to get dry goods and cheese.
To Check
Filling order
Filling order
When all products for an order have been picked, the tub is pushed into the center conveyor and goes to check.
I was wondering why you had three conveyors. That's clever.
Yes, it gets orders quickly down the line.
That's true, but more importantly, you reduce wasted effort by preventing pickers from handling orders that are already complete.
That's an interesting point... I had not thought about it in that way.

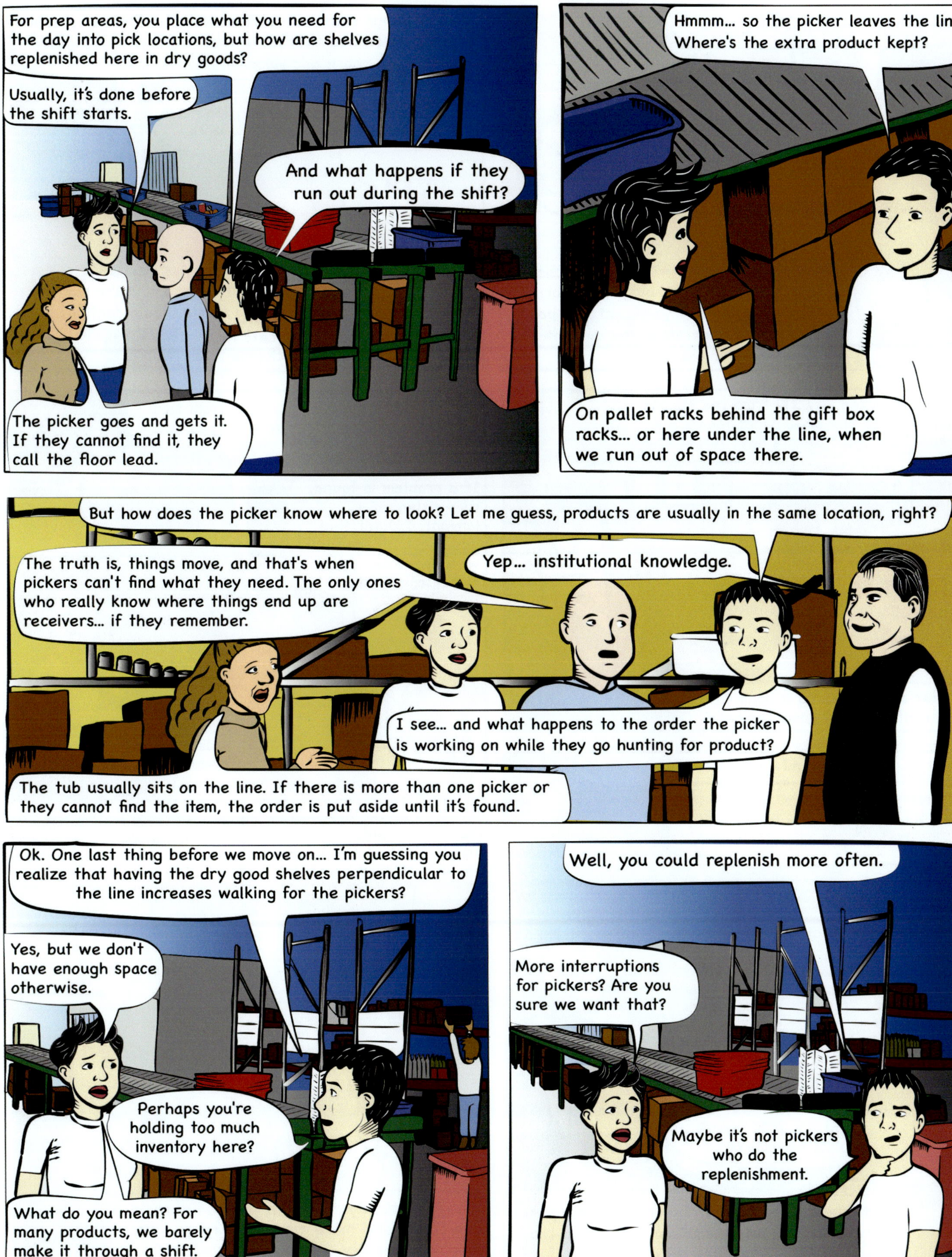
For prep areas, you place what you need for the day into pick locations, but how are shelves replenished here in dry goods?
Usually, it's done before the shift starts.
And what happens if they run out during the shift?
The picker goes and gets it. If they cannot find it, they call the floor lead.
Hmmm... so the picker leaves the line. Where's the extra product kept?
On pallet racks behind the gift box racks... or here under the line, when we run out of space there.
But how does the picker know where to look? Let me guess, products are usually in the same location, right?
The truth is, things move, and that's when pickers can't find what they need. The only ones who really know where things end up are receivers... if they remember.
Yep... institutional knowledge.
I see... and what happens to the order the picker is working on while they go hunting for product?
The tub usually sits on the line. If there is more than one picker or they cannot find the item, the order is put aside until it's found.
Ok. One last thing before we move on... I'm guessing you realize that having the dry good shelves perpendicular to the line increases walking for the pickers?
Yes, but we don't have enough space otherwise.
Perhaps you're holding too much inventory here?
What do you mean? For many products, we barely make it through a shift.
Well, you could replenish more often.
More interruptions for pickers? Are you sure we want that?
Maybe it's not pickers who do the replenishment.

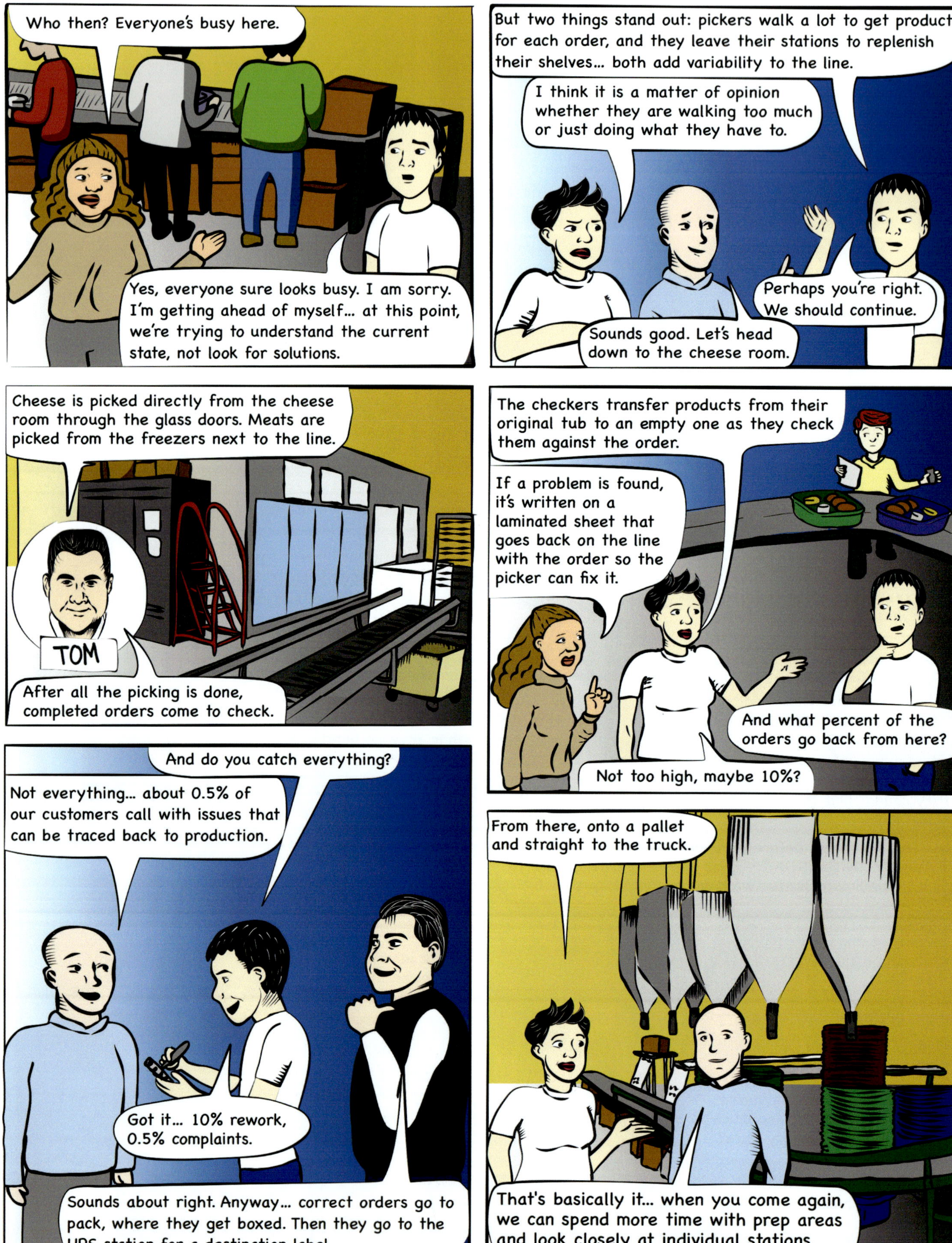

Who then? Everyone's busy here.
Yes, everyone sure looks busy. I am sorry. I'm getting ahead of myself... at this point, we're trying to understand the current state, not look for solutions.
But two things stand out: pickers walk a lot to get product for each order, and they leave their stations to replenish their shelves... both add variability to the line.
I think it is a matter of opinion whether they are walking too much or just doing what they have to.
Perhaps you're right. We should continue.
Sounds good. Let's head down to the cheese room.
Cheese is picked directly from the cheese room through the glass doors. Meats are picked from the freezers next to the line.
TOM
After all the picking is done, completed orders come to check.
The checkers transfer products from their original tub to an empty one as they check them against the order.
If a problem is found, it's written on a laminated sheet that goes back on the line with the order so the picker can fix it.
And what percent of the orders go back from here?
Not too high, maybe 10%?
And do you catch everything?
Not everything... about 0.5% of our customers call with issues that can be traced back to production.
Got it... 10% rework, 0.5% complaints.
Sounds about right. Anyway... correct orders go to pack, where they get boxed. Then they go to the UPS station for a destination label.
From there, onto a pallet and straight to the truck.
That's basically it... when you come again, we can spend more time with prep areas and look closely at individual stations.

What do you think? Can Lean help?
I see many opportunities... let's go back to the office and discuss how to proceed.
Office
We're excited to try this! What should we implement first?
That's great! But we should talk about a few things before you commit...
My research at UM is about developing Lean in places where people think it won't work. I chose to focus on companies dealing with high variability.
We got that box ticked!
Good. Now, I'm convinced Lean can help you. However, Toyota's methods apply to its situation. We will have to modify them to apply to yours.
I can see that. When Mo showed me the Toyota Way book, I was doubtful we could learn from it.
TOYOTA SOLUTIONS
ZINGERMAN'S PROBLEMS
We can certainly learn from the principles of the Toyota Way. But we will have to develop our own approach for ZMO.
This sounds even more interesting!
And we will discover what works by trying things out as we tackle the problems we identify.
When do we start?
Almost there...
There are three implications to this approach.
First, I know about Lean, but you're the experts in your process. We'll have to work together to develop a Lean approach that fits your organization.
Sounds good. I worry when outsiders think they have all the answers.

Second, the changes we make will not always work the first time. We will need perseverance to keep refining the solution until it works. And even then, improvement never really ends.
Sounds like a long journey, but I think this approach fits us. We've built everything here by trying new ideas and keeping the ones that work.
Great! This brings me to the third implication. Lean is about solving problems, which depends on surfacing them quickly. We need to develop a no-blame environment.
A what?
An environment where people are not penalized for failing. We will not be implementing Lean solutions, but rather, finding our way. We're going into uncharted territory, where the only certainty is that there will be failures. And yet, we need your people to willingly try new ideas and admit when they are not working as expected.
Think about it... how many of you would experiment with new ideas if every time one failed, you were punished?
I wouldn't. I would stay well within my comfort zone.
Exactly! No one would take risks. And the saddest part is that we learn most when we fail. When we succeed, we confirm what we already know. When we fail, we can learn something new and correct our assumptions.
EXPECTATION (Delicious!)
REALITY (Burnt)
Why?
What can I learn so it's better next time?
Makes sense. The good news is that we may already have a no-blame environment... I think.
Our culture is very people centered. But I'm not sure we allow enough room for failure. I mean, we've all been taught growing up that success is good, and failure is to be avoided. Should we now encourage people to fail?

EDUARDO
Well, we don't really want them to fail. In fact, everyone around this table should support the people so they can succeed. What we want is for people to feel safe knowing there are no negative consequences for failing... as long as they learn and don't repeat the mistake.
Your actions as owners and managers are the key. Make successes about the people and celebrate their efforts. But always make failures about the process, and focus on improving it.
Actual
Plan
Great job! What worked well that we should standardize?
Plan
Actual
Where did the process fail? Let's work together to improve it!
That's deep...
When there's a problem, don't go on a witch hunt looking for someone to blame. Instead, focus on improving the process to prevent the failure from happening again.
But certainly people make mistakes and do things they shouldn't.
Yes, but that's usually because they lack training or the process is imposing requirements that are hard to satisfy successfully. In general, people want to do the right thing.
That's also at the core of our culture... we strongly believe people want to do a good job.
So, we're on our way to this no-blame environment, but we have work to do... especially in this group. What else?
Well, the end objective is to achieve your goals for the business and your customers by evolving a sustainable Lean system. And to do this, we must address the process, people, and culture.
Sounds like a lot... Where do we start?
Perhaps we should follow in Toyota's footsteps and use the approach that resulted in TPS and the Toyota Way: identify problems and solve them one by one in a way that prevents their recurrence.
THE TOYOTA WAY

But everyone has problems. If we go to the warehouse, every person will tell you ten things they don't like.
I'm not talking about likes or dislikes. We'll use a stricter definition. A problem is a gap between the current condition and a desired state.
DESIRED CONDITION
GAP=PROBLEM
CURRENT CONDITION
Interesting. That will disqualify a lot of complaints and force everyone to clarify their 'problems'.
That's exactly the point. Once you identify this gap, it's easier for others to understand what you're talking about. It also facilitates later conversations about finding root causes and testing countermeasures.
Root causes? Testing? You make us sound like scientists in a lab.
Yes. A root cause is the underlying reason behind a problem. If you deal with it, the problem will not come back. However, we may not be certain of the root cause, and much less of the solutions. We'll have to act like scientists and experiment. It's fun.
At Toyota, they get closer to the root cause by asking 'why' five times, going deeper into the problem each time.
We're late for school.
Why?
We woke up late.
Why?
We went to bed late.
Why?
We had to finish homework.
Why?
We did not do it before.
Why?
We were watching videos and playing games.
Hmmm...
Perhaps we should do the homework first...
I guess we'll learn more about this...
We will. Now, to develop a customized Lean system, I propose we clarify your business objectives and identify gaps to your current condition. We can then put on our lab coats and pull improvements as needed by experimenting and testing possible countermeasures for your biggest problems.
We have not talked about this, but the idea of 'pulling' instead of 'pushing' is a core Lean concept. Pulling improvements thus seems like the right approach to implement Lean. Don't you think?
If you say so... but I'm getting lost.
Don't worry... the point is, it makes more sense to identify a problem and solve it by testing our ideas with the team, rather than starting with the 'Lean solution' and pushing it on people who may not have a use for it.

Seems reasonable... I guess it also reduces people's natural resistance to change.
Yes! Especially if we're working on a problem they helped identify...
...and more so if solving it makes their lives easier.
EDUARDO
Precisely! Pushing solutions onto an organization is like force feeding geese. You shove solutions down everyone's throats and then wonder why they resist the changes.
Hadn't thought about that, but it's certainly a colorful analogy.
You know, I think the Zingerman's change process is similar to what you describe. It always starts with a need.
That's great. It's usually easier to build on what you already have than to start from scratch.
Ok, we're in total agreement. What else?
EDUARDO
Eventually, we can expect others to contribute more, but at first this group will need to drive the process.
Come help!
A P C D
I think that's well within our expectations.
Good. We'll lead, but early on, we'll have to engage the people doing the work. We need to bring them along for the ride, or improvements will be short lived. At the very least, people must understand what we're doing, and they must be involved in testing things out so they experience the changes first hand.
Leadership at Zingerman's is more about enabling others than telling them what to do, so people will expect to be involved... and will have an opinion!
And very strong ones sometimes...
But all this will take time, and people on the line are constantly rushing. When are they going to do all this?
Need to improve!
Need to pick products!

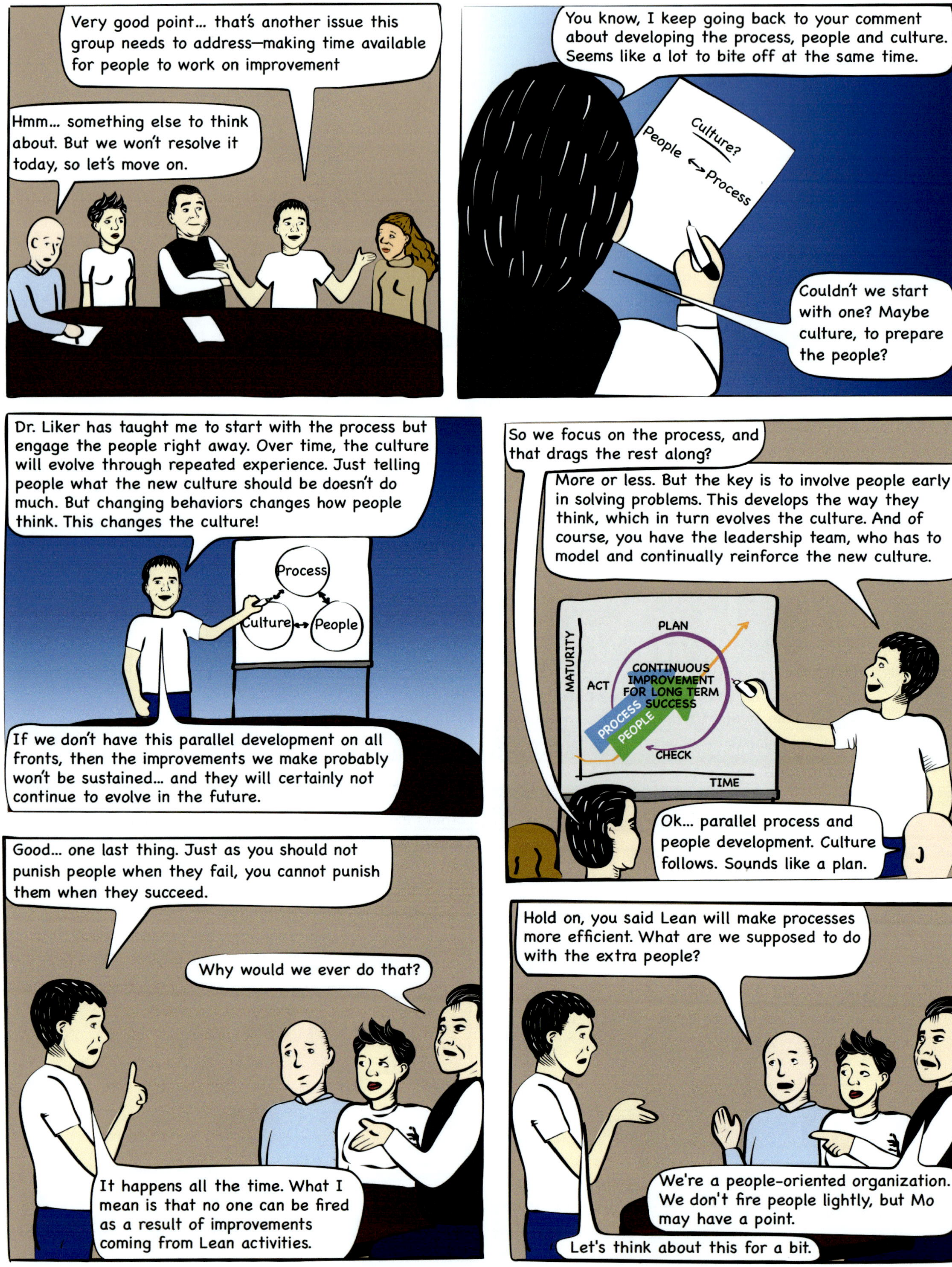
Very good point... that's another issue this group needs to address—making time available for people to work on improvement
Hmm... something else to think about. But we won't resolve it today, so let's move on.
You know, I keep going back to your comment about developing the process, people and culture. Seems like a lot to bite off at the same time.
Culture?
People ↔ Process
Couldn't we start with one? Maybe culture, to prepare the people?
Dr. Liker has taught me to start with the process but engage the people right away. Over time, the culture will evolve through repeated experience. Just telling people what the new culture should be doesn't do much. But changing behaviors changes how people think. This changes the culture!
Process
Culture
People
If we don't have this parallel development on all fronts, then the improvements we make probably won't be sustained... and they will certainly not continue to evolve in the future.
So we focus on the process, and that drags the rest along?
More or less. But the key is to involve people early in solving problems. This develops the way they think, which in turn evolves the culture. And of course, you have the leadership team, who has to model and continually reinforce the new culture.
PLAN
MATURITY
ACT
CONTINUOUS IMPROVEMENT FOR LONG TERM SUCCESS
PROCESS
PEOPLE
CHECK
TIME
Ok... parallel process and people development. Culture follows. Sounds like a plan.
Good... one last thing. Just as you should not punish people when they fail, you cannot punish them when they succeed.
Why would we ever do that?
It happens all the time. What I mean is that no one can be fired as a result of improvements coming from Lean activities.
Hold on, you said Lean will make processes more efficient. What are we supposed to do with the extra people?
We're a people-oriented organization. We don't fire people lightly, but Mo may have a point.
Let's think about this for a bit.

Let me interrupt for a bit and highlight some important points we discussed here:

- Don't copy Toyota... their problems are different from yours, so most probably their solutions will not be a good fit for your company. You need to experiment to develop a Lean system customized to the needs of your organization.
- Simultaneously develop the processes and the people. In fact, develop people through problem solving, by coaching them as they test ideas to improve their own processes. The culture will evolve through repeated experience.
- Surface problems and use them to pull improvements where needed, when needed... do not force feed the goose!
- Initial solutions may not work or produce only marginal improvements. Multiple cycles of improvement will be needed to get the desired results. Perseverance is key!
- Drive out fear: develop a no-blame environment where people can take risks and learn from their failures. And never, ever fire someone as a result of making improvements.

A people-centered culture at Zingerman's

Continuing with Eduardo's visit in 2004, it's now our turn to explain the history and culture of Zingerman's.

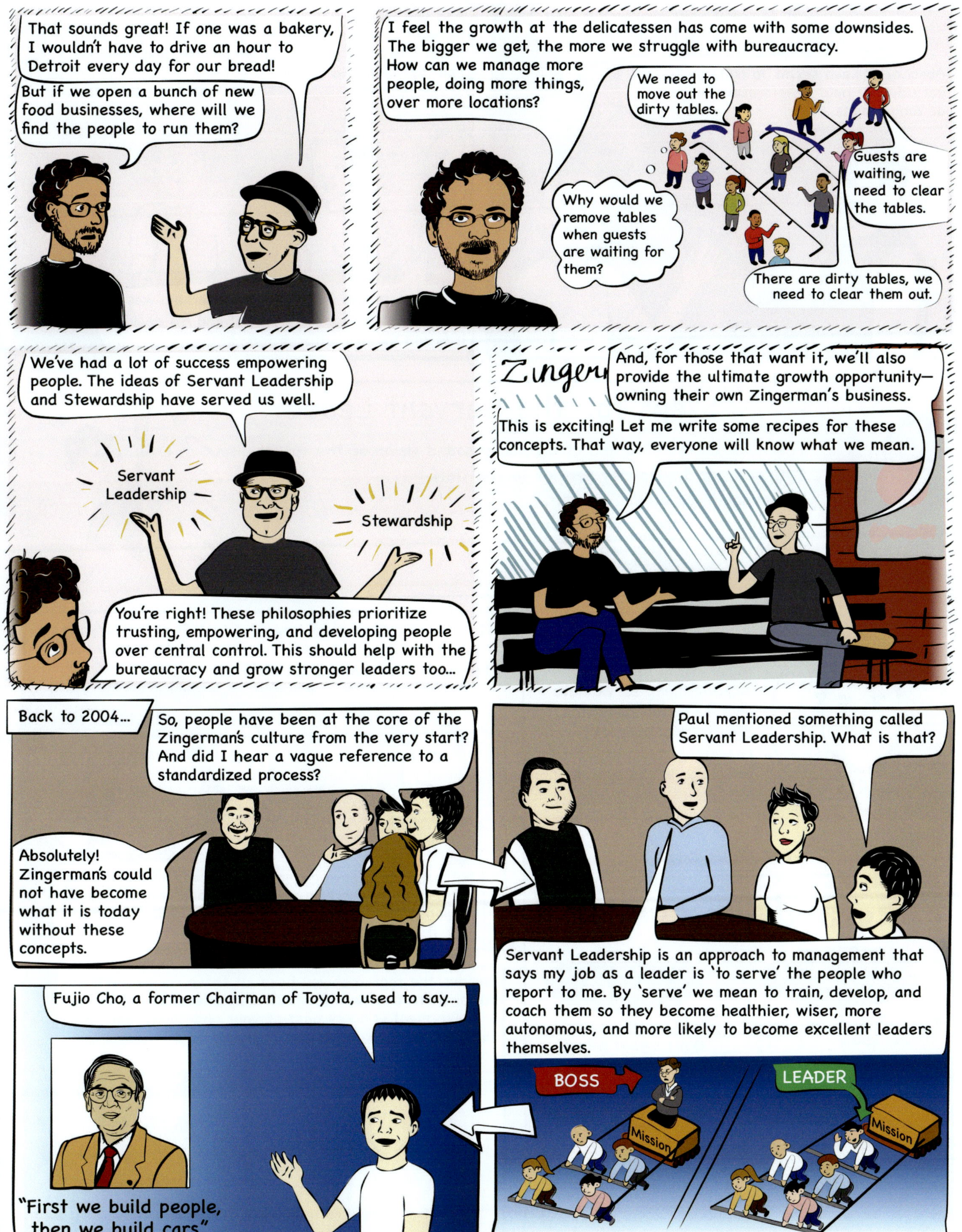
That sounds great! If one was a bakery, I wouldn't have to drive an hour to Detroit every day for our bread!
But if we open a bunch of new food businesses, where will we find the people to run them?
I feel the growth at the delicatessen has come with some downsides. The bigger we get, the more we struggle with bureaucracy.
How can we manage more people, doing more things, over more locations?
We need to move out the dirty tables.
Guests are waiting, we need to clear the tables.
Why would we remove tables when guests are waiting for them?
There are dirty tables, we need to clear them out.
We've had a lot of success empowering people. The ideas of Servant Leadership and Stewardship have served us well.
Servant Leadership
Stewardship
You're right! These philosophies prioritize trusting, empowering, and developing people over central control. This should help with the bureaucracy and grow stronger leaders too...
And, for those that want it, we'll also provide the ultimate growth opportunity—owning their own Zingerman's business.
This is exciting! Let me write some recipes for these concepts. That way, everyone will know what we mean.
Back to 2004...
So, people have been at the core of the Zingerman's culture from the very start? And did I hear a vague reference to a standardized process?
Absolutely! Zingerman's could not have become what it is today without these concepts.
Paul mentioned something called Servant Leadership. What is that?
Servant Leadership is an approach to management that says my job as a leader is 'to serve' the people who report to me. By 'serve' we mean to train, develop, and coach them so they become healthier, wiser, more autonomous, and more likely to become excellent leaders themselves.
BOSS
Mission
LEADER
Mission
Fujio Cho, a former Chairman of Toyota, used to say...
"First we build people, then we build cars."

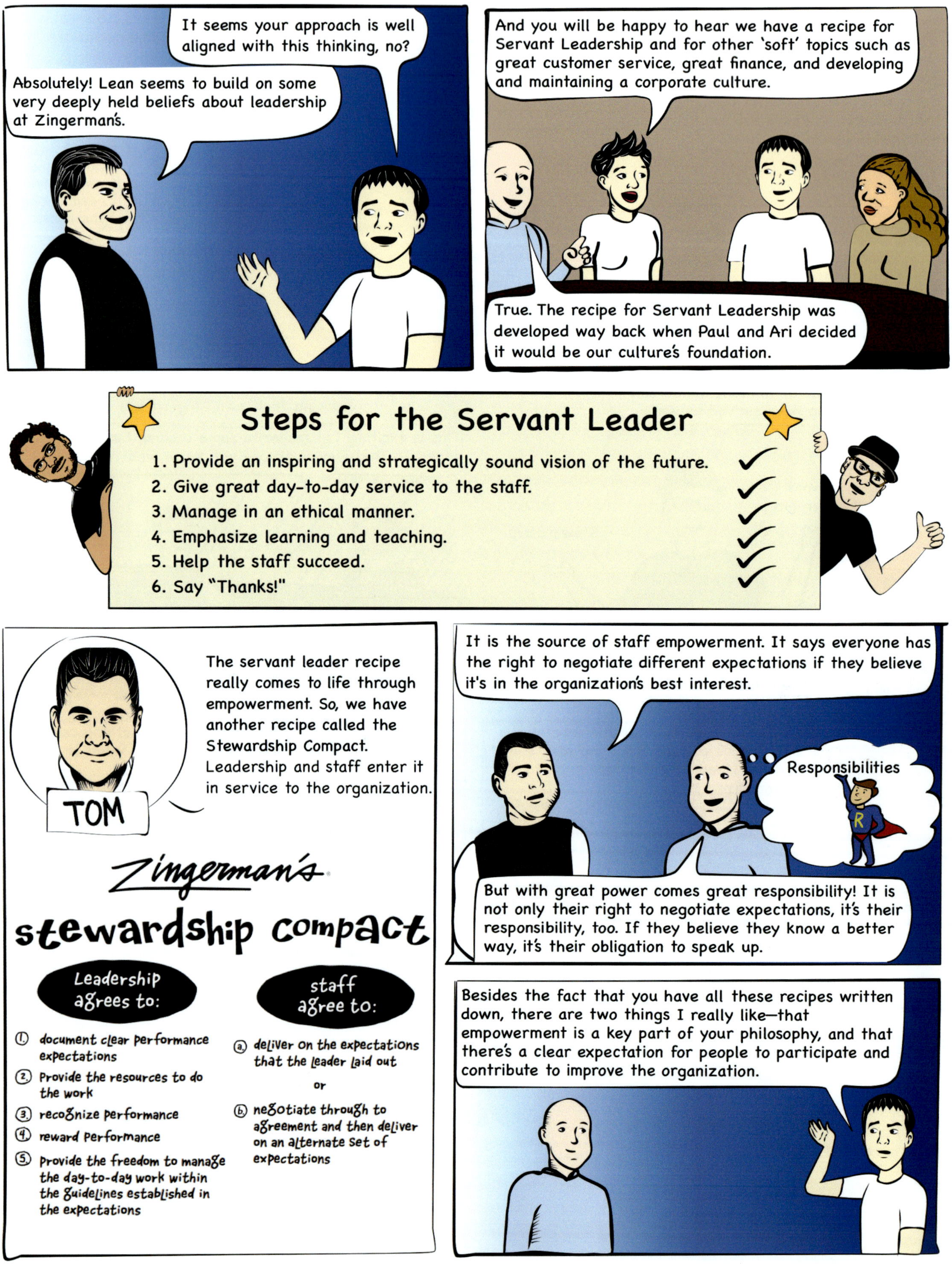
It seems your approach is well aligned with this thinking, no?
Absolutely! Lean seems to build on some very deeply held beliefs about leadership at Zingerman's.
And you will be happy to hear we have a recipe for Servant Leadership and for other 'soft' topics such as great customer service, great finance, and developing and maintaining a corporate culture.
True. The recipe for Servant Leadership was developed way back when Paul and Ari decided it would be our culture's foundation.
Steps for the Servant Leader
1. Provide an inspiring and strategically sound vision of the future.
2. Give great day-to-day service to the staff.
3. Manage in an ethical manner.
4. Emphasize learning and teaching.
5. Help the staff succeed.
6. Say "Thanks!"
TOM
The servant leader recipe really comes to life through empowerment. So, we have another recipe called the Stewardship Compact. Leadership and staff enter it in service to the organization.
Zingerman's
stewardship compact
Leadership agrees to:
① document clear performance expectations
② provide the resources to do the work
③ recognize performance
④ reward performance
⑤ provide the freedom to manage the day-to-day work within the guidelines established in the expectations
staff agree to:
ⓐ deliver on the expectations that the leader laid out
or
ⓑ negotiate through to agreement and then deliver on an alternate set of expectations
It is the source of staff empowerment. It says everyone has the right to negotiate different expectations if they believe it's in the organization's best interest.
Responsibilities
R
But with great power comes great responsibility! It is not only their right to negotiate expectations, it's their responsibility, too. If they believe they know a better way, it's their obligation to speak up.
Besides the fact that you have all these recipes written down, there are two things I really like—that empowerment is a key part of your philosophy, and that there's a clear expectation for people to participate and contribute to improve the organization.

Servant Leadership has been part of Zingerman's DNA from day one. Now, 25 years after the Deli started, there is a whole solar system of Zingerman's businesses—all committed to the same philosophical keystones of Servant Leadership, Stewardship, and Service to our customers, our vendors, and each other.

As you will see, Servant Leadership and Lean are indeed a good match. They form a virtuous cycle where improvements are naturally made in support of the people so they can better serve customers, each other, and the organization.

Where do we go from here?
N
W
E
S
Where to?
You have a very interesting culture. Now it's time to decide where to start.
Finally! This will have been one productive day if we start making improvements already.
Well, I doubt we'll get that far today. But we should be able to reach a shared understanding of the main problems and define a general direction.
That would still make for a very productive day.
Yes, it would. Now, can I ask why you want to do this? What's the purpose of a Lean transformation at ZMO?
Well, we're in the business of providing our customers an exceptional experience. A large portion of that comes down to being able to fulfill their orders, and every year in December, we have this huge peak where all hell breaks lose.
You can say that again!
It's very chaotic, and it threatens to affect our customers. In part, it comes from lack of space, but I think there's more to it.
If we had more space, we could organize things better and it would not be so chaotic.
Ok, but the truth is, we have the space we need for a year or so after we move to a new location. But a couple of years down the road, we're bursting at the seams again. Should we just bite the bullet and focus on getting better at moving?
1998
2000
2002
2004

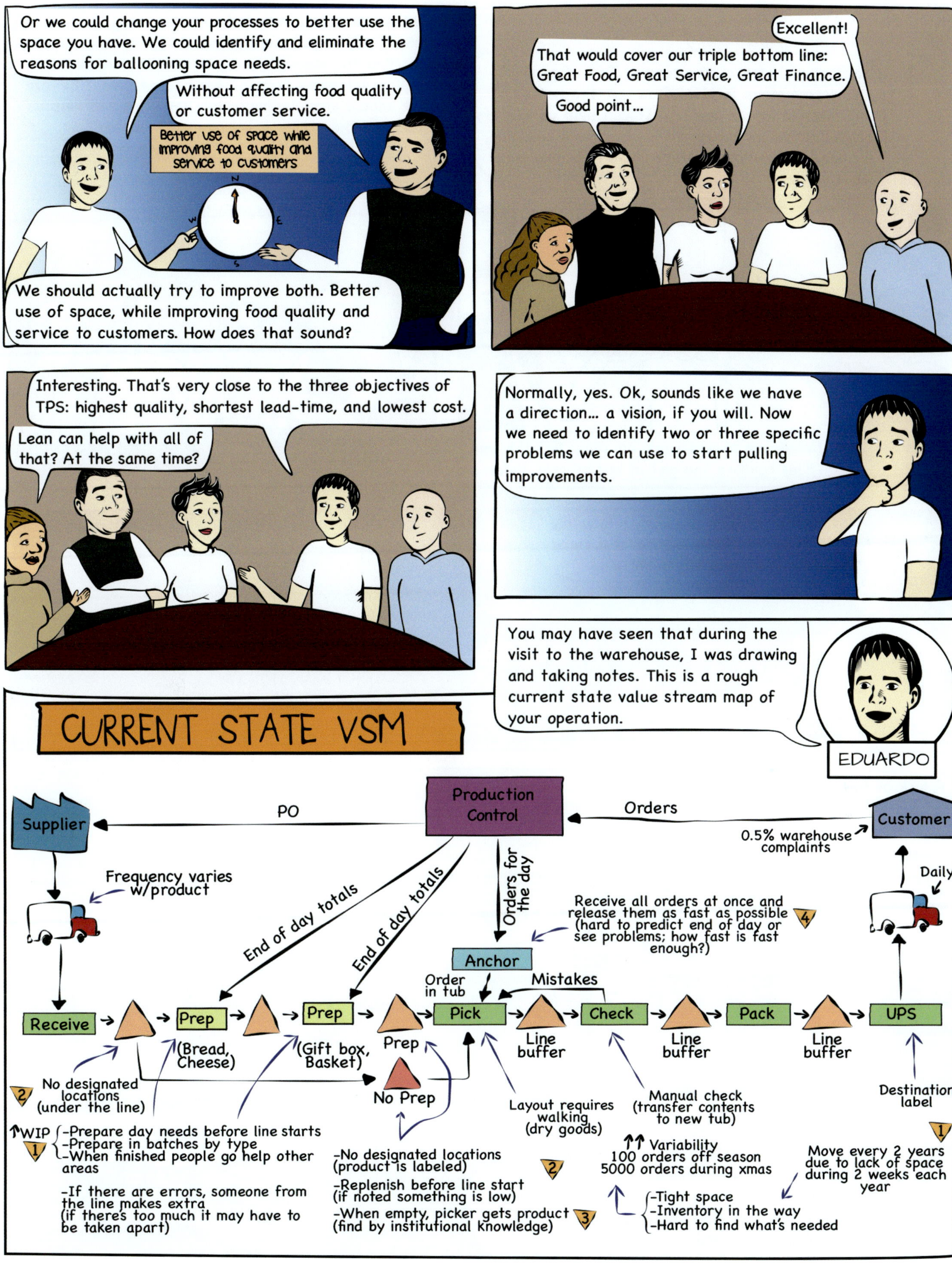
Or we could change your processes to better use the space you have. We could identify and eliminate the reasons for ballooning space needs.
Without affecting food quality or customer service.
Better use of space while improving food quality and service to customers
N
W
E
S
We should actually try to improve both. Better use of space, while improving food quality and service to customers. How does that sound?
Excellent!
That would cover our triple bottom line: Great Food, Great Service, Great Finance.
Good point...
Interesting. That's very close to the three objectives of TPS: highest quality, shortest lead-time, and lowest cost.
Lean can help with all of that? At the same time?
Normally, yes. Ok, sounds like we have a direction... a vision, if you will. Now we need to identify two or three specific problems we can use to start pulling improvements.
You may have seen that during the visit to the warehouse, I was drawing and taking notes. This is a rough current state value stream map of your operation.
EDUARDO
CURRENT STATE VSM
Production Control
Supplier
PO
Orders
Customer
0.5% warehouse complaints
Frequency varies w/product
End of day totals
End of day totals
Orders for the day
Daily
Receive all orders at once and release them as fast as possible (hard to predict end of day or see problems; how fast is fast enough?)
4
Anchor
Order in tub
Mistakes
Receive
Prep
(Bread, Cheese)
Prep
(Gift box, Basket)
Prep
No Prep
Pick
Line buffer
Check
Line buffer
Pack
Line buffer
UPS
2
No designated locations (under the line)
↑WIP
1
-Prepare day needs before line starts
-Prepare in batches by type
-When finished people go help other areas
-If there are errors, someone from the line makes extra (if there's too much it may have to be taken apart)
-No designated locations (product is labeled)
-Replenish before line start (if noted something is low)
-When empty, picker gets product (find by institutional knowledge)
2
3
Layout requires walking (dry goods)
Manual check (transfer contents to new tub)
↑↑ Variability
100 orders off season
5000 orders during xmas
-Tight space
-Inventory in the way
-Hard to find what's needed
Destination label
1
Move every 2 years due to lack of space during 2 weeks each year

Great overview of our process. Is this a roadmap for improvement?
No, just a sketch of the current flow of product and information. Product flows at the bottom, and information at the top. It can help us identify opportunities for improvement, but for a roadmap, we need to develop a future state map showing what we want to achieve.
Supplier
PO
Orders
Customer
0.5% warehouse complaints
Daily
End of day totals
Prep
(Bread, Cheese)
(Gift box, Basket)
No Prep
Check
Pack
Line buffer
Well, we should work on that. But this one does capture the gist of our process today.
I hope so. I also included notes on things I observed, or you mentioned during the tour. And I marked the main problems I see with inverted yellow triangles. From a Lean perspective, I believe we should start by improving flow. This will help us identify the problems we need to work on.
Flow? What do you mean?
The flow of product through your facility.
Ideally we want product to flow like a river, constantly moving at a steady pace from receiving to shipping.
A lack of flow causes a good portion of your space issue.
Sorry, but we're a warehouse... we store product for when customers want it. How can the product be constantly flowing?
Right... the ideal condition is continuous flow, but no one has achieved that fully. In reality everyone operates as a series of connected lakes. Products flow through processes and then stagnate in lakes of inventory.

So we will reduce inventory to improve flow?
In some cases we will. But that's not the main driver. We want to have the right amount of inventory to ensure your operation runs well. Later on, we can reduce inventory by dealing with the underlying reasons for needing it.
But won't we run out more often if we reduce inventory?
Not really. The father of TPS was Taiichi Ohno, and one of his sayings was...
"The more inventory you have, the more likely you will not have what you really need."
You said it yourself at the warehouse. During peak days, you build all those gift boxes and baskets, resulting in lots of inventory, but frequently some are missing when you need them.
That's true...
I need A!
D
C
E
B
A
What usually happens is that you have too much of some items and not enough of others.
Anyway, let's focus first on the line. What's currently your biggest impediment to flow? What creates the biggest lake of inventory?
Definitively the prep work. That generates so much inventory that you can hardly walk in this place when the line is about to start.
Ok, so what can we do to improve flow?

But wait, we need those items to fulfill the orders.
Well, do you need everything ready before you start the first order?
No, we only need what's on that order.
Correct.
G-WEE
order G-WEE
But we don't know what the first order will require. That's why we prepare everything in advance.
Yes, that's your current approach, but what if we could find a way to prep only what is needed for the next few orders?
Hmm... we would need less space if items are consumed as they are being prepared.
Less inventory means smaller lakes and better flow... did I get that right?
Absolutely!
But how? The weekender needs to be available when the order comes down the line... and to make it, we need bagged bread. How can everything happen at the same time?
I don't Know.
We don't need solutions yet. Perhaps we went too far already. Remember, we're just trying to identify the top two or three problems we will focus on initially.
Ok, so we have the first one: too much space is used by inventory generated before the line starts. What's the second problem?

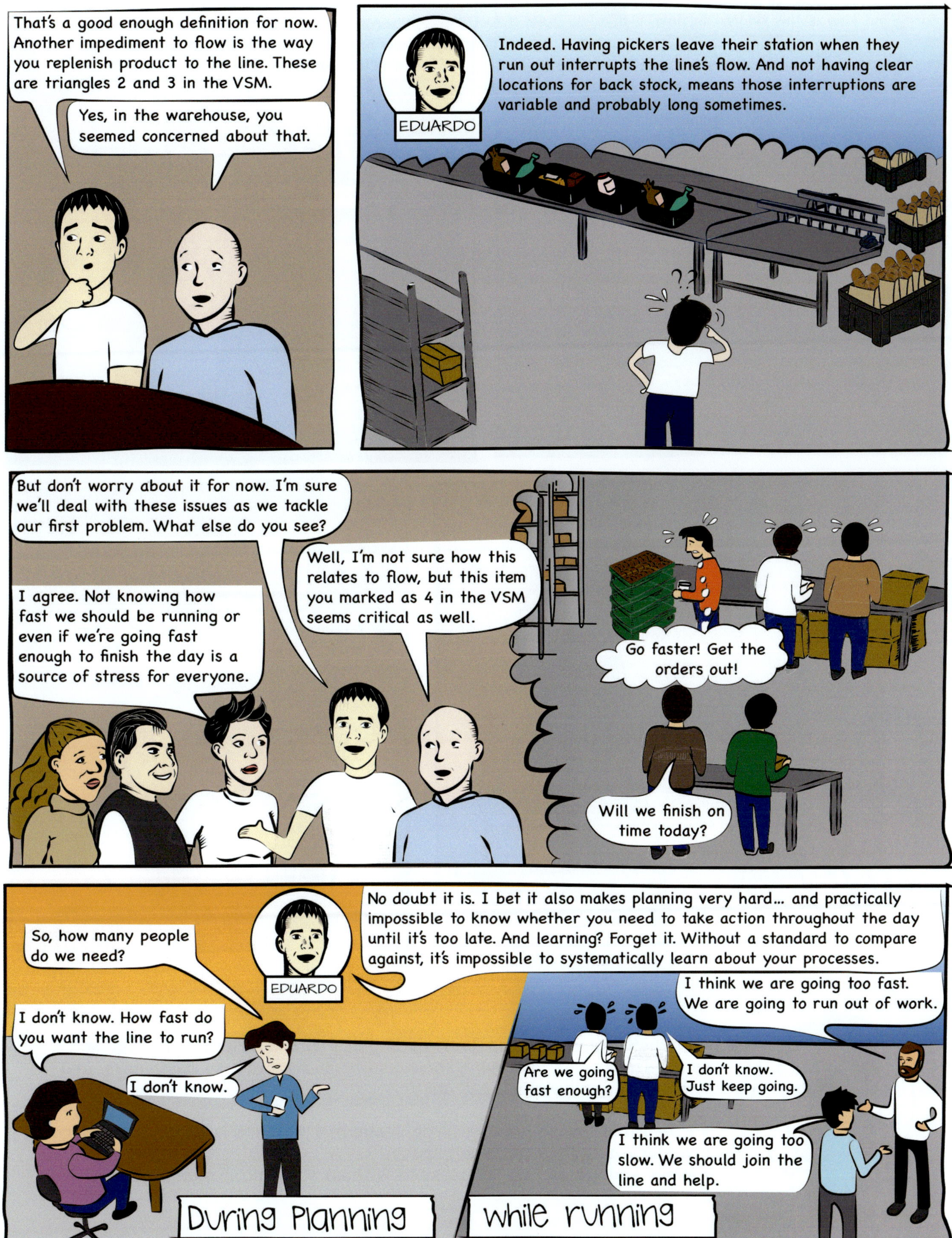
That's a good enough definition for now. Another impediment to flow is the way you replenish product to the line. These are triangles 2 and 3 in the VSM.
Yes, in the warehouse, you seemed concerned about that.
EDUARDO
Indeed. Having pickers leave their station when they run out interrupts the line's flow. And not having clear locations for back stock, means those interruptions are variable and probably long sometimes.
But don't worry about it for now. I'm sure we'll deal with these issues as we tackle our first problem. What else do you see?
Well, I'm not sure how this relates to flow, but this item you marked as 4 in the VSM seems critical as well.
I agree. Not knowing how fast we should be running or even if we're going fast enough to finish the day is a source of stress for everyone.
Go faster! Get the orders out!
Will we finish on time today?
EDUARDO
No doubt it is. I bet it also makes planning very hard... and practically impossible to know whether you need to take action throughout the day until it's too late. And learning? Forget it. Without a standard to compare against, it's impossible to systematically learn about your processes.
So, how many people do we need?
I don't know. How fast do you want the line to run?
I don't know.
During Planning
I think we are going too fast. We are going to run out of work.
Are we going fast enough?
I don't know. Just keep going.
I think we are going too slow. We should join the line and help.
While running

And that's how our Lean journey began... with a direction to reduce space used, while improving food quality and service to customers, and two specific issues to focus on:

- Preparation work done in large sequential batches results in too much inventory and uses too much space.
- Work is done as fast as possible without knowing if that's good enough.

Experimenting with flow just in time for Christmas

After that first meeting, Eduardo came to ZMO a few times per week and taught us about observing the process deeply. Toyota calls this Genchi Genbutsu—go and see to learn. It takes patience and is especially hard if you think you already know the process. The trick is to observe the flow of product and the cycle of work over and over to understand the general behavior and all the things that go wrong. Is the output steady? Is the quality always the same? As we observe, we discover the facts of the process.

As a starting point, we focused on creating a smoothly flowing process. Things rarely worked exactly as expected, though. We tried something, learned from it, and continued to tweak it. This experimentation is the essence of kaizen. Gaining a deep understanding through direct observation and working out how to make and evaluate a change are time consuming and sometimes hard, but this is what gets you to excellent processes and exceptional people. Patience and perseverance are critical!

Now let's look at the early planning phase. Remember how prep happened before the line started running? Here we are in a meeting, figuring out how to run both simultaneously.

Which means we need a lot of space to store all the prepped items before we start using them—very expensive space!
IDEAL:
ONE-PIECE-FLOW
Correct. Now, the ideal situation would be for items to become available just as they are needed. Remember the TPS house? Just in time is one of the pillars.
Mmm, kind of like Star Trek?
Beam it down, Scotty!
Sounds good, but how do we do it in real life? We need bread ready to make gift boxes. And we need both ready when an order for them comes along. The same goes for cheese, pastries, and baskets.
We don't need all solutions at once. Let's break the problem down and take a first step. Which of the items you prep requires the most space to store?
Boxes and baskets for sure!
Great! Let's start there. For now, let's assume other items are prepped in advance, and let's focus on developing a process to prepare boxes and baskets JIT. Any ideas?
Well, we could synchronize the release of the order with the production of the gift box. This way, the order arrives at the picker as the gift box gets to the rack.
A Weekender coming in five orders!
Weekender... coming up!
That might work, but synchronization can be hard. Let's take a step back... do gift boxes need to be ready in advance for the pickers?
Of course! Otherwise, what will they pick when an order asks for a gift box?
Betty, that assumes you will pick gift boxes from inventory. Is that the only way to do it?
Well, either we make things in advance and have them available when we need them, or... we make them when we need them? Like they make sandwiches at the deli.
Made to order
Pick from inventory
CONVENIENCE STORE

Now that's an idea! How can we put it in practice?
I still don't see it! Preparing gift boxes and baskets takes much longer than picking them. How will we keep up with the pace needed? Not likely!
I feel the same way... seems impossible.
With your current set up, I agree. Impossible! But we're dreaming about the future now.
Sounds good. But in that dream, do we have a magic wand that creates gift boxes instantaneously? As Betty said, they take a long time to prepare.
The time it takes is a capacity issue—we just need the right number of people preparing them.
What do you mean?
Let's say that based on customer demand, you want one packed box going into the truck every minute. Then 60 seconds is the takt time for the line. Remember we talked about it earlier?
60s = Takt Time
Yes, you mentioned Toyota uses it to set up the speed of the assembly line to match demand.
Exactly! It's part of the JIT column in the TPS house.
Now, let's further assume gift boxes on average take 3 minutes to assemble and all your orders include one. With this, we can figure out the number of people needed by dividing the 3 minutes... or 180s of work content by the 60s output rate. And... you will need 3 people making gift boxes to keep the line running at a 60s takt.
60s = Takt Time
Number of people = Cycle time / Takt time
= 180s / 60s = 3 people
I'm beginning to like this takt time. Simple and powerful! It can help us define the design requirements for the line and its stations. Remarkable...
It sounds simple in theory, but I'm not sure I trust these numbers.
Why not? The explanation seemed pretty clear...
Wait, she has a point. First of all, the result is only as good as the underlying data. If it takes 4 minutes instead of 3 to make a gift box, we would need more people.

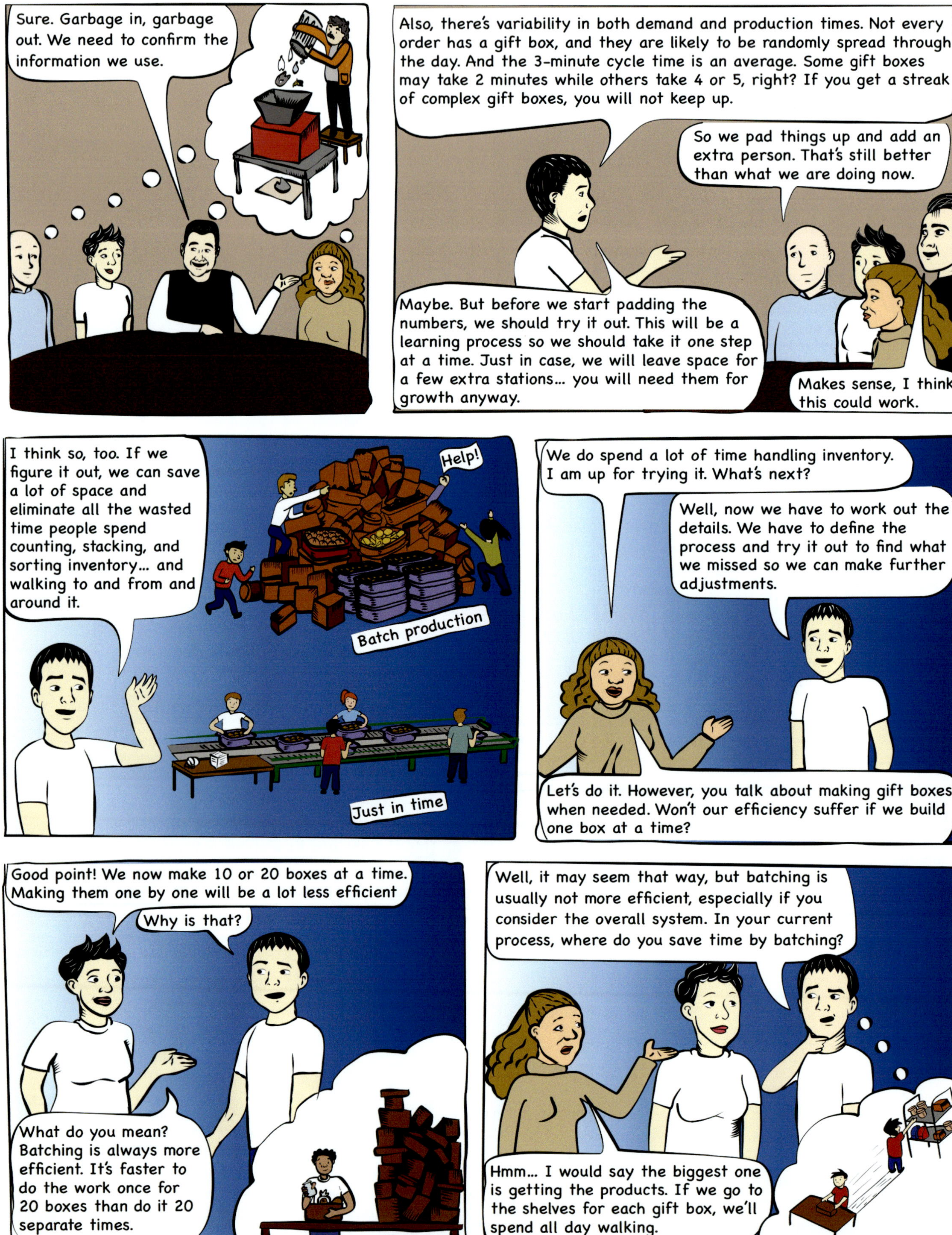

Sure. Garbage in, garbage out. We need to confirm the information we use.
Also, there's variability in both demand and production times. Not every order has a gift box, and they are likely to be randomly spread through the day. And the 3-minute cycle time is an average. Some gift boxes may take 2 minutes while others take 4 or 5, right? If you get a streak of complex gift boxes, you will not keep up.
So we pad things up and add an extra person. That's still better than what we are doing now.
Maybe. But before we start padding the numbers, we should try it out. This will be a learning process so we should take it one step at a time. Just in case, we will leave space for a few extra stations... you will need them for growth anyway.
Makes sense, I think this could work.
I think so, too. If we figure it out, we can save a lot of space and eliminate all the wasted time people spend counting, stacking, and sorting inventory... and walking to and from and around it.
Help!
Batch production
Just in time
We do spend a lot of time handling inventory. I am up for trying it. What's next?
Well, now we have to work out the details. We have to define the process and try it out to find what we missed so we can make further adjustments.
Let's do it. However, you talk about making gift boxes when needed. Won't our efficiency suffer if we build one box at a time?
Good point! We now make 10 or 20 boxes at a time. Making them one by one will be a lot less efficient
Why is that?
What do you mean? Batching is always more efficient. It's faster to do the work once for 20 boxes than do it 20 separate times.
Well, it may seem that way, but batching is usually not more efficient, especially if you consider the overall system. In your current process, where do you save time by batching?
Hmm... I would say the biggest one is getting the products. If we go to the shelves for each gift box, we'll spend all day walking.

Perfect! You have identified precisely the problem we need to solve. We need high efficiency, but we also need to build one by one. How can we do this?
What if someone else does the picking?
Have a picker bring ingredients to the box maker? Hmm...
You already have a pick process. Couldn't those people pick the ingredients for the boxes and baskets as well?
And then what? Have people building gift boxes further down the line?
Why not? It would be similar to how we pack at the end of the line. In-line gift box and basket assembly... I like it!
2. Make box
1. Pick
Wait, what happens when the customer orders a gift box and something else? How does the box maker know what to put in the box and what to leave out?
Good catch. Don't you have standard recipes?
We do... but everything at ZMO is customizable. If the customer wants to add, remove, or replace something, we'll do it... so the standard is not so standard.
Besides, that would create a situation where people could make mistakes.
Good point. We want processes where mistakes are impossible or at least hard to make. At Toyota they call this
Poke-Yoke which means mistake proofing.
Well, what if we build the boxes and baskets before picking the rest of the products? If we process an order with a Weekender and a loaf of bread, the Weekender's ingredients would get picked and the gift box assembled, before it would travel the line to the bread station, where the loaf would be added.
1. Make box
2. Pick
That would ensure we don't put the wrong product in the gift box.

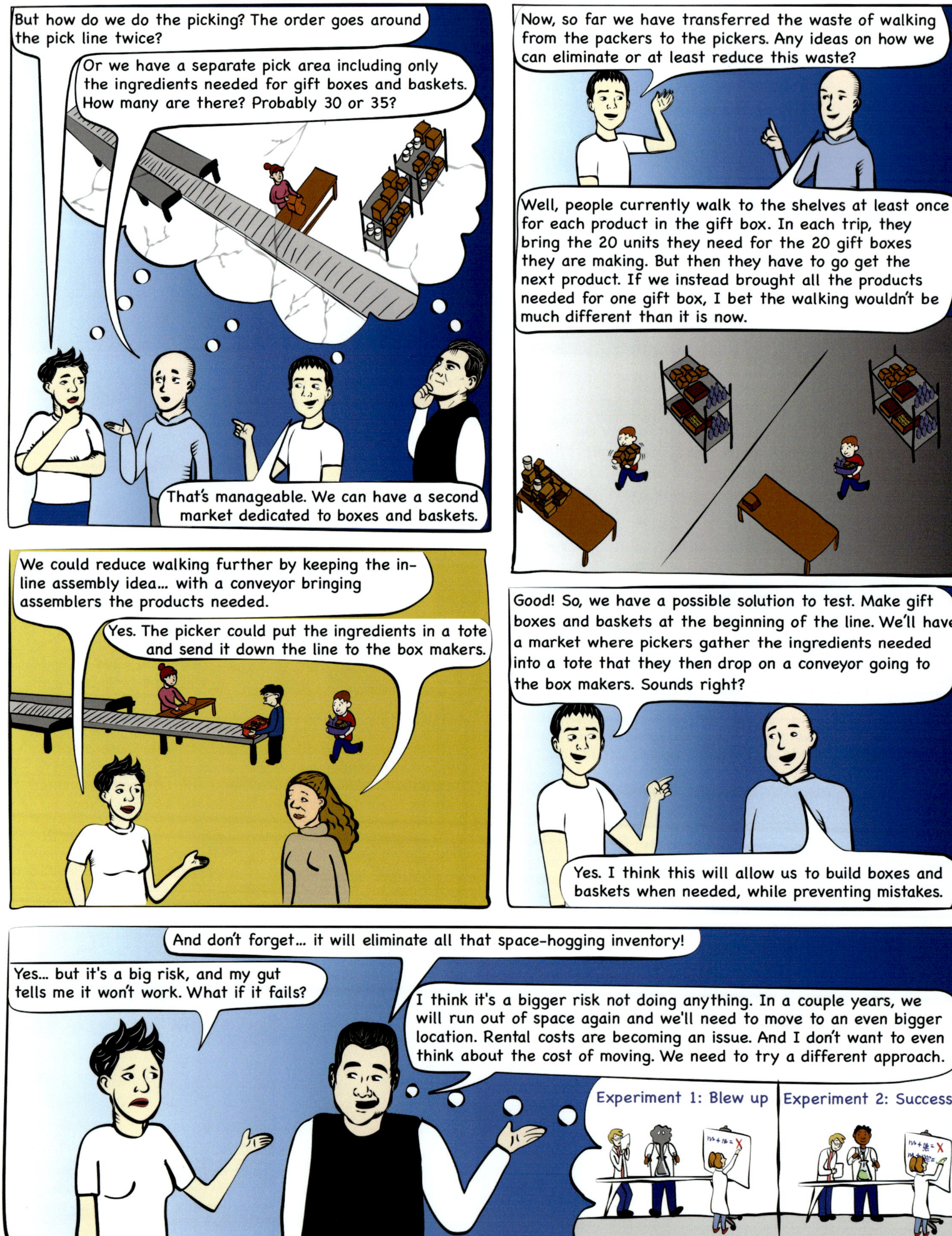

But how do we do the picking? The order goes around the pick line twice?
Or we have a separate pick area including only the ingredients needed for gift boxes and baskets. How many are there? Probably 30 or 35?
That's manageable. We can have a second market dedicated to boxes and baskets.
Now, so far we have transferred the waste of walking from the packers to the pickers. Any ideas on how we can eliminate or at least reduce this waste?
Well, people currently walk to the shelves at least once for each product in the gift box. In each trip, they bring the 20 units they need for the 20 gift boxes they are making. But then they have to go get the next product. If we instead brought all the products needed for one gift box, I bet the walking wouldn't be much different than it is now.
We could reduce walking further by keeping the in-line assembly idea... with a conveyor bringing assemblers the products needed.
Yes. The picker could put the ingredients in a tote and send it down the line to the box makers.
Good! So, we have a possible solution to test. Make gift boxes and baskets at the beginning of the line. We'll have a market where pickers gather the ingredients needed into a tote that they then drop on a conveyor going to the box makers. Sounds right?
Yes. I think this will allow us to build boxes and baskets when needed, while preventing mistakes.
And don't forget... it will eliminate all that space-hogging inventory!
Yes... but it's a big risk, and my gut tells me it won't work. What if it fails?
I think it's a bigger risk not doing anything. In a couple years, we will run out of space again and we'll need to move to an even bigger location. Rental costs are becoming an issue. And I don't want to even think about the cost of moving. We need to try a different approach.
Experiment 1: Blew up
Experiment 2: Success

This illustrates our discussions. They were not always as neat, but the improvement process usually followed a similar pattern:

1. Identify and agree on the problem, which requires understanding the current condition through a lot of go and see, data gathering, and sometimes even experimentation.
2. Define a desired direction by trying to understand how the ideal process would look from a Lean perspective.
3. Discuss possible options and work through the details (deep into the process) to address issues the team may have. Select one workable solution to try.
4. Test and implement and test and refine... this part never ends. We may let things run for a while, but at some point, we come back and refine them further. It's the essence of continuous improvement.

The purpose of such discussions was to engage the people, not determine the perfect solution. We knew we would not get it right the first time. As we make changes, we learn, refine the approach, and continue making progress... a process that also develops the people involved.

Feed the line by pulling products as needed

We took a risk and redesigned the entire process for gift boxes and baskets, all at once, just before Christmas. I was confident it would work. After a few more meetings with Eduardo, we had worked out the layout. Boxes and baskets would each have their own assembly line. Orders would be given to pickers, who would gather the ingredients into a tote and drop them on the correct line. Once assembled, they would flow to the main line and follow the usual process... pick, check, pack, and ship.

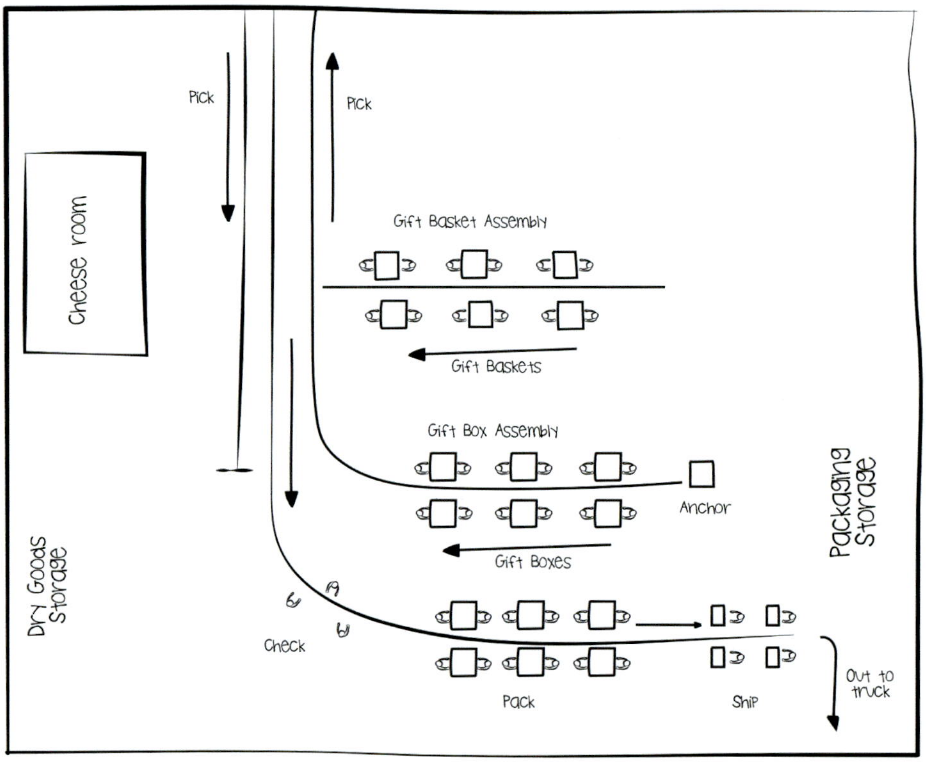

We are now on the warehouse floor to discuss other improvements needed to support the new layout.

Let's start by understanding the current situation. Can you describe what happens now? How does product go from the dock to the point at which it is picked?
Sure. Product is unloaded at the dock. At some point, it's received and moved into storage. It can be put directly into a pick location, if there's space. More often, it goes into an open location in back stock.
Or under the line...
Yes... for some products. Especially during December.
Truck
Receive
Unload
Take to Back Stock
What happens afterwards?
Product in back stock is taken to the pick location when needed.
As you know, we try to refill the shelves at the beginning of the shift... if there's time. Otherwise, the picker gets it when the pick location runs out.
Ok. Something like this?

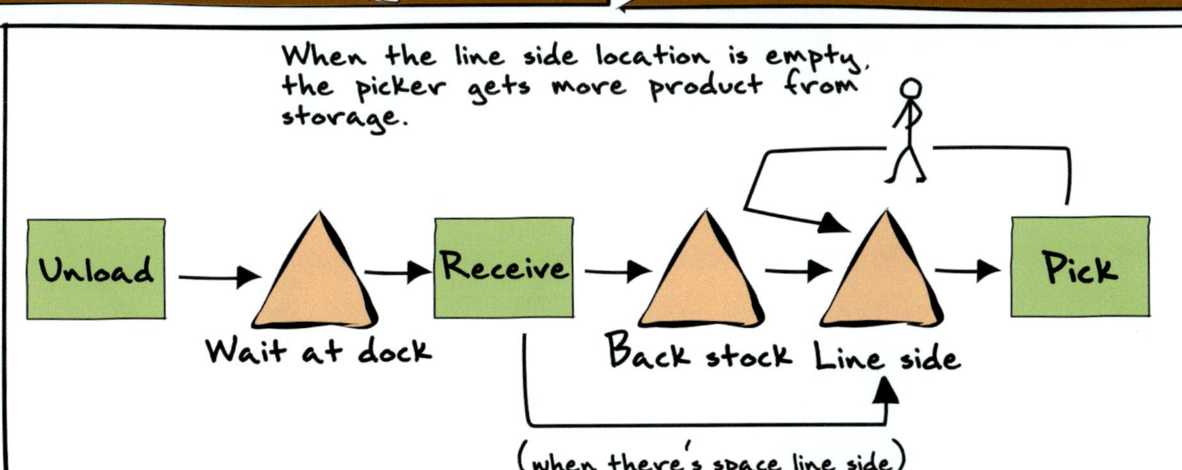
When the line side location is empty, the picker gets more product from storage.
Unload
Wait at dock
Receive
Back stock
Line side
Pick
(when there's space line side)

There are small variations for different types of products, but in general, this looks correct.
Good. Today, we'll focus on the flow of product to the pick location. Ideally, items should always be available when the picker needs them. How can we do this?
If we had enough space, we could fill the shelves with enough inventory to last the whole shift. Then we would not run out.
But we already do that, and it doesn't work. Even for slow movers where we have plenty of inventory, we run out because someone forgot to replenish them or was too busy. Besides, we want to reduce space used, not increase it.
Reduce inventory and not run out... seems like a contradiction.
In your current system it is. Now, imagine needing 80 units of a product in a shift, but it's bulky, and you can only fit 15 at the line. How could you ensure you don't run out?
Well, if we replenish the line side location before the last unit is picked, there will always be inventory in the market.
That's right! And that's the purpose of routes. A material handler comes at fixed intervals, bringing a few cases of multiple products to replenish the market. They can use a cart for this.
Lineside
Back stock

But how do they know what to bring? Do they come check and then go get it?
Lineside
Back stock
That would work, but it seems like an awful lot of walking. Any other ideas?
We know what's in the orders, so in theory we could predict what will be used and bring it to the line.
Why can't the warehouse ever do what the system tells them to?
?
MRP
That's another possibility. That's a 'push' system and is basically what computer scheduling systems like MRP do. In theory, they are great. In practice however, predictions are not right, and variability messes things up. In the end, you require a lot of inventory to keep things running smoothly.
Probably not what we want, then.
Indeed. Let's go back to your idea, Lisa. In a 'pull' system, replenishment happens in response to consumption. No predictions needed. And responding to actual demand takes care of variability. Toyota has had great success with simple pull systems.
Except for the walking...hmm. What if the route runner wrote down what was low when he brought inventory to the line? He could then bring the items needed the next time around.
Perfect. That would minimize walking. However, I suggest we use kanban instead of looking at what's low and making a list.
Use what?
Kanban. It's just a signal to tell the route runner more product is needed. It can take many forms, but it's frequently a card indicating the item, quantity needed, and addresses for where it comes from and where it should go to.
Kanban
Pick
Backstock
Routes
Lineside market

If I understand correctly, the kanban sits in a case at the market and gets triggered when all the items in the case are picked, right?
Yes. When the pickers use up a case, they place the kanban in a collection point signaling 'please refill me.' When the route runners come around, they deliver product and take the kanban that have accumulated since their last visit. This tells them what to bring next.
We'll need to try this. But how do we figure out how much product we need in the market?
If you look up kanban calculation, you will find many equations that use slightly different assumptions. They are often complicated. I prefer to keep it simple. Let's break it down.
Let's take the bulky item from before. Say you need 80 units in an 8-hour shift. How much should you hold at the line?
Well, wouldn't it depend on how often we replenish the market?
Very good point. Say we replenish once per hour.
Then you need 10 per hour, so you should have at least 10 in the market.
Inventory Behavior
Inventory Level
Demand
With zero variability we can bring a fixed amount at the end of each cycle (there is no need for additional information)
Time
Replenish
Replenish
Replenish
Replenish
Time Between Replenishment
Right. If there was no variability, 10 would be just enough. We would consume exactly 10 per hour, so we would bring 10 units to the market every hour. That's the amount needed to cover demand between replenishments.

So we need another 10 units in the market?
Now, since we pick the kanban in one cycle and deliver the product in the next, there will usually be some kanban in transit.
Replenish
Replenish
Replenish
Replenish
Yes. We need kanban to represent another 10 units, which is the consumption over the delay period. Note that we would need 20 additional units if instead of delivering one cycle after picking the kanban, it took two cycles to deliver.
Inventory Behavior
Replenish amount indicated by Kanban picked in previous cycle
Inventory Level
Demand
Pick Kanban
Replenish and pick Kanban
Replenish and pick Kanban
Replenish and pick Kanban
Time
Time Between Replenishment
And finally, we need a bit extra to cover variability. For a market you will replenish multiple times a day from a nearby stock, you can add one more cycle, or 10 more units.
That makes 30 units in the market. So, we need three times the average demand between replenishments.
Wait, I thought you said the market could only hold 15 units of this bulky product?
Inventory Behavior
Replenish amount indicated by Kanban picked in previous cycle
Inventory Level
Demand
Safety stock
Pick Kanban
Replenish and pick Kanban
Replenish and pick Kanban
Replenish and pick Kanban
Time
Time Between Replenishment
You're right. What can we do?

Over the next few months, we designed the gift box and basket stations and the market to feed them. As we grew comfortable with the new concepts, we added markets for bread and pastry. We built custom stations and markets using Fastube®, and then we changed the layout over a long weekend. On November 1st, 2004, we ran the new process for the first time. We had scarcely a month to get used to it before holiday orders started piling up.

Sequence orders to level workload

The new line has been running for a few days, and the crew is getting used to it. We expected a rough start and we are making adjustments as we learn. Eduardo is back with some new topics to discuss.

Good prediction, Betty. However, we do not want people to remove orders from the line. This only hides the underlying problems.
But sometimes we have no option. In December, we sometimes need to do it to keep the line running.
Ok, and what happens when you do so?
What do you mean? We put the orders aside and feed them back to the line when it's flowing better.
And the next day? Do you remove orders from the line again?
Depending on what's going on, but frequently we have to.
That's my concern. In Lean, we strive to get to the root cause of the problem so it does not come back. We want a system where problems are clearly visible. Keeping the orders on the line and forcing people to stop working creates awareness and will get everyone thinking about how to solve the real problem.
EDUARDO
Clever. You want us to feel the pain as motivation to improve the system.
But this pain may result in delays to the customer. We cannot allow that.
Well, I hope it doesn't come to that. Either way, the idea is to help your customers. Having to remove orders from the line is a symptom of an unreliable process. Every day you operate that way, you risk missing a shipment and disappointing your customers.
Hmm… that's an interesting perspective. Working around our problems does not help improve the system for our customers in the long run.
Great insight! What we need is to highlight the issues so the team can focus on each problem and address the underlying cause.

And this will strengthen the system and make it less likely we ship late to a customer in the future. I like it!
It's a short-term risk that will result in a better process and lower risk of failure long-term.
PERFORMANCE IMPROVEMENT
Right. Besides, moving tubs off the line consumes time and adds no value. And, ergonomically, it's not good for your people to do all that bending down. Anyway, this is just one example. In general, we want to highlight problems instead of working around them.
It makes sense. If we can see a problem, we may be able to solve it. No one can do anything about problems that remain hidden.
Exactly! Now, let's go back to observing the line. I think we can tackle one of those underlying issues today. Besides the struggle to get baskets onto the main line, what else do you see further down? Remember, we want a steady flow of orders.
Well, the pickers seem to alternate between feast and famine.
True. Sometimes they are overwhelmed with orders, while other times they just stand around.
Too much work
No work

Good observation. Why do you think that is?
It seems to have something to do with the type of order… and perhaps with the way those orders arrive.
Good points, but what drives that arrival sequence?
Well, it must come from how orders are released. We print them in the sequence in which they were taken, and that's how they go to the line.
True, but they also get mixed up a bit on the line depending on how long boxes and baskets take to be picked and assembled.
Ok… so what can we do to get a smoother flow into pick?
We could release orders differently. But how do we create a better mix?
Good question… and that gets us to heijunka, which means creating a leveled workload—another key concept in TPS. When people think about Lean, what usually comes to mind is reducing muda, or waste. At Toyota, it's just as important to reduce variability, which is called mura in Japanese.
More Japanese words? I'm not sure I can remember them all.
You're right, let's stick to English. Heijunka is simply leveling, and the goal is to reduce the ups and downs in workload and in the amount of products used. Variability is the enemy of a smooth flow. By leveling, we smooth sharp peaks and valleys into soft rolling hills.
W/O Leveling
W/ Leveling
Are you suggesting that changing the way we release orders to the line will smooth the flow in pick, so we won't have to remove orders from the line in December?
A better release of orders will help level the workload for the whole line and minimize the chance that it will get blocked, yes.
I still don't see how we do it, though.

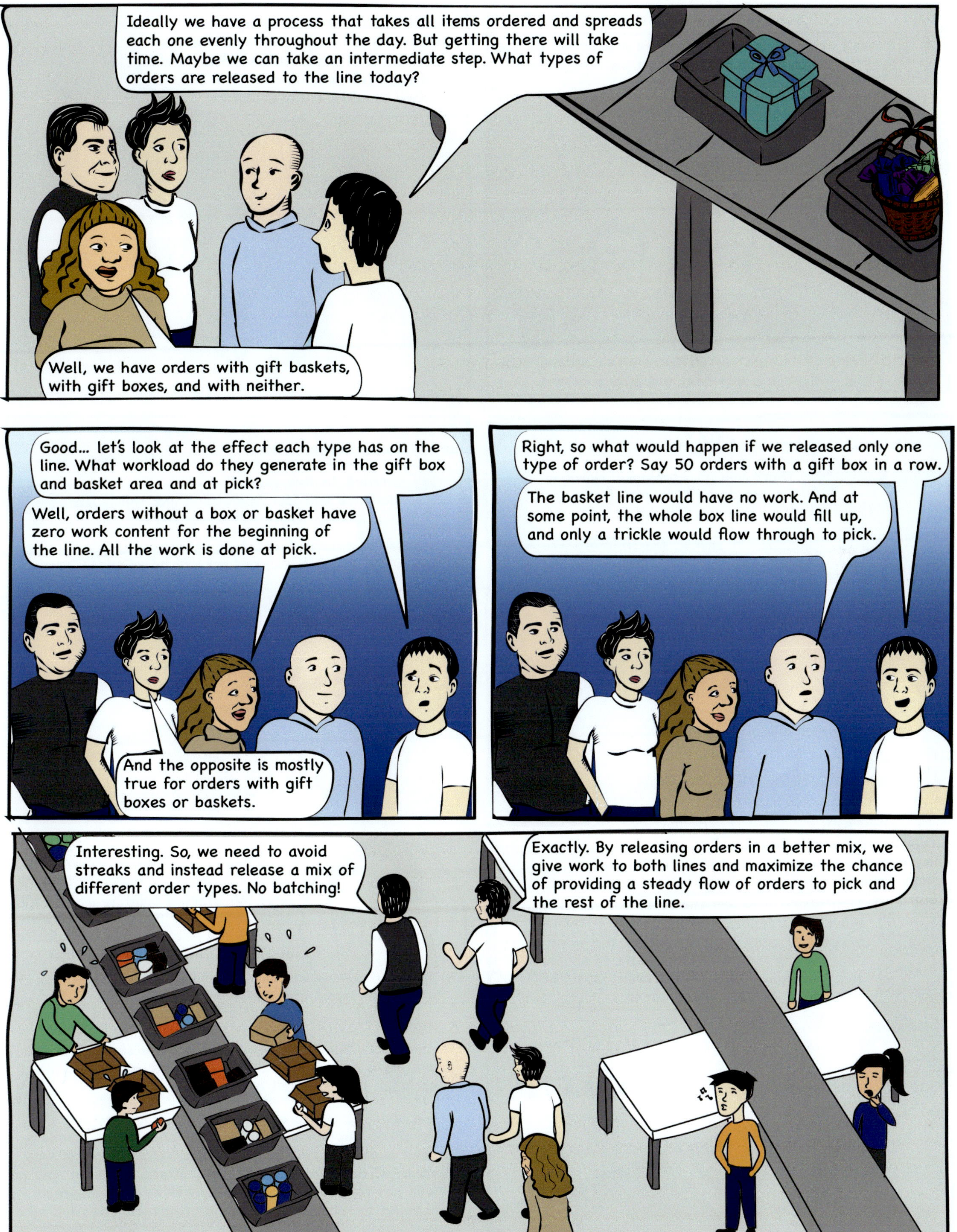
Ideally we have a process that takes all items ordered and spreads each one evenly throughout the day. But getting there will take time. Maybe we can take an intermediate step. What types of orders are released to the line today?
Well, we have orders with gift baskets, with gift boxes, and with neither.
Good... let's look at the effect each type has on the line. What workload do they generate in the gift box and basket area and at pick?
Well, orders without a box or basket have zero work content for the beginning of the line. All the work is done at pick.
And the opposite is mostly true for orders with gift boxes or baskets.
Right, so what would happen if we released only one type of order? Say 50 orders with a gift box in a row.
The basket line would have no work. And at some point, the whole box line would fill up, and only a trickle would flow through to pick.
Interesting. So, we need to avoid streaks and instead release a mix of different order types. No batching!
Exactly. By releasing orders in a better mix, we give work to both lines and maximize the chance of providing a steady flow of orders to pick and the rest of the line.

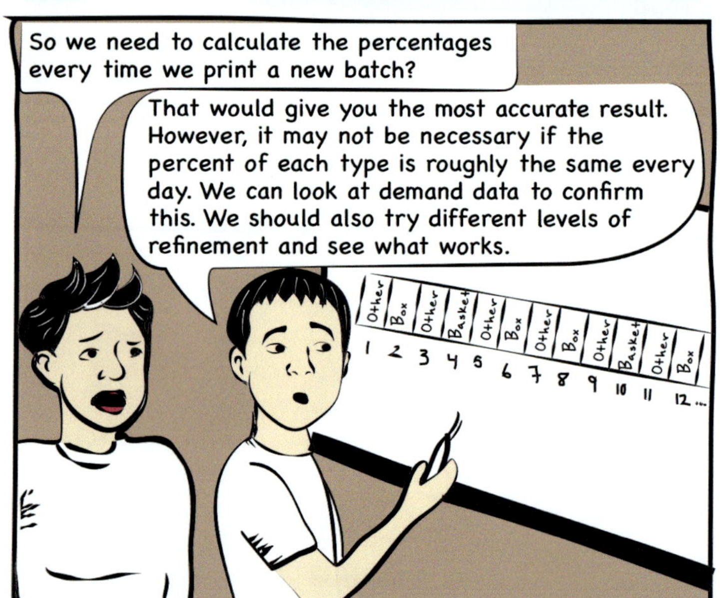

That began our leveling experiment... which continues to evolve 15 years later. We started printing orders by type and delivering three different piles to the Anchor table. The desired mix would then be released by grabbing orders from the three piles as needed.

The effect was clear from day one. The box and basket lines ran constantly. The flow into pick was more stable and the mix more balanced. And the workload, although still variable, lost its feast or famine behavior.

We also started to appreciate Eduardo's teaching style. He asked questions to draw ideas and get us thinking, then explained new concepts at critical times. He was clearly guiding us, but in a very interactive way. And he was not forcing us into a preconceived mold. Instead, he seemed to follow some guiding principles, but read what was going on and customized his ideas to our needs.

Takt defines the standard speed for the line

It's now late November, and the redesigned line has run for three weeks… or perhaps I should be more accurate: it's been three weeks of learning and tweaking, while the line runs. And all while we hire hundreds of people for Christmas. It's been hectic, and tensions are high, but the team is beginning to feel confident in the new process.

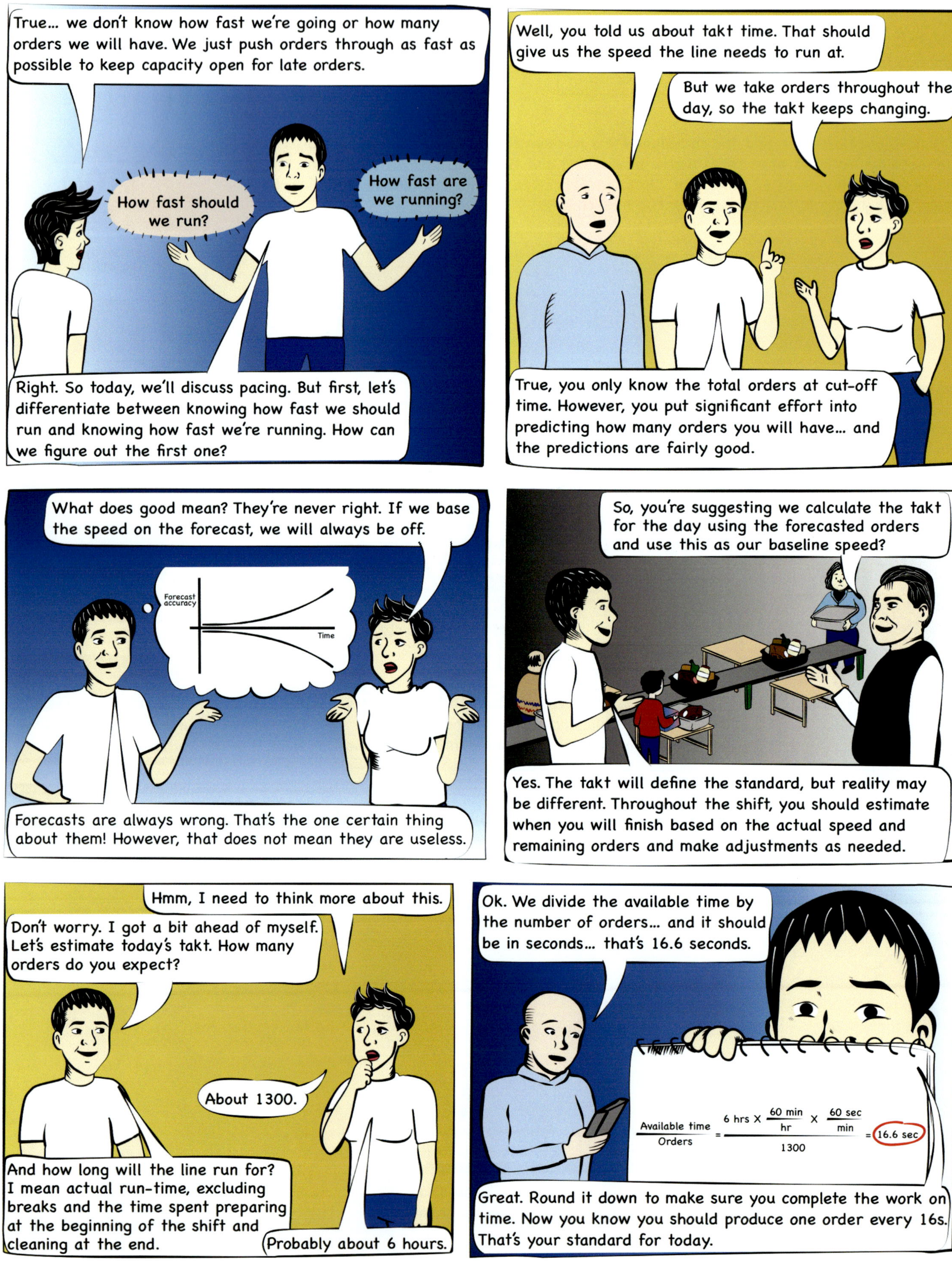
True... we don't know how fast we're going or how many orders we will have. We just push orders through as fast as possible to keep capacity open for late orders.
How fast should we run?
How fast are we running?
Right. So today, we'll discuss pacing. But first, let's differentiate between knowing how fast we should run and knowing how fast we're running. How can we figure out the first one?
Well, you told us about takt time. That should give us the speed the line needs to run at.
But we take orders throughout the day, so the takt keeps changing.
True, you only know the total orders at cut-off time. However, you put significant effort into predicting how many orders you will have... and the predictions are fairly good.
What does good mean? They're never right. If we base the speed on the forecast, we will always be off.
Forecast accuracy
Time
Forecasts are always wrong. That's the one certain thing about them! However, that does not mean they are useless.
So, you're suggesting we calculate the takt for the day using the forecasted orders and use this as our baseline speed?
Yes. The takt will define the standard, but reality may be different. Throughout the shift, you should estimate when you will finish based on the actual speed and remaining orders and make adjustments as needed.
Hmm, I need to think more about this.
Don't worry. I got a bit ahead of myself. Let's estimate today's takt. How many orders do you expect?
About 1300.
And how long will the line run for? I mean actual run-time, excluding breaks and the time spent preparing at the beginning of the shift and cleaning at the end.
Probably about 6 hours.
Ok. We divide the available time by the number of orders... and it should be in seconds... that's 16.6 seconds.
Available time / Orders = (6 hrs X 60 min/hr X 60 sec/min) / 1300 = 16.6 sec
Great. Round it down to make sure you complete the work on time. Now you know you should produce one order every 16s. That's your standard for today.

But how is this helpful? What do we do with this?
I guess we need the second part... how fast we're running.
That's right. How can we figure that out?
If we pick a spot on the line and count the orders that go by in a given amount of time, we can calculate it.
1
2
3
4
Yes, that gives us the local speed of the line at that time. Depending on the situation, this may or may not represent the overall speed, which is what we need to compare to the takt.
We can count completed orders at the end of the line. Since we know how long the line has been running for, we can figure out the average speed, right?
Right. Another easy place to count is at the beginning of the line. Would one be better than the other?
8,9,10...
Before we answer that, is counting orders the only way to know the speed of the line?
Hmmm... either we measure it, or we somehow know it...
Know it from how we release orders... is that what you mean by pacing?
16s, release order...
16s, release order...
Exactly! If we know how fast we should be running, given by the takt, we can release orders at that rate and pace the line to match the speed we want.
That seems like an oversimplification. Just because I want to release an order every 16s doesn't mean the line can work at that speed.
Wait for 16s...
You're probably right. Most of the time the line will want to run at a different speed. What would happen then? Say the line could run faster. What would you see?
The line would be empty, and people would be waiting for work.

Ok, and what could you do?
Release orders faster.
Yes, you could do that and get ahead. Or you could continue to release at takt and use excess people for other work. Either way, it would be an intentional decision, and you would know you're ahead of plan if you chose to run faster.
Now, what if the line was running slower than the 16s takt?
The opposite. The line would fill up, and the Anchor would not be able to put orders on it.
16s, release order...
The reaction in this case is harder though. We would want to speed up the line. How to do it is the question.
That's right. By comparing to the takt time, you would realize you're running slower than planned and would want to correct it. So, what could we do?
Well, in a sequential line like ours, the bottleneck... the slowest station... defines the overall speed. If we identify where the bottleneck is, we can add capacity there to speed up the whole line.
Perfect! However, your bottleneck shifts depending on the mix of orders. Leveling helps, but it's not good enough yet. If you get 5 or 6 high workload gift boxes in a row, the gift box line gets blocked. If the gift boxes are small, but the orders include many other items, then pick becomes the bottleneck.
We can't take action if we don't know where to act...
We know we need to act on the bottleneck. We just need to find it.
Ok, so how do we do it? What should we look for on the line?
Order tubs? Orders would back up at the slowest station.
Orders will accumulate upstream of the bottleneck and the line will be empty downstream. The line will tell us!

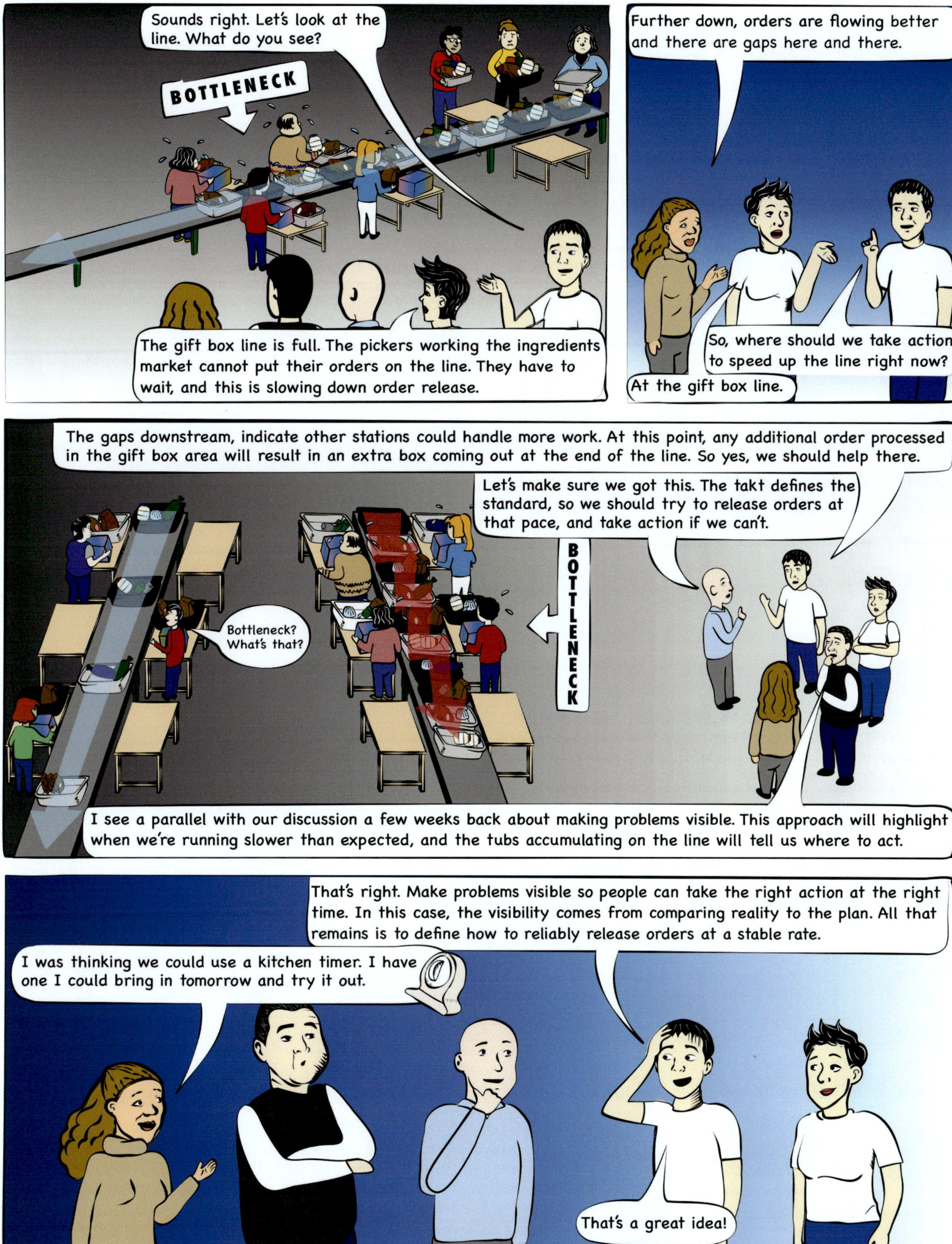
Sounds right. Let's look at the line. What do you see?
BOTTLENECK
The gift box line is full. The pickers working the ingredients market cannot put their orders on the line. They have to wait, and this is slowing down order release.
Further down, orders are flowing better and there are gaps here and there.
So, where should we take action to speed up the line right now?
At the gift box line.
The gaps downstream, indicate other stations could handle more work. At this point, any additional order processed in the gift box area will result in an extra box coming out at the end of the line. So yes, we should help there.
Let's make sure we got this. The takt defines the standard, so we should try to release orders at that pace, and take action if we can't.
Bottleneck? What's that?
BOTTLENECK
I see a parallel with our discussion a few weeks back about making problems visible. This approach will highlight when we're running slower than expected, and the tubs accumulating on the line will tell us where to act.
That's right. Make problems visible so people can take the right action at the right time. In this case, the visibility comes from comparing reality to the plan. All that remains is to define how to reliably release orders at a stable rate.
I was thinking we could use a kitchen timer. I have one I could bring in tomorrow and try it out.
That's a great idea!

Year 2: Small experiments lead to second big Christmas experiment

It's now January 2005. With Christmas over, the first big test for Lean is behind us. The process was so successful it transformed the team from doubters into believers. Betty is now a complete convert and thirsty for more. The group has come together to reflect on what happened.

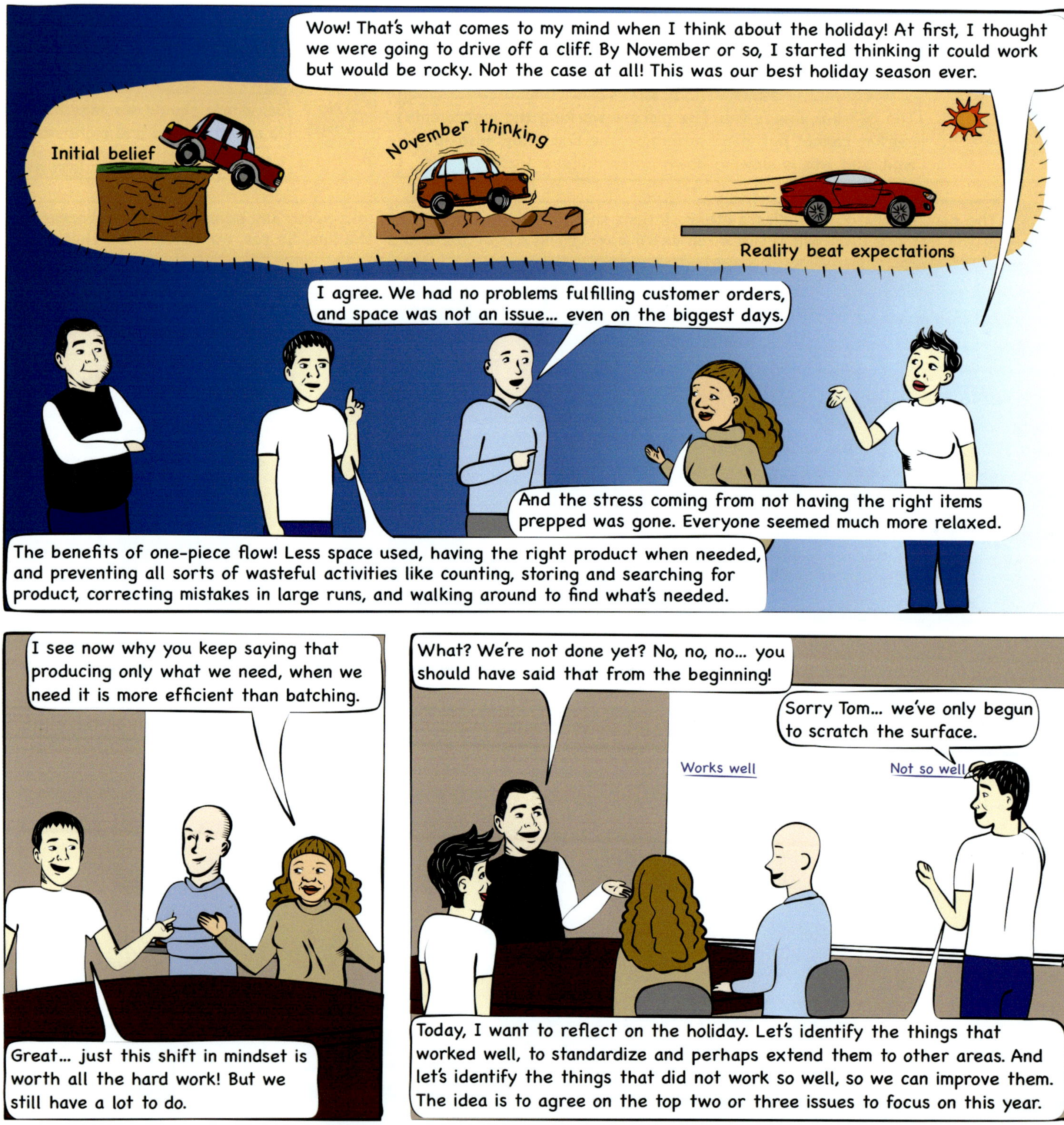

Works well
Not so well
- One-piece flow
- Simultaneous run of prep and line
- Markets and routes
For what worked, you can write down this one-piece flow thing... and also running prep simultaneously with the line.
Also, markets and routes. The gift box ingredients and the line side bread markets worked very well. Especially compared to dry goods, where pickers still did their own replenishment. The interruptions to the line's flow there were a constant hassle.
Works well
Not so well
- One-piece flow
- Simultaneous run of prep and line
- Markets and routes
- Accurate release to takt
Good point. I guess extending the use of markets to dry goods and cheese is an easy next step.
We should definitely do that. Regarding the struggles, we should take another look at the whole takt thing. The stop watch that replaced the original kitchen timer worked a bit better, but I'm not convinced the Anchor always released on time.
I agree. On several occasions, I saw her skip a sequence. She would then try to catch up by releasing orders before the alarm went off. Anything else wrong with the takt process?
Well, if we're not sure about the release speed, then the conclusions we draw from it, like the end of day estimation, are also doubtful. How accurate were we on this?
Usually we were within 15 minutes or so of our calculation. Maybe not perfect, but if the alternative is guessing as before... no comparison!
Right... A bigger issue, though, was using takt to evaluate performance throughout the day and taking appropriate action. I don't think we have a good process for this. And I don't think it happened regularly enough.
Ok, we have some work to do on takt. We need to improve the accuracy of release and define a better process to use that information.
Not so well
- Accurate release to takt
- Reaction to deviations from standard line speed

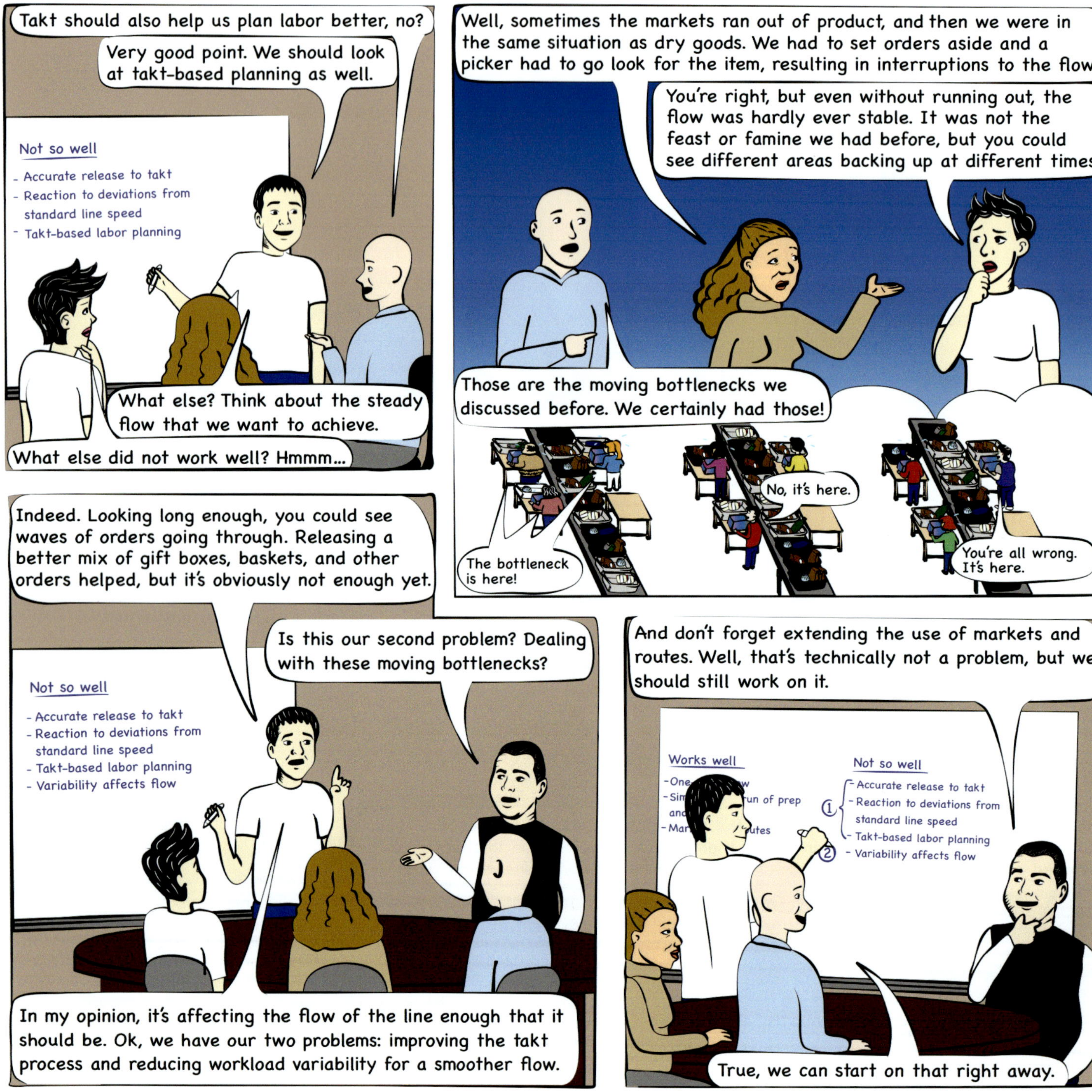

With Eduardo's help, we started extending markets and routes to dry goods and cheese, and later on to other areas that required regular replenishments. We built markets, estimated their size, defined routes, and used kanban to feed the line everything it needed. This work extended through most of the year, while the management team focused on improving takt and dealing with variability, as we will soon see.

To takt or not to takt
The new markets and routes are working well, and we continue to expand to new areas. Shouldn't we start working on the other problems we identified in our holiday reflection?
Absolutely! I'm glad you brought it up. I suggest we start with takt, as it will stabilize the line further and help us identify new opportunities for improvement.
The issue is ensuring orders are released at the right rate, correct?
That's one problem, but more generally, we're just not using takt to its full potential.
True, but let's start with the release rate. I'm concerned about the poor souls who release orders. It's an intermittent and boring job. The person gets distracted and releases the order late, or skips one entirely and then tries to catch up.
And the alarm? It drives me crazy, going off every 15 seconds... or whatever the takt happens to be. I can't stay near that station for long.
You're both right. We're failing our people with this process... and we get variability when we want stability.
Exactly! You all know I am an IT guy at heart. I've been thinking about automating the process. With some coding, I think EVE can choose which orders to release and print them at the line at the rate we tell her to.
EVE keeps time... so no more alarm? Plus, printing at the line would save time for the folks in the office. Seems like a win-win.

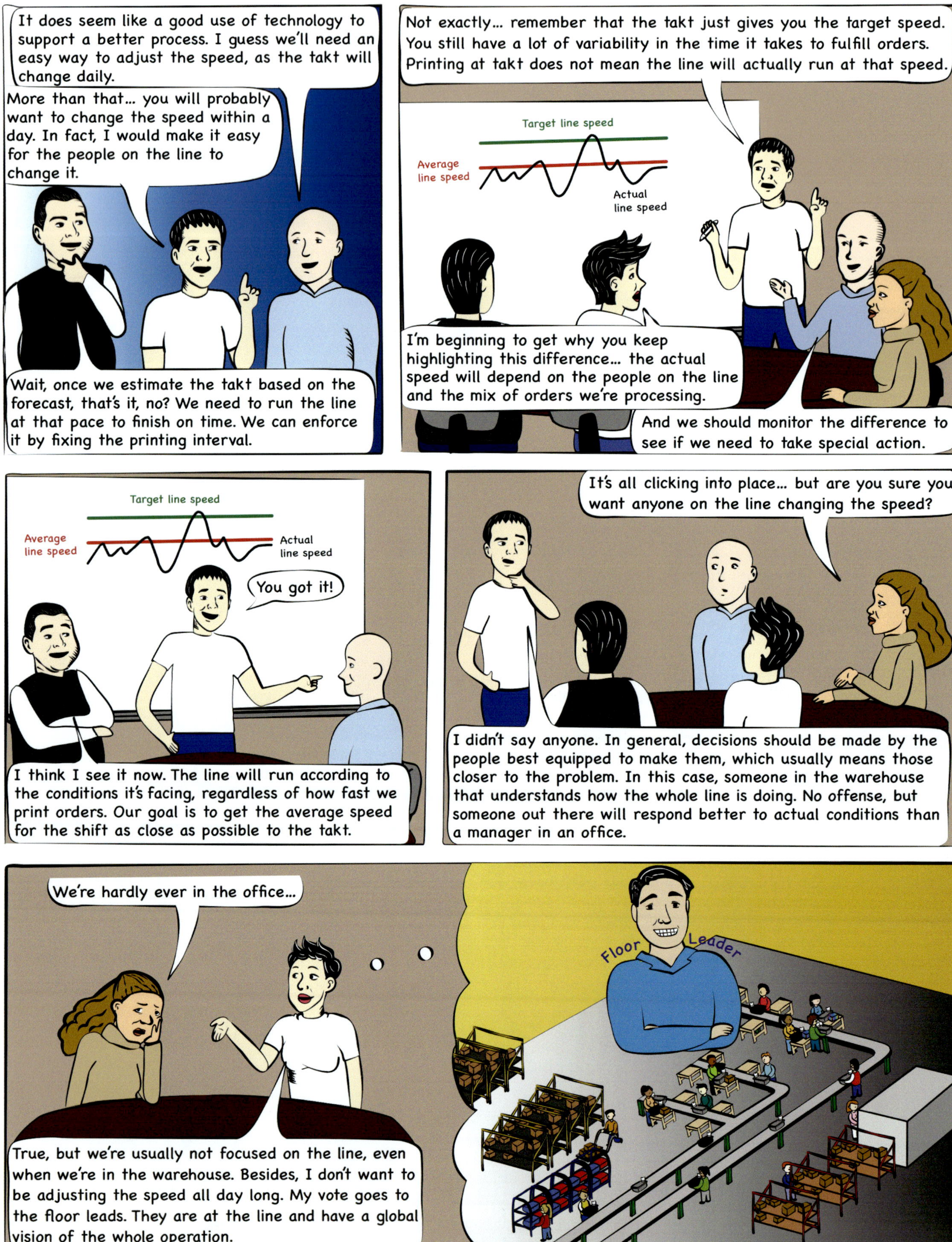
It does seem like a good use of technology to support a better process. I guess we'll need an easy way to adjust the speed, as the takt will change daily.
More than that... you will probably want to change the speed within a day. In fact, I would make it easy for the people on the line to change it.
Wait, once we estimate the takt based on the forecast, that's it, no? We need to run the line at that pace to finish on time. We can enforce it by fixing the printing interval.
Not exactly... remember that the takt just gives you the target speed. You still have a lot of variability in the time it takes to fulfill orders. Printing at takt does not mean the line will actually run at that speed.
Target line speed
Average line speed
Actual line speed
I'm beginning to get why you keep highlighting this difference... the actual speed will depend on the people on the line and the mix of orders we're processing.
And we should monitor the difference to see if we need to take special action.
Target line speed
Average line speed
Actual line speed
You got it!
I think I see it now. The line will run according to the conditions it's facing, regardless of how fast we print orders. Our goal is to get the average speed for the shift as close as possible to the takt.
It's all clicking into place... but are you sure you want anyone on the line changing the speed?
I didn't say anyone. In general, decisions should be made by the people best equipped to make them, which usually means those closer to the problem. In this case, someone in the warehouse that understands how the whole line is doing. No offense, but someone out there will respond better to actual conditions than a manager in an office.
We're hardly ever in the office...
Floor Leader
True, but we're usually not focused on the line, even when we're in the warehouse. Besides, I don't want to be adjusting the speed all day long. My vote goes to the floor leads. They are at the line and have a global vision of the whole operation.

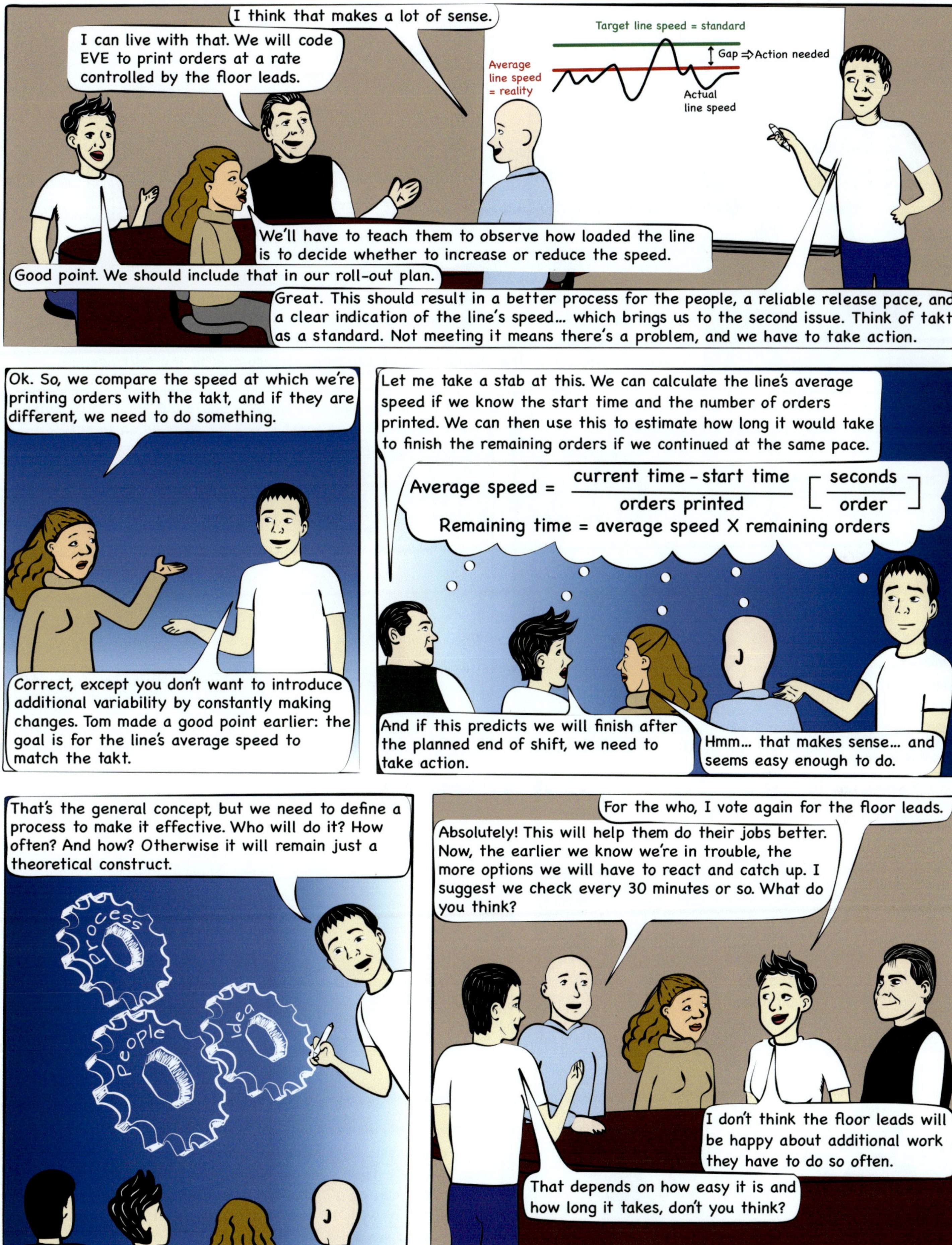
I can live with that. We will code EVE to print orders at a rate controlled by the floor leads.
I think that makes a lot of sense.
Target line speed = standard
Average line speed = reality
Gap ⇒ Action needed
Actual line speed
We'll have to teach them to observe how loaded the line is to decide whether to increase or reduce the speed.
Good point. We should include that in our roll-out plan.
Great. This should result in a better process for the people, a reliable release pace, and a clear indication of the line's speed... which brings us to the second issue. Think of takt as a standard. Not meeting it means there's a problem, and we have to take action.
Ok. So, we compare the speed at which we're printing orders with the takt, and if they are different, we need to do something.
Correct, except you don't want to introduce additional variability by constantly making changes. Tom made a good point earlier: the goal is for the line's average speed to match the takt.
Let me take a stab at this. We can calculate the line's average speed if we know the start time and the number of orders printed. We can then use this to estimate how long it would take to finish the remaining orders if we continued at the same pace.
Average speed = current time - start time / orders printed [seconds / order]
Remaining time = average speed X remaining orders
And if this predicts we will finish after the planned end of shift, we need to take action.
Hmm... that makes sense... and seems easy enough to do.
That's the general concept, but we need to define a process to make it effective. Who will do it? How often? And how? Otherwise it will remain just a theoretical construct.
Process
People
Idea
For the who, I vote again for the floor leads.
Absolutely! This will help them do their jobs better. Now, the earlier we know we're in trouble, the more options we will have to react and catch up. I suggest we check every 30 minutes or so. What do you think?
I don't think the floor leads will be happy about additional work they have to do so often.
That depends on how easy it is and how long it takes, don't you think?

How can you make a calculation eas... never mind. I bet you have an idea.
Orders processed
Planned start time
Planned end of day
Total orders for the shift
Takt = standard
12:00 1:00 2:00 3:00 4:00 5:00
Time
Well, I like to make things visual whenever possible. We could have a chart with time on the bottom and orders processed on the vertical axis. At the beginning of the day, we can draw the plan... which is just a straight line from zero orders at the start, to the forecasted amount at the planned end of day. This corresponds to the takt needed.
All the floor leads need to do is mark the cumulative number of orders released every 30 minutes.
Planned start time
Planned end of day
Whitout action we will finish late
Total orders for the shift
Takt = standard
Average line speed
Gap ⇒ need to take action
Time
Nice. That's a simple process and results in a clear visual.
Very clear... when we're under the planned line, we need to take action. Easy!
Let's try it out! We still need to figure out what to do when we're behind, but at least it will be clear when to act.
Sounds like we have a plan. Now, we also talked about using takt to plan labor. How are we doing on that?
Well, it's great to know how fast we should run, but translating that into the number of people needed is not so easy.
What do you mean?
We need to run at a 20 second takt.
Should we use 15 people or 20?
I'm not sure... let's try 18.
Since there is so much variability in the orders, we don't know how to estimate how many people we need for any given takt.
Right, and basing it on what we see at the line is very hard since the takt itself changes often. Today it's 20 seconds, tomorrow it can be 17, and the day after, 21. Let's say we ran well today with 15 people for a 20s takt. How many people would we need for tomorrow's 17 second takt?

You should be able to calculate it. 17s is 15% faster, so you need 15% more people, no? That's... 2.25 more people.
Ok, but we cannot add a quarter of a person. Do we add two and risk not having enough capacity, or three, knowing it will be too much?
Go with three. That would give us the possibility of taking additional orders... and we can always end the day early if the line runs too fast.
Good. That lets us scale labor between different takt values. However, it's critical to know how many people we really need at a certain takt before we scale it.
Yes... we're back at the beginning. Our reality is that the number and content of orders are constantly changing, so the takt and the people needed to achieve it change constantly as well.
Tue → 20s takt
Wed → 22s takt
Why did we need so many people?
The first bit is a fact. The implication of constantly changing takt, maybe not.
What do you mean?
Takt time = available time / orders
Needed time = standard takt time x orders
The takt calculation has two components. One is the number of orders... which is constantly changing. The other is the production time. What if we adjusted the shift length to get a constant takt?
So instead of adding 15% more people, we would run a 15% longer shift?
But we cannot push the end of day too far. We need to finish before the carrier picks up the orders.
We can figure out when to start the shift to finish in time... but I think we have too much variability in the number of orders per day to have a single takt.
Thanks for bringing that up, Tom. You're absolutely right. If we run a Friday with 100 orders at the same speed we run a Monday with 1000, we'll either have a very long Monday or a very short Friday.
True. So, what can we do?
Maybe we can select a few takt values that cover our whole range of orders?
Great idea, Betty! Let's decide on a fixed set of standard takt levels.

Let's select them so they are easy to scale. A 10 second takt is twice as fast as a 20, so we just need to double the people.
10s
20s
Good point. I think those two are in. During Christmas we need a 10, and 20 is a logical progression.
Seems like a pretty big gap.
I think so, too. We should include a 15. And doubling it gets us to 30.
10s
15s
20s
30s
60s
I would add a 60 for the slowest days.
That probably does it… we have our standard takt levels. Let's take them for a test run!
Great! Now we need the corresponding standard labor numbers. We can calculate a starting point, but given order content variability, we'll need to fine-tune the numbers by experimenting at the line.
Takt level
Labor?
10s
15s
20s
30s
60s
No issue there. If we run the same takt repeatedly and record the number of people, the station they were at, and the results, we should be able to define fairly well the staffing levels needed. Give us a couple of weeks.
Shall we call it a day? We have plenty to do. I'll start working with IT to print orders on takt at the line.
I'll work with the floor leads to set up the chart showing the daily takt plan, so we can track performance and know when to take action.
Takt level
Labor?
10s
15s
20s
30s
60s
Lisa, how about you and I work on the standard labor for the standard takt levels?

Responding to moving bottlenecks – HYN

In year 2 of our Lean journey, the concepts that got us through last Christmas continue to evolve. It is June 2005, and we're about to go into summer sale. We're using kanban to feed all product locations and we're extending it to feed packing stations with boxes and tape. We have also done our first tests printing orders at the line, at the speed defined by takt. We're working on the problems we found, so I'm confident we can go live after summer sale ends. Other aspects of takt are also progressing well...

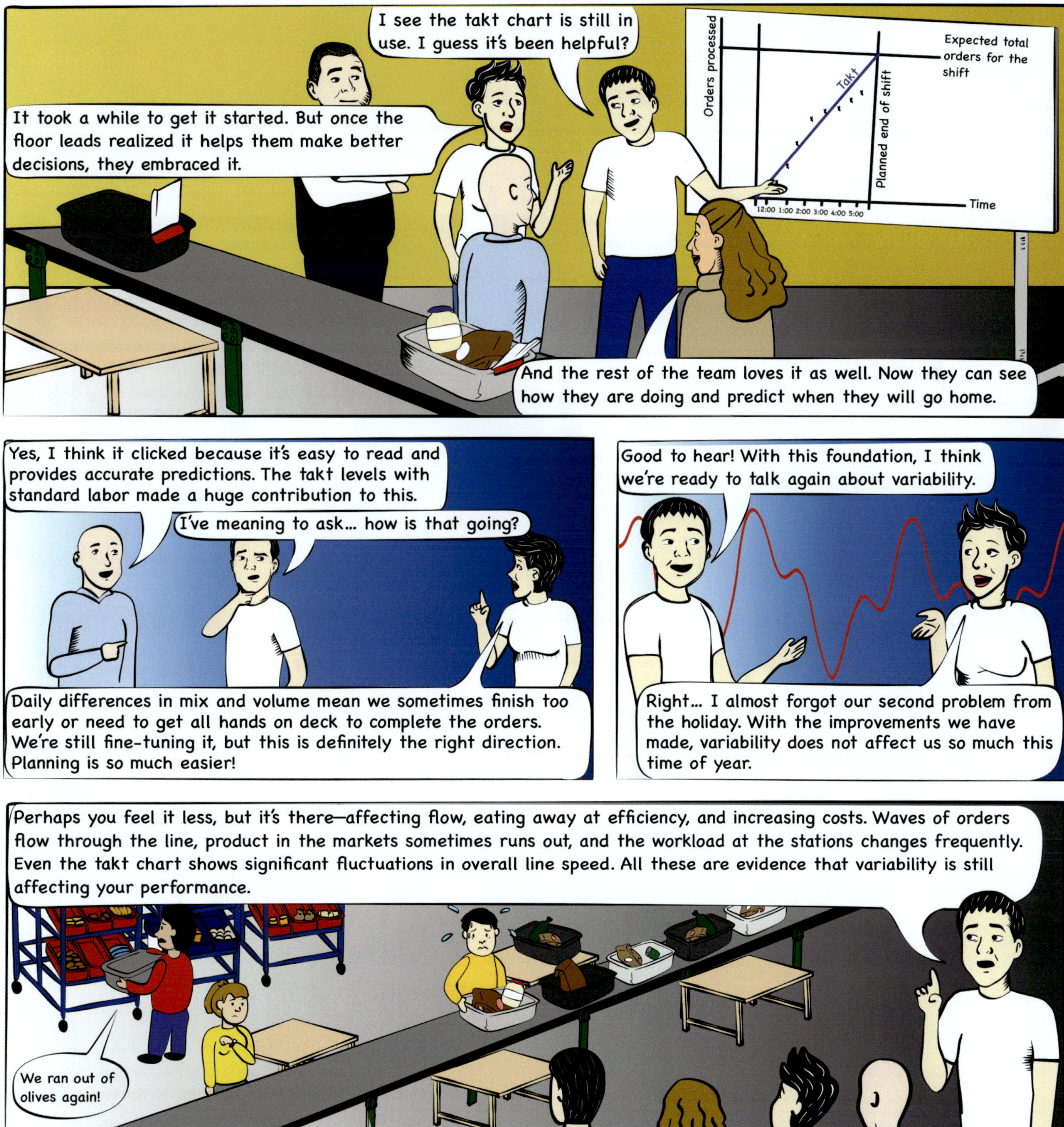

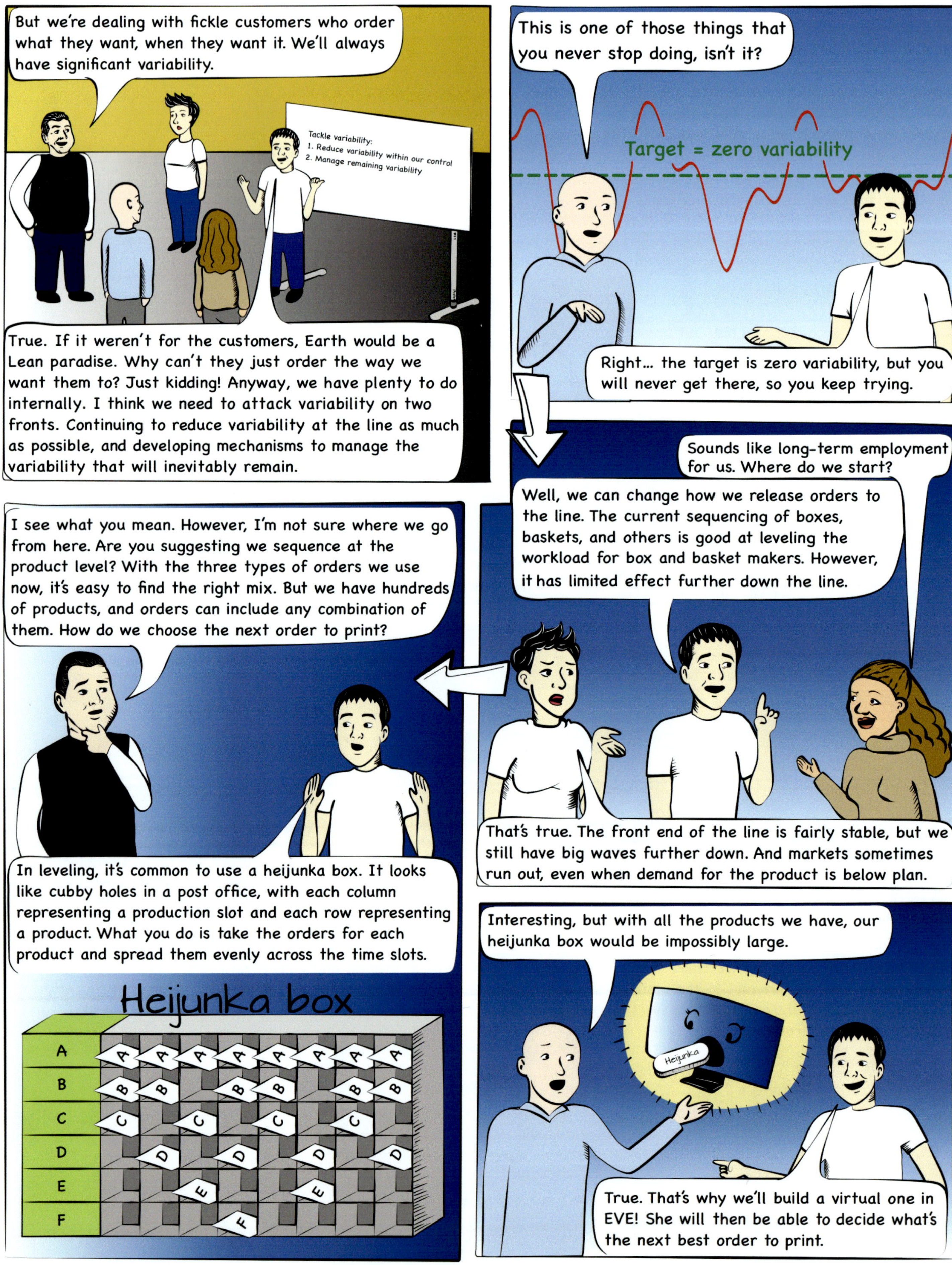

But we're dealing with fickle customers who order what they want, when they want it. We'll always have significant variability.
Tackle variability:
1. Reduce variability within our control
2. Manage remaining variability
True. If it weren't for the customers, Earth would be a Lean paradise. Why can't they just order the way we want them to? Just kidding! Anyway, we have plenty to do internally. I think we need to attack variability on two fronts. Continuing to reduce variability at the line as much as possible, and developing mechanisms to manage the variability that will inevitably remain.
This is one of those things that you never stop doing, isn't it?
Target = zero variability
Right... the target is zero variability, but you will never get there, so you keep trying.
Sounds like long-term employment for us. Where do we start?
Well, we can change how we release orders to the line. The current sequencing of boxes, baskets, and others is good at leveling the workload for box and basket makers. However, it has limited effect further down the line.
That's true. The front end of the line is fairly stable, but we still have big waves further down. And markets sometimes run out, even when demand for the product is below plan.
I see what you mean. However, I'm not sure where we go from here. Are you suggesting we sequence at the product level? With the three types of orders we use now, it's easy to find the right mix. But we have hundreds of products, and orders can include any combination of them. How do we choose the next order to print?
In leveling, it's common to use a heijunka box. It looks like cubby holes in a post office, with each column representing a production slot and each row representing a product. What you do is take the orders for each product and spread them evenly across the time slots.
Heijunka box
A
B
C
D
E
F
Interesting, but with all the products we have, our heijunka box would be impossibly large.
Heijunka
True. That's why we'll build a virtual one in EVE! She will then be able to decide what's the next best order to print.

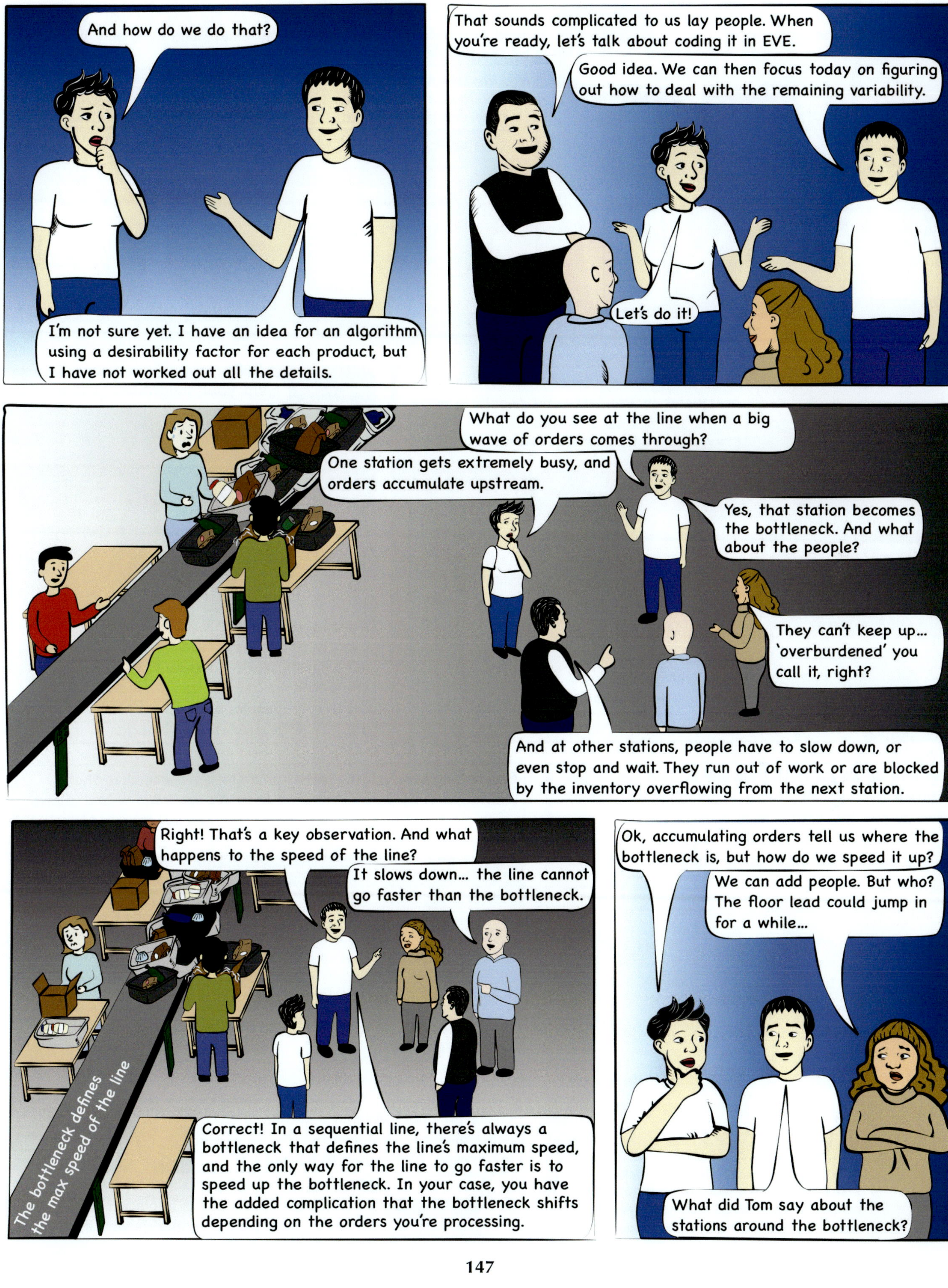
And how do we do that?
I'm not sure yet. I have an idea for an algorithm using a desirability factor for each product, but I have not worked out all the details.
That sounds complicated to us lay people. When you're ready, let's talk about coding it in EVE.
Good idea. We can then focus today on figuring out how to deal with the remaining variability.
Let's do it!
What do you see at the line when a big wave of orders comes through?
One station gets extremely busy, and orders accumulate upstream.
Yes, that station becomes the bottleneck. And what about the people?
They can't keep up... 'overburdened' you call it, right?
And at other stations, people have to slow down, or even stop and wait. They run out of work or are blocked by the inventory overflowing from the next station.
Right! That's a key observation. And what happens to the speed of the line?
It slows down... the line cannot go faster than the bottleneck.
The bottleneck defines the max speed of the line
Correct! In a sequential line, there's always a bottleneck that defines the line's maximum speed, and the only way for the line to go faster is to speed up the bottleneck. In your case, you have the added complication that the bottleneck shifts depending on the orders you're processing.
Ok, accumulating orders tell us where the bottleneck is, but how do we speed it up?
We can add people. But who? The floor lead could jump in for a while...
What did Tom say about the stations around the bottleneck?

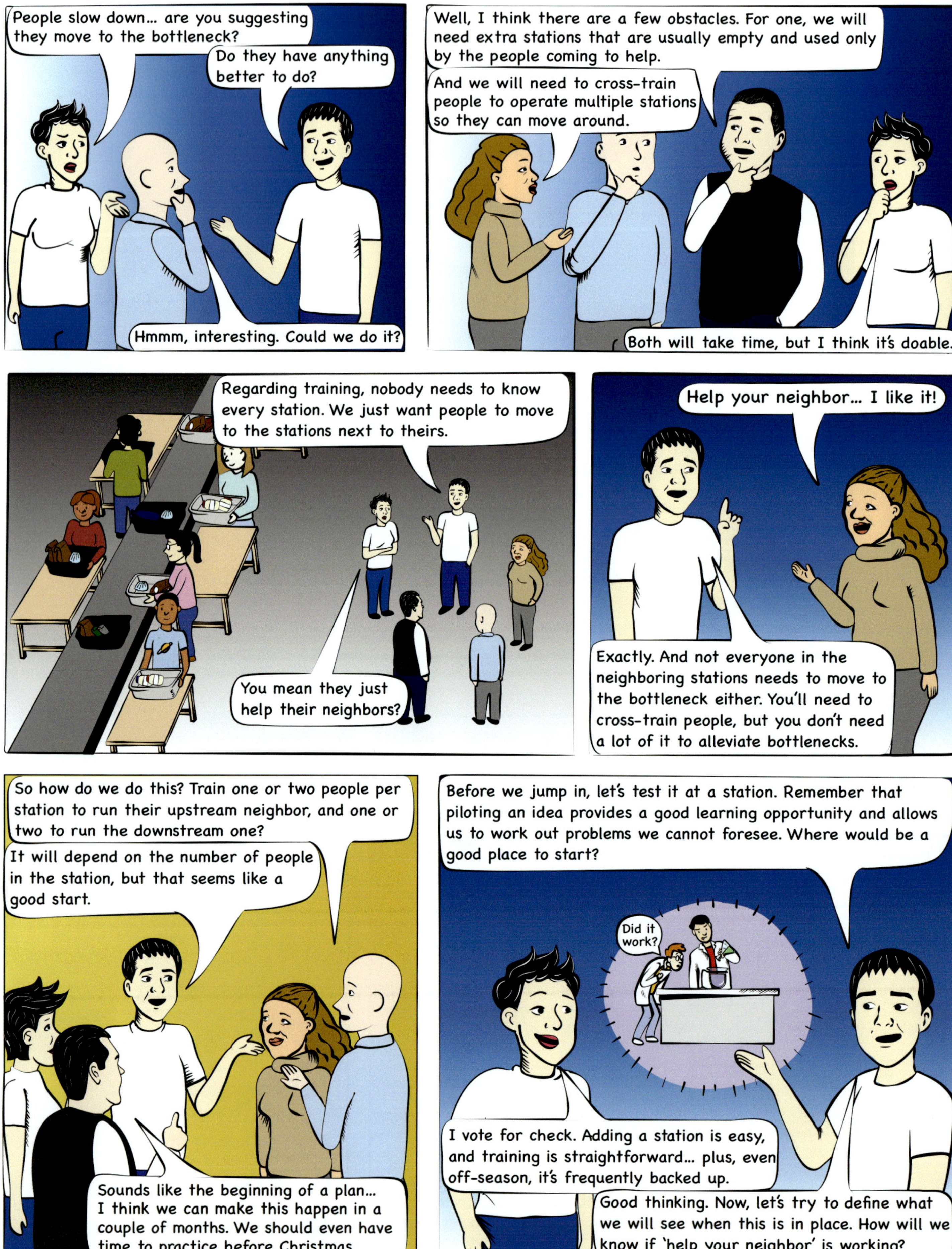

People slow down... are you suggesting they move to the bottleneck?
Do they have anything better to do?
Hmmm, interesting. Could we do it?
Well, I think there are a few obstacles. For one, we will need extra stations that are usually empty and used only by the people coming to help.
And we will need to cross-train people to operate multiple stations so they can move around.
Both will take time, but I think it's doable.
Regarding training, nobody needs to know every station. We just want people to move to the stations next to theirs.
You mean they just help their neighbors?
Help your neighbor... I like it!
Exactly. And not everyone in the neighboring stations needs to move to the bottleneck either. You'll need to cross-train people, but you don't need a lot of it to alleviate bottlenecks.
So how do we do this? Train one or two people per station to run their upstream neighbor, and one or two to run the downstream one?
It will depend on the number of people in the station, but that seems like a good start.
Sounds like the beginning of a plan... I think we can make this happen in a couple of months. We should even have time to practice before Christmas.
Before we jump in, let's test it at a station. Remember that piloting an idea provides a good learning opportunity and allows us to work out problems we cannot foresee. Where would be a good place to start?
Did it work?
I vote for check. Adding a station is easy, and training is straightforward... plus, even off-season, it's frequently backed up.
Good thinking. Now, let's try to define what we will see when this is in place. How will we know if 'help your neighbor' is working?

Well, the line will run faster.
True... if we speed up the bottleneck, the line will necessarily run faster. However, I think that will be hard to see, as it will be confounded with the speed defined by the mix of orders you're processing.
LEAN
SUCCESS?
You lost me there...
I think Eduardo is saying we will see the line running at a certain speed, but we won't know how fast it would have run if people were not helping each other.
Exactly. If we look at data over many days, we may see a shift in average speed, but there are probably other things we can observe directly at the line. What else should we look for?
Well, we should not see people standing idle.
Right. Some people will go help the bottleneck, so they won't be idle. And, the ones that remain at their stations should have work to do as more orders go through the bottleneck. Anything else?
Check should not back up as badly, and the waves of orders should become smaller.
That's certainly what we want. Those two are easy to observe: busier people and fewer backups at check. I would say that's success... if we see both.
I have a question. How will people know when to go help their neighbor?
Very good point. We're asking them to leave their main job and go do someone else's work, so they need a way to define when that's the right thing to do.
Well, when there's a bottleneck, stations downstream starve for work, and stations upstream get blocked by orders on the line. A simple rule could be to go help the station upstream when you run out of work, and go help the station downstream when you're blocked.
Go upstream to get work when starved and downstream to open space when blocked... seems simple enough.
Go help to open space for your work
Go help to get work for yourself
BLOCKED
WORKING
STARVED
Shall we try it?

Year 3: Learn and try again

It's January 2006, and the second Lean Christmas was again successful beyond expectations. We're back together to dissect the holiday processes and define a direction for 2007.

I think HYN worked well, but you make two interesting points, Betty. As Lean brings structure to your process, leaders should change from firefighters giving orders, to planners coaching others to solve their own problems. Now, regarding the inconsistencies, any ideas on why this happens?
Works well
-Takt levels for planning
-Print orders at takt
-Planned takt vs actual comparison
-HYN
Not so well
-Inconsistencies in HYN
It could be the people… but you have told us people fail because the process allows them to. So, we should focus on the process.
Good recovery!
Maybe we could improve training, but I think some areas just lend themselves better to HYN than others. In some areas, it's harder to see what's happening and react correctly.
Yeah… maybe we need better signals.
Ok… training and signals. We should consider these for the next HYN improvements. What else?
Works well
-Takt levels for planning
-Print orders at takt
-Planned takt vs actual comparison
-HYN
-Kanban, markets, and routes
Not so well
-Inconsistencies in HYN
-Duplication of line side markets
I think markets and kanban worked well even in the areas we recently expanded into. However, we're starting to have a lot of duplication between the pick market for gift boxes and baskets and the pick market for the rest.
Good point. As your range of gift boxes and baskets increases and space becomes tighter, you may need a different layout for the line.
With all we're learning and as sales continue to grow, I have no doubt the layout will have to evolve… hopefully we'll be able to do it in this building.
-Print orders at takt
-Planned takt vs actual comparison
-HYN
-Kanban, markets,
routes
-Space usage
-Duplication of line side markets
I can see that happening. Without Lean, we would probably be moving to a bigger place next year, but space did not feel tight at all.
Mostly true, but not for cheese. During the peak days, we had a team working outside the cheese room, and sometimes we still struggled to keep up.
Pfff… the line is out of Gouda again!
Not so well
-Duplication of line side markets
-Not enough space in cheese room

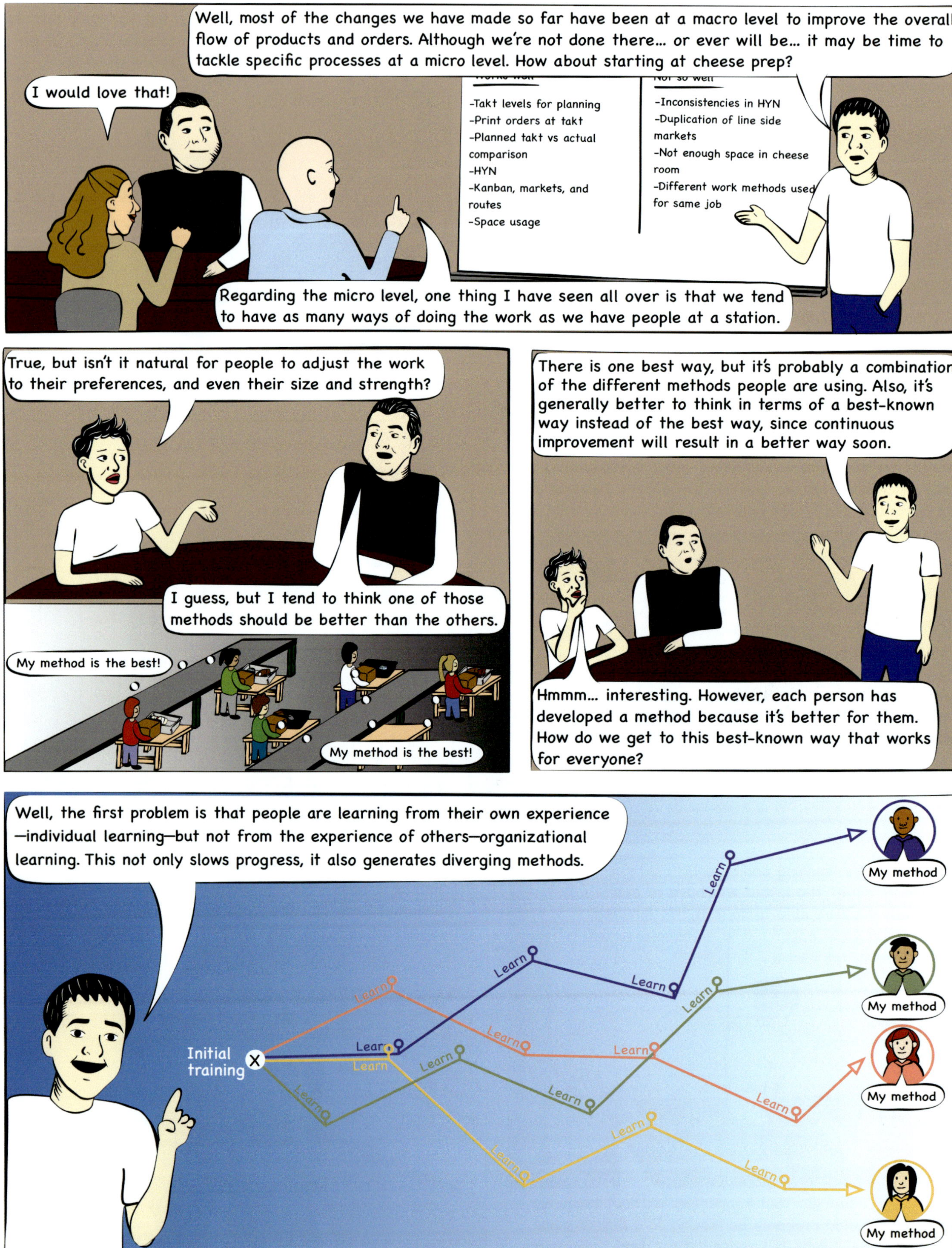
Well, most of the changes we have made so far have been at a macro level to improve the overall flow of products and orders. Although we're not done there... or ever will be... it may be time to tackle specific processes at a micro level. How about starting at cheese prep?
I would love that!
-Takt levels for planning
-Print orders at takt
-Planned takt vs actual comparison
-HYN
-Kanban, markets, and routes
-Space usage
-Inconsistencies in HYN
-Duplication of line side markets
-Not enough space in cheese room
-Different work methods used for same job
Regarding the micro level, one thing I have seen all over is that we tend to have as many ways of doing the work as we have people at a station.
True, but isn't it natural for people to adjust the work to their preferences, and even their size and strength?
I guess, but I tend to think one of those methods should be better than the others.
My method is the best!
My method is the best!
There is one best way, but it's probably a combination of the different methods people are using. Also, it's generally better to think in terms of a best-known way instead of the best way, since continuous improvement will result in a better way soon.
Hmmm... interesting. However, each person has developed a method because it's better for them. How do we get to this best-known way that works for everyone?
Well, the first problem is that people are learning from their own experience —individual learning—but not from the experience of others—organizational learning. This not only slows progress, it also generates diverging methods.
Initial training
Learn
My method
My method
My method
My method

Let me see if I got this... you're saying that by converting individual learning into organizational learning, people will learn from each other, and together they will develop this best-known way that works for everyone?
There's a bit more to it, but basically, yes.
Ok, so how do we do this organizational learning?
In a nutshell, we need to capture what individuals learn into standards others can use. There are basically three ways. We can change the physical process so people have to use the new method. We can codify the learnings into standard operating procedures that define how to do the job. Or we can share the new knowledge widely so others can tackle similar issues.
Learn
Improve process
Individual Learning
Organizational Learning
Structured knowledge
Tacit knowledge
Learning is embedded in the process or codified in documents (such as standardized work)
Learning is widely shared
Seems complicated.
Not really. In fact, you're already doing it. When you changed the line's layout, you embedded changes that prevented pre-building of gift boxes and baskets. When you introduced markets and routes, you changed the picker's job.
But all those people still use different methods. Look at two gift box assemblers, and you will see differences in how they work.
You're right. We made macro level changes that define how and when they can do the work. That still leaves a lot of room for each person to develop the details of their own method.
So now we need to capture the micro level detail at each station...
...and we do it in a standard operating procedure. I think that's what we call recipes.
Recipes... I like it. At the micro level, we can also make physical changes, such as standardizing how gift box stations are set up.
Anyway, it seems we have one of the problems we will focus on this year. What else?
comparison
-HYN
Not so well
-Inconsistencies in HYN
-Duplication of line side markets
-Workload variations
-Run out of products in markets
I want to go back to the variability issue. HYN softens the bottlenecks by enabling people to move to where they are most needed. However, workload fluctuations are still significant, and we continue to run out of product in the markets too often.

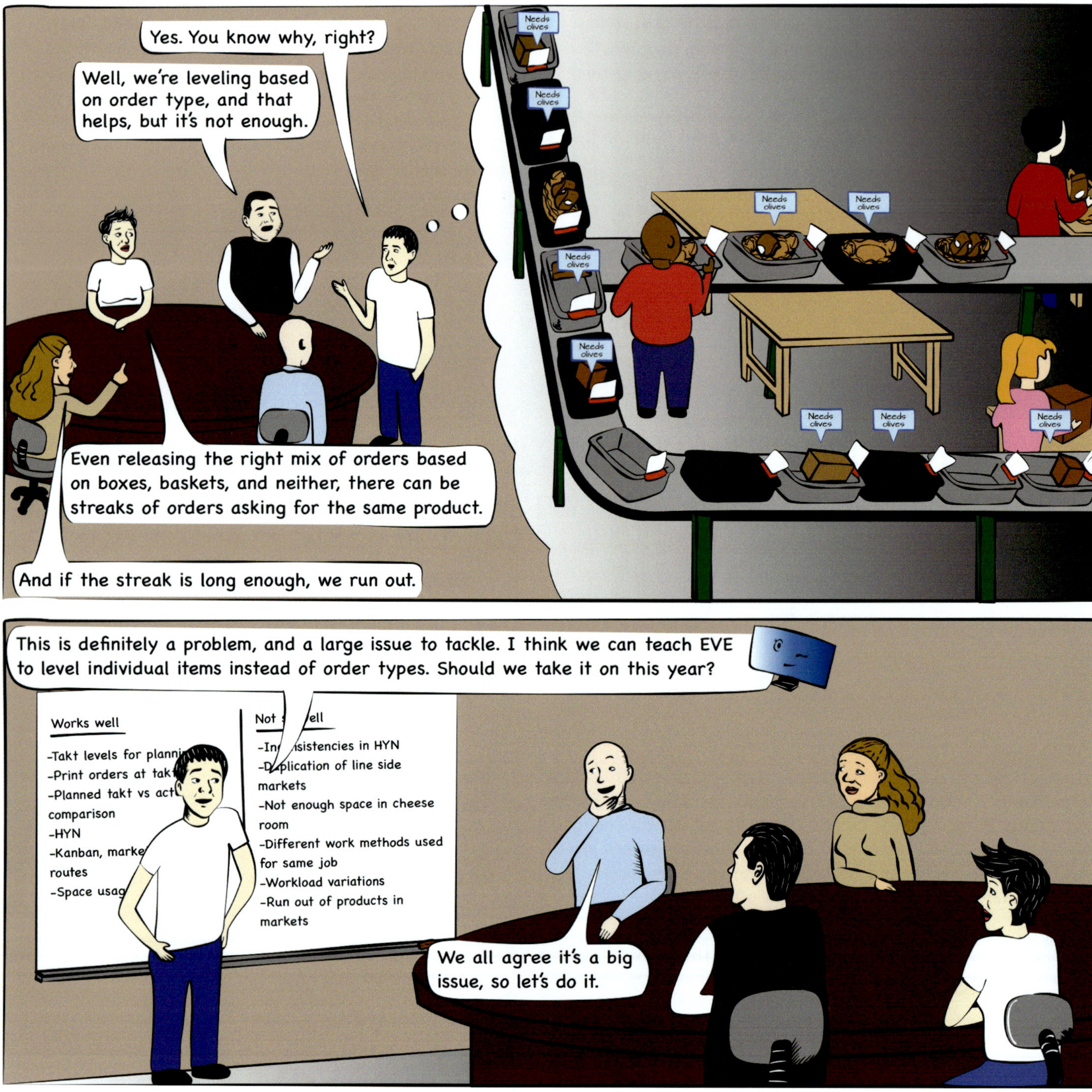

Another successful holiday and more reflection to focus our work. The main two problems for top management are standardizing work methods, starting at cheese prep, and improving leveling. We will also experiment with better signals and training to improve the consistency of HYN. We're still far from true continuous improvement, but as we work on the bigger problems, we also learn to see and tackle some of the smaller ones constantly nagging at us. In fact, to make progress on those, we should probably start involving more people in improvement activities.

Standardize to learn faster

Today starts a new phase in our Lean journey. We're beginning to develop standardized work, or what we in the food business call recipes. This is exciting. Of course we want better results, but it's more than that. We think this will be a way to engage our team members in managing and improving their areas. And since we hire so many temps for the holidays, we suspect this will make training a lot easier. The team is now meeting with the people that run the cheese room.

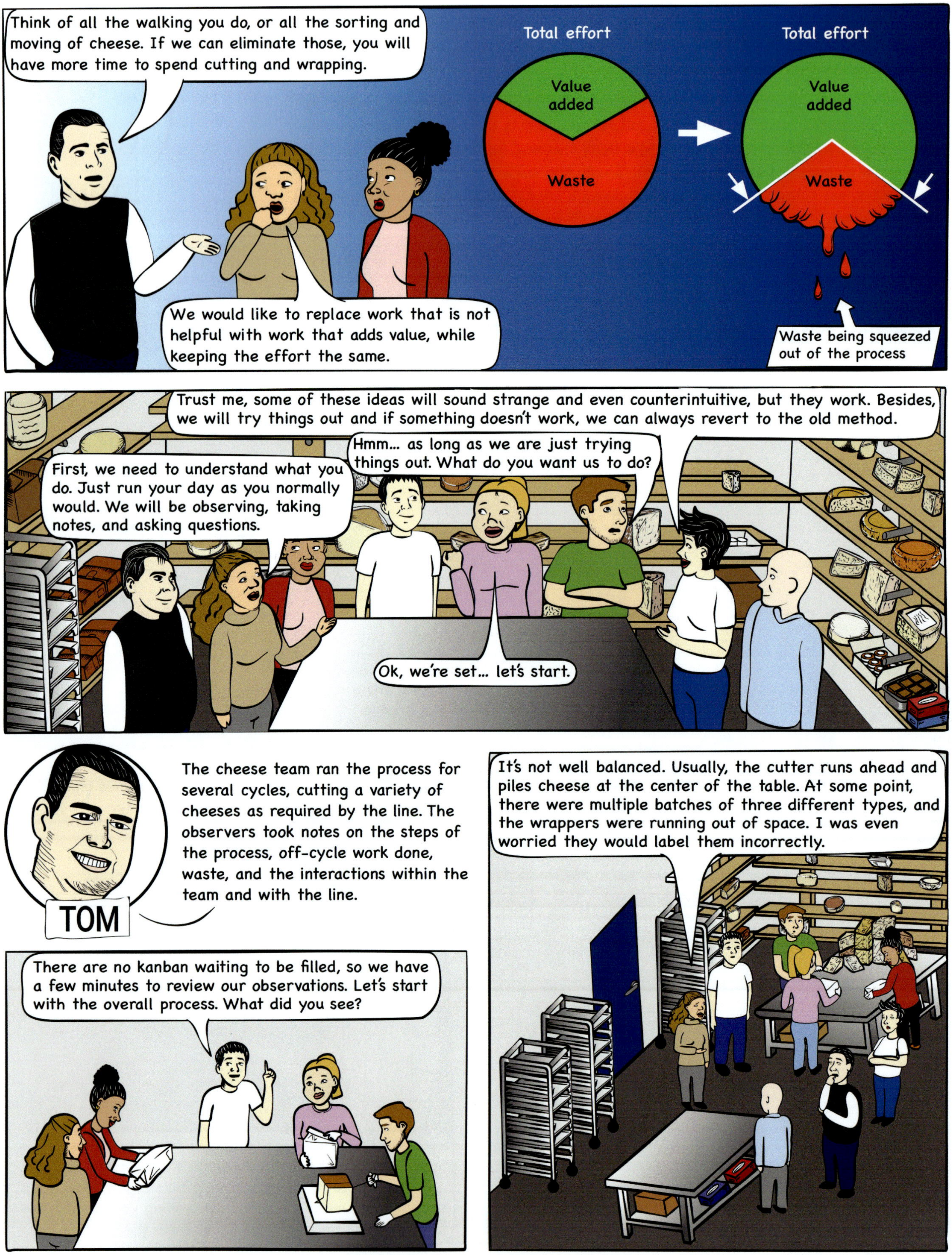
Think of all the walking you do, or all the sorting and moving of cheese. If we can eliminate those, you will have more time to spend cutting and wrapping.
Total effort
Value added
Waste
Total effort
Value added
Waste
We would like to replace work that is not helpful with work that adds value, while keeping the effort the same.
Waste being squeezed out of the process
Trust me, some of these ideas will sound strange and even counterintuitive, but they work. Besides, we will try things out and if something doesn't work, we can always revert to the old method.
Hmm... as long as we are just trying things out. What do you want us to do?
First, we need to understand what you do. Just run your day as you normally would. We will be observing, taking notes, and asking questions.
Ok, we're set... let's start.
TOM
The cheese team ran the process for several cycles, cutting a variety of cheeses as required by the line. The observers took notes on the steps of the process, off-cycle work done, waste, and the interactions within the team and with the line.
It's not well balanced. Usually, the cutter runs ahead and piles cheese at the center of the table. At some point, there were multiple batches of three different types, and the wrappers were running out of space. I was even worried they would label them incorrectly.
There are no kanban waiting to be filled, so we have a few minutes to review our observations. Let's start with the overall process. What did you see?

Yes, for some cheeses, it's a lot faster to cut than to wrap.
It's taking so long...
But then came the streak of hard cheeses, and the cutter became the bottleneck. Opening the wheel of parm took a long time, and the wrappers ran out of work and had to wait.
That was one long changeover.
But that's the nature of the work. Some cheeses are easier to cut than others, and we do not control what the line requests.
Both are true, Brian, but perhaps we can make a change so the work between you and the wrappers is a little more balanced. Any ideas?
What about bringing HYN... Help Your Neighbor into the cheese room? I think if the cutter and wrappers help each other we will see less inventory and less waiting.
I was thinking along the same lines, but how do we do it? We need a signal to tell them when to help.
What provides the signal at the line?
The buffers... when they are full or empty.
Go help to open space for your work
Go help to get work for yourself
BLOCKED
WORKING
STARVED
We can define a max number of pieces allowed on the table. When the limit is reached, the cutter helps wrap.
And when the table is empty, the wrappers help the cutter. They can get the next cheese, wrap the previous one, or wipe down the cutting board.

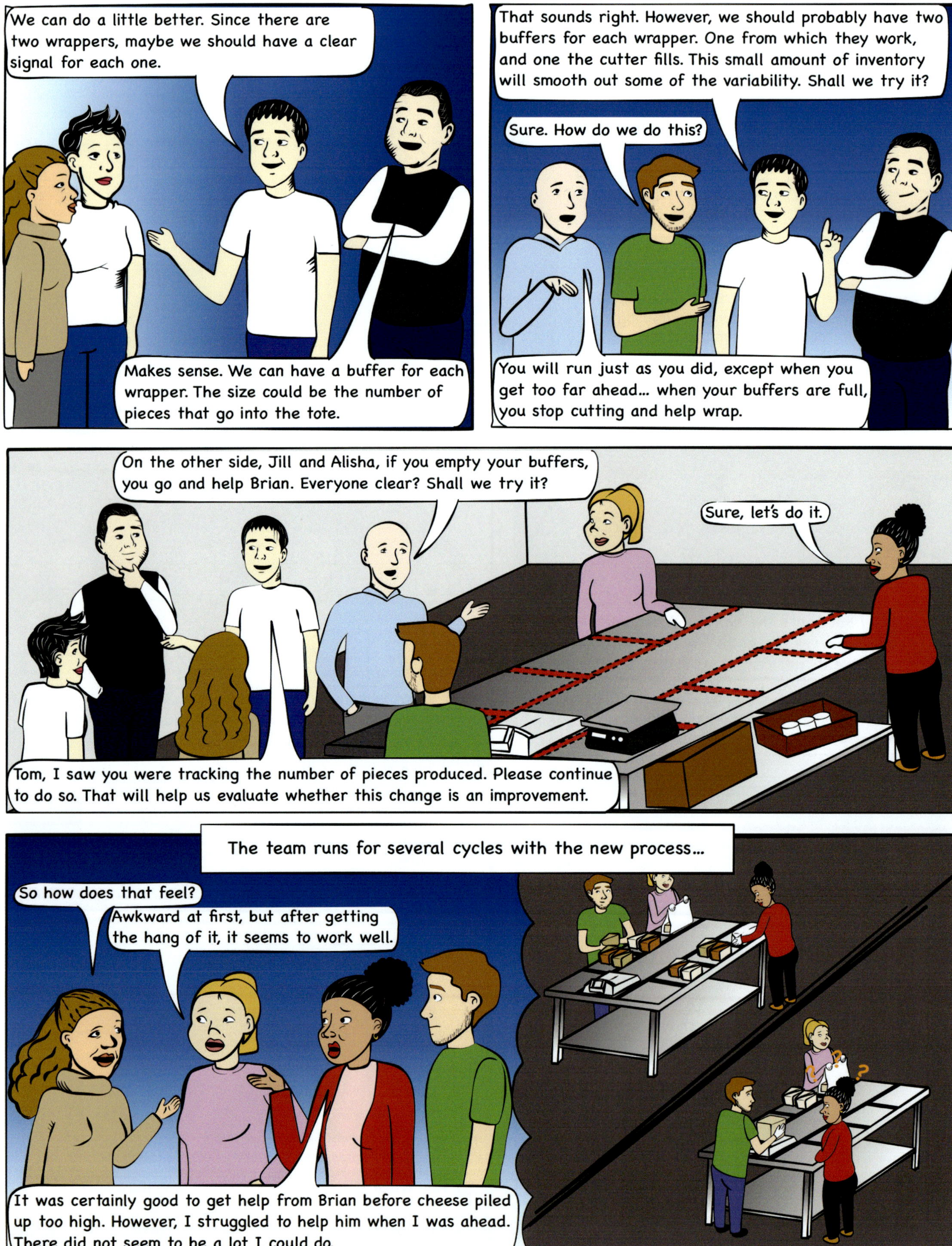
We can do a little better. Since there are two wrappers, maybe we should have a clear signal for each one.
Makes sense. We can have a buffer for each wrapper. The size could be the number of pieces that go into the tote.
That sounds right. However, we should probably have two buffers for each wrapper. One from which they work, and one the cutter fills. This small amount of inventory will smooth out some of the variability. Shall we try it?
Sure. How do we do this?
You will run just as you did, except when you get too far ahead... when your buffers are full, you stop cutting and help wrap.
On the other side, Jill and Alisha, if you empty your buffers, you go and help Brian. Everyone clear? Shall we try it?
Sure, let's do it.
Tom, I saw you were tracking the number of pieces produced. Please continue to do so. That will help us evaluate whether this change is an improvement.
The team runs for several cycles with the new process...
So how does that feel?
Awkward at first, but after getting the hang of it, it seems to work well.
It was certainly good to get help from Brian before cheese piled up too high. However, I struggled to help him when I was ahead. There did not seem to be a lot I could do.

We need to define HYN better in that direction... maybe set up a second cutting station? Anyway, considering it's your first try, you did a great job!
Average seconds / piece
67
59
Initial
HYN
And the numbers confirm it. Before, we had one finished piece every 67 seconds on average. Now it dropped to 59 seconds.
Definitely an improvement! And what about workload? Did you feel you were working harder?
Quite the opposite. Before, when cut cheese piled up, we had to reorganize it to make space, and we had to reach across the table to get the remaining pieces we were wrapping. All of that was gone.
I feel the same way. I don't have to move cheese around to push more onto the table. And I also don't feel the pressure to stay ahead, since I will get help if I fall behind.
Just as we hoped. More production, less effort, less stress... seems like a winner.
Indeed it does. Shall we make it part of our regular process?
Of course. Why wouldn't we?
Great! Now, I would like to do two more things, and we're already halfway through the shift. I want to tackle one more issue, and then let's try to capture what we learned today. I see a lot of time is wasted finding the right label for the cheese. And that does not even include when you run out and go print a new roll.
I'm glad you bring that up. I always struggle to find the labels I need.
I hate it too, but what can we do? We have a lot of different cheeses, and that means a lot of labels.
Having many different cheeses certainly makes the problem worse. The question though, is how can we reduce the time spent looking for the label needed, given that you have these many.

Maybe we could organize them alphabetically?
What if we printed the labels when we needed them? Then we would not have the clutter of rolls, and we would not run out, either.
I like where you're going. Let's schedule a time to look at this in more detail. However, for now, let's look for a quick fix we can test today.
Hmmm... what if we store the labels with the cheese, and Brian picks them when he gets the next cheese to cut? He could then give them to Jill and Alisha along with the cut pieces.
That's thinking outside the box! It would be a bit more work for the cutter, but a huge help for the wrappers.
Could we try it now?
Why not? Can you reorganize the labels while we continue to supply the line? It will only take a few minutes.
Let's do it!
Tom, can you continue to track the pieces produced once we make the change?
After reorganizing the labels and running the new process for several cycles...
So, what do you think?
No more looking for labels... I love it!
I agree. This makes a huge difference.

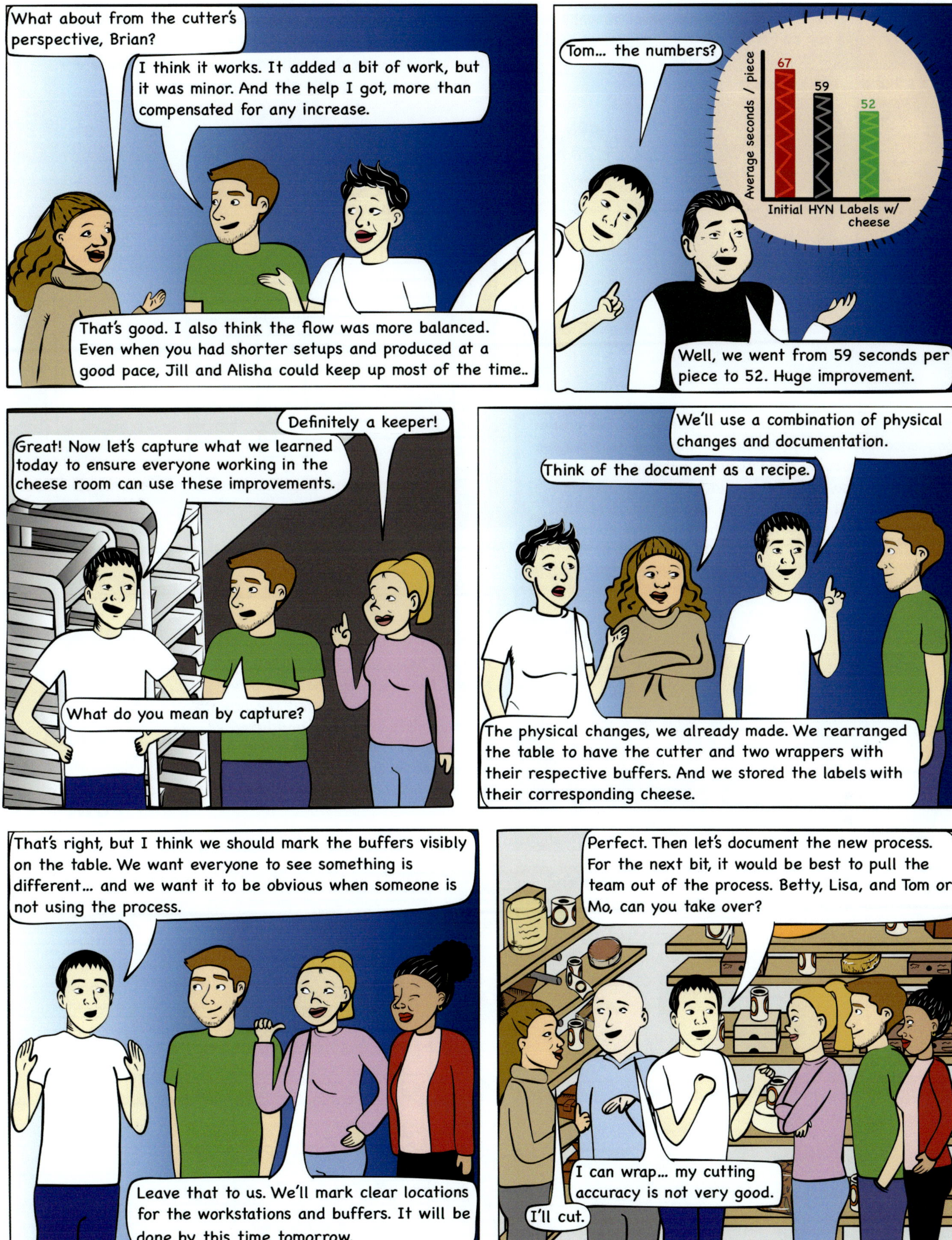
What about from the cutter's perspective, Brian?
I think it works. It added a bit of work, but it was minor. And the help I got, more than compensated for any increase.
That's good. I also think the flow was more balanced. Even when you had shorter setups and produced at a good pace, Jill and Alisha could keep up most of the time..
Tom... the numbers?
Average seconds / piece
67
59
52
Initial
HYN
Labels w/ cheese
Well, we went from 59 seconds per piece to 52. Huge improvement.
Great! Now let's capture what we learned today to ensure everyone working in the cheese room can use these improvements.
Definitely a keeper!
What do you mean by capture?
We'll use a combination of physical changes and documentation.
Think of the document as a recipe.
The physical changes, we already made. We rearranged the table to have the cutter and two wrappers with their respective buffers. And we stored the labels with their corresponding cheese.
That's right, but I think we should mark the buffers visibly on the table. We want everyone to see something is different... and we want it to be obvious when someone is not using the process.
Leave that to us. We'll mark clear locations for the workstations and buffers. It will be done by this time tomorrow.
Perfect. Then let's document the new process. For the next bit, it would be best to pull the team out of the process. Betty, Lisa, and Tom or Mo, can you take over?
I can wrap... my cutting accuracy is not very good.
I'll cut.

Betty, can you please wrap as well? Tom, you can track if they perform as well as Brian, Jill, and Alisha.
I like it... I get the easy job.
Now, Brian, you'll create the Standard Operating Procedure for the cutting job. We're going to use a standardized work sheet. First, write down all the steps needed. These are actions, so they usually start with a verb.
Standardized Work
Process:
Created by: Date created: Last modified by: Date modified:
Step Tips Time Inv after Work flow Diagram
1 2 3 4 5 6 7 8 9 10
Total:
Like get the next cheese?
Yes, but think in detail about each step and the proper sequence. For example, before getting the next cheese to cut, you probably need to see what the line is requesting. Also, in the tips column, you can include advice that will help others do the action correctly... maybe indicate where to find the totes coming back from the line. Let's focus on those two columns for now.
And we do the same for wrapping?
Absolutely.
As Lisa, Betty, and Mo continued to supply the line with cheese, Alisha, Jill, and Brian documented the process. By the shift's end, they had listed all the steps in the right sequence, and some even included tips.
TOM
Ok, the shift is over. Let's get back together and see where we are. How are the documents coming?
Standardized Work
Created by: John Date created: 7 mar 2006
Step Tips
1 Identify next cheese to be cut
Get the next tote coming back from the line. The kanban indicates type of cheese, size, and quantity needed.
2 Get the cheese and corresponding labels
Cut the number of labels needed from the roll and leave the roll on the shelf.
3 Unwrap the cheese
4 Weigh the cheese
5 Estimate the size to cut to get the desired weight
6 Cut cheese and weigh to confirm size
Cut as many pieces as indicated in the kanban.
Place cut pieces and corresponding labels into a wrapper's buffer
8 Wrap remaining cheese and return it to the shelf
9 Wipe wire cutter to prepare for next cheese
10 If there's an empty buffer for the wrappers, start the process again; if not, go help wrap

I think we're done. We included the improvements we made with HYN and label locations.
Perfect. Now we have an SOP everyone can use. In the work-flow diagram area, you can add sketches or pictures of the cheese room and/or the stations to give others a better image of the standard layout and the process in general.
What about time and inventory?
The time, you can ignore... at least for now. Every type of cheese takes a different amount, so defining a single standard for all won't help. The inventory is defined by the buffers. You are allowed only two totes' worth of cut pieces for each wrapper.
So, what happens now?
Well, this captures the best-known way Eduardo told us about. Now we have to use it. We train everyone with it and make sure they follow it.
That's right. If everyone uses the new process, we gain about 15s per piece in productivity without working harder. But more importantly, if people do not use it, we lose the advantages of organizational learning and return to slower progress and diverging methods.
Initial training
Learn
My method
I have a question about that. Do we have to stick exactly to the SOP? Normally, as we work, we find small changes that work better for us. Are we not supposed to do that anymore?
That's a very good point. We absolutely want you to try different things... that's how the process will continue to improve. However, when you find a better method, you need to capture it by changing the physical process or the SOP or both.
Our method
Our method
Our method
Our method
Learn
Learn
Learn
Learn
Learn
SOP

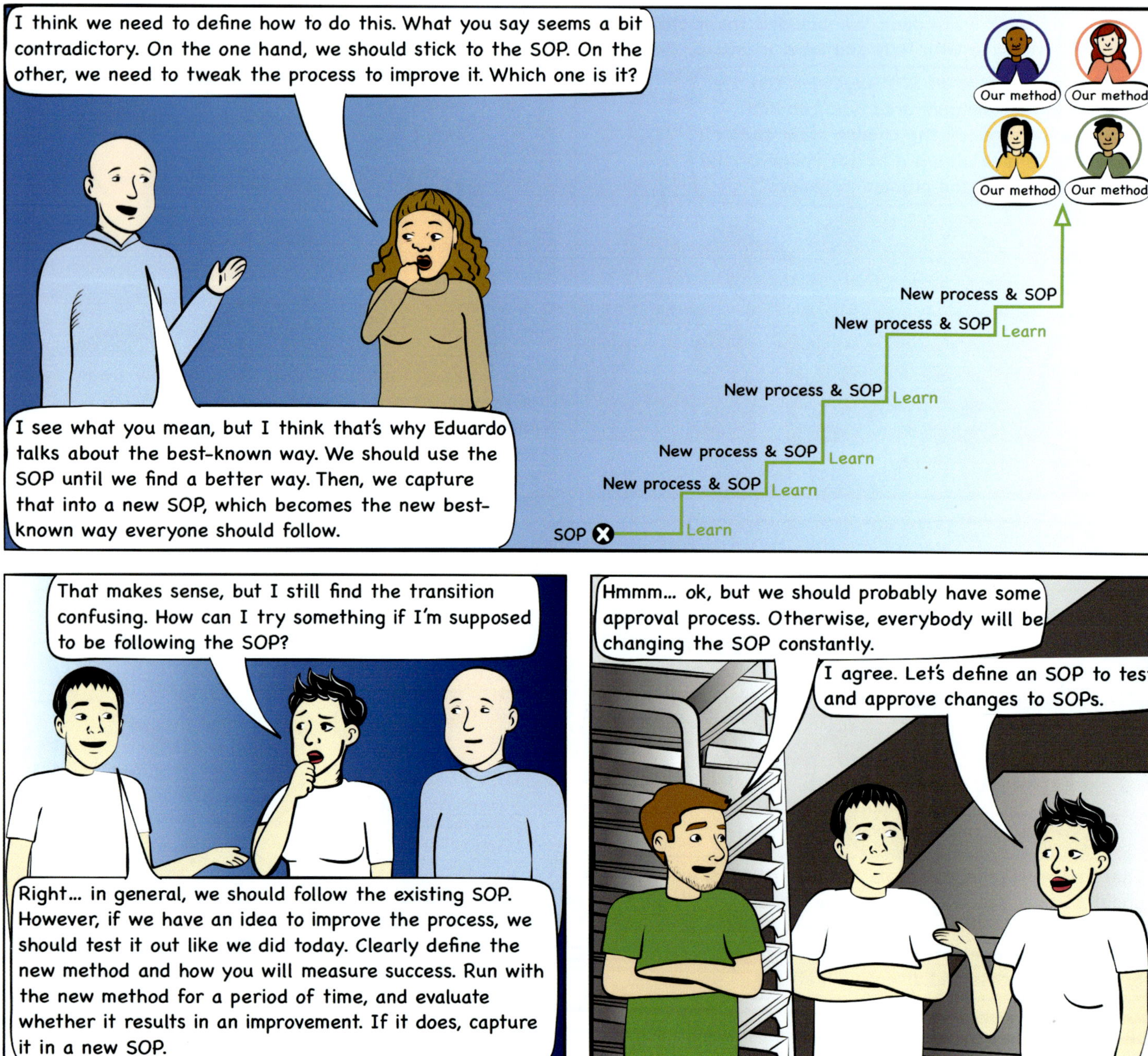

With that, we introduced SOPs into our Lean journey. I would like to say that from there it spread like wildfire, but I would be lying. It took a lot of hard work. In many cases, we had to push hard to get an SOP written. Some people thought it would make the job too strict. Others were not comfortable doing this kind of work. And then when there was an SOP, not everybody followed it, so we introduced regular audits and had an open discussion when we found a discrepancy.

Fourteen or so years later, SOPs are simply part of ZMO's way of doing business. Everyone in the warehouse expects to have one for every job they are asked to do. But getting there took years. By the 2007 holidays, we only had SOPs for about half the stations on the line.

ZMO continues alone

It's February 2007, and the holidays were again better than ever. Leveling now happens by item instead of order type. This has improved flow at the line by reducing workload variability and has stabilized consumption from markets. We're even looking at reducing the inventory held at the line, which of course would result in significant space savings. SOPs were also a success. Their value became especially clear to the core crew when training the holiday staff. Anyway, Eduardo has wrapped up his research with us and is now presenting at the university. Let's go see.

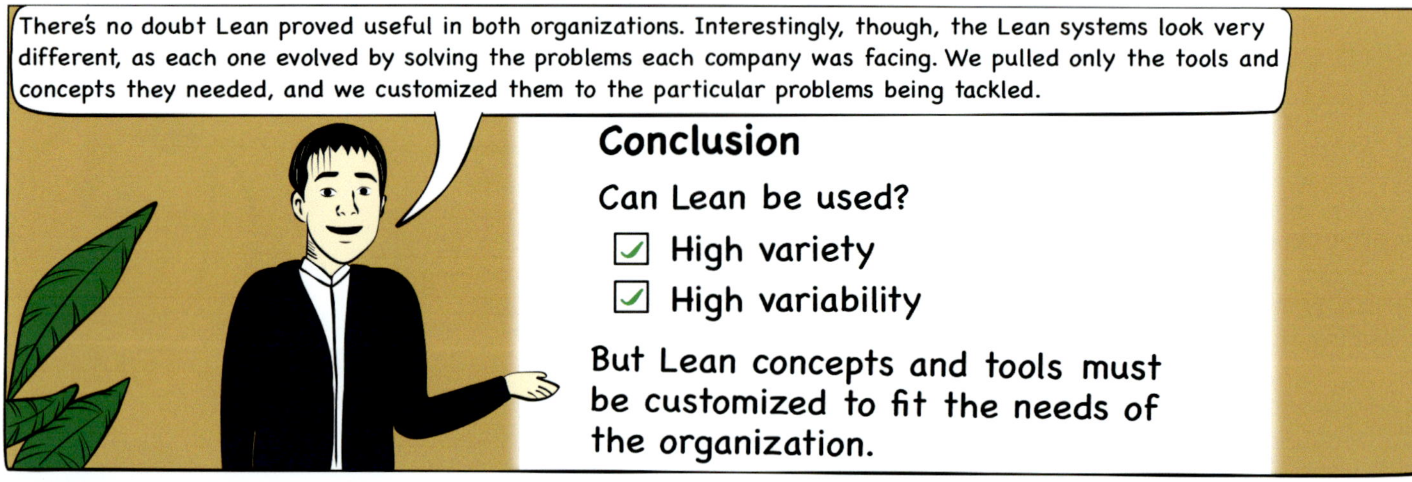
There's no doubt Lean proved useful in both organizations. Interestingly, though, the Lean systems look very different, as each one evolved by solving the problems each company was facing. We pulled only the tools and concepts they needed, and we customized them to the particular problems being tackled.
Conclusion
Can Lean be used?
High variety
High variability
But Lean concepts and tools must be customized to fit the needs of the organization.

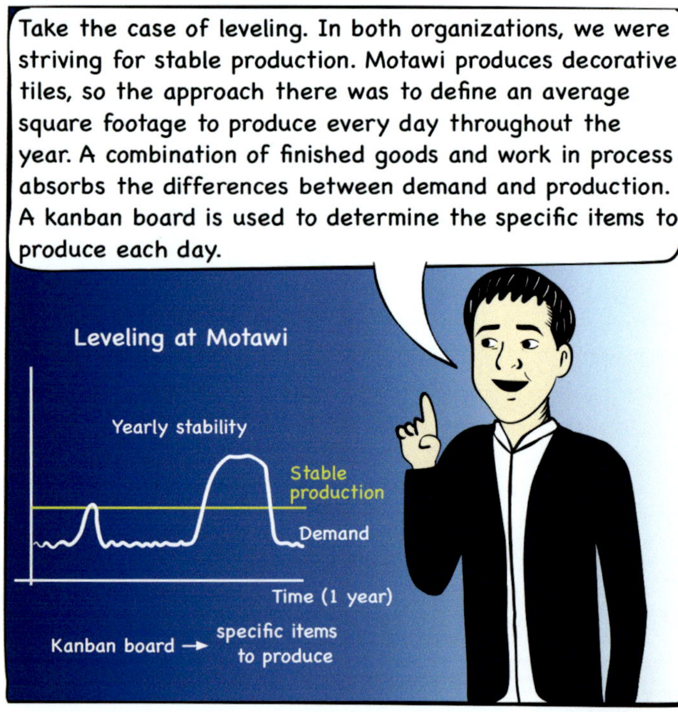
Take the case of leveling. In both organizations, we were striving for stable production. Motawi produces decorative tiles, so the approach there was to define an average square footage to produce every day throughout the year. A combination of finished goods and work in process absorbs the differences between demand and production. A kanban board is used to determine the specific items to produce each day.
Leveling at Motawi
Yearly stability
Stable production
Demand
Time (1 year)
Kanban board → specific items to produce

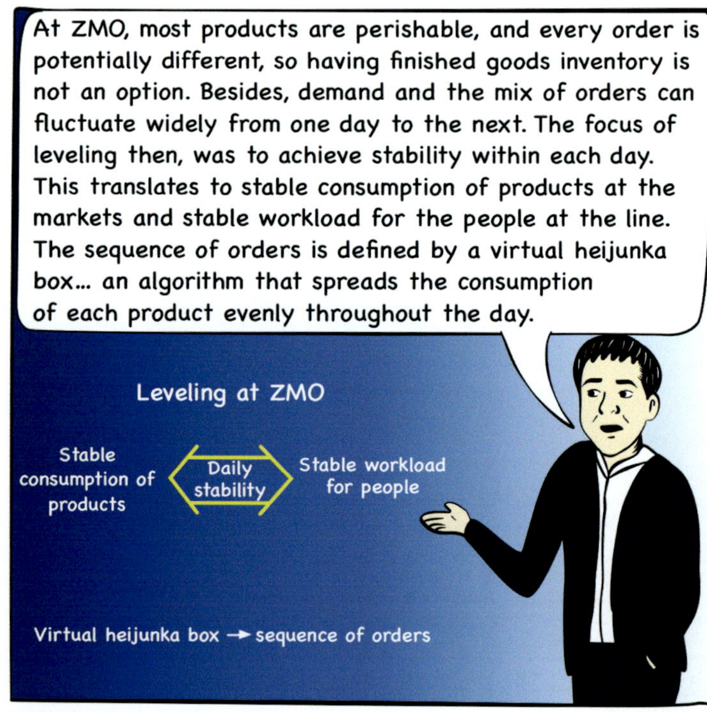
At ZMO, most products are perishable, and every order is potentially different, so having finished goods inventory is not an option. Besides, demand and the mix of orders can fluctuate widely from one day to the next. The focus of leveling then, was to achieve stability within each day. This translates to stable consumption of products at the markets and stable workload for the people at the line. The sequence of orders is defined by a virtual heijunka box… an algorithm that spreads the consumption of each product evenly throughout the day.
Leveling at ZMO
Stable consumption of products
Daily stability
Stable workload for people
Virtual heijunka box → sequence of orders

I came to the University of Michigan to learn about Lean and how to use it to improve performance in organizations. After working for three years with ZMO and four years with Motawi under Professor Liker's guidance, I'm convinced that to develop sustainable Lean systems, we must identify problems in the organization and pull the improvements needed to address them. Pushing Lean solutions on people only generates resistance. Furthermore, the concepts and tools we use must be customized to fit the specific problem being tackled. We must also involve people early on to use their expertise, develop their thinking, and give them control over the processes they will manage. And finally, we must have the perseverance to continue tweaking the countermeasures as we continue to learn. Rarely will the first solution we try result in the improvements we want.
Conclusion
To develop sustainable and durable Lean systems:
1. Identify problems preventing us from operating as desired
2. Pull improvements as needed to tackle those problems
3. Customize the concept or tool to fit the specific problem
4. Make a change, evaluate results, learn and try again until reaching the desired condition
5. Engage people early and develop them and the process simultaneously
6. Create a learning organization where new knowledge is captured for others to use

Trying to develop a Lean system by copying exactly what Toyota does will likely be ineffective, unless we're facing the exact same problems they faced.
This concludes my presentation. Many thanks to all for coming.
After some deliberation among the dissertation committee...
Thank you, and congratulations, Doctor Lander. You are now Doctor of Engineering.
Back at ZMO a few weeks later
We have called this meeting as Doctor Lander is leaving to join Toyota's Technical Center in Brussels, and we need to continue our Lean journey.
You know what to do... continue identifying and solving problems. Strive to improve flow, and at the process level, look for and eliminate waste.
Use problems to pull improvements
Desired condition
Gap = Problem
Current condition
P1
P2
P3
P4
Strive to improve flow
Waste
Eliminate waste
That's useful, Eduardo, and we will continue to do that. However, we would like to define our main priorities for the next two or three years. I think we should look at both process issues and higher level systemic issues.
What do you mean by systemic issues?
Well, so far Eduardo has guided us in selecting problems and helped us pull the right improvements. How will we do this on our own?
Also, how do we maintain the speed of progress or maybe even accelerate it? We all see plenty of opportunities, but never seem to have time to tackle them all.
Ok, I think I understand... it's all interrelated, but let's start with the easier bit of selecting the main themes to focus on. Themes, like leveling, are bigger than specific problems.
Workload
With HYN
After leveling
Orders coming from customers
Time
I never thought I would say this, but on the variability side, I think we're doing ok. Leveling orders by individual items resulted in a much more stable flow, and Help Your Neighbor handles the rest.

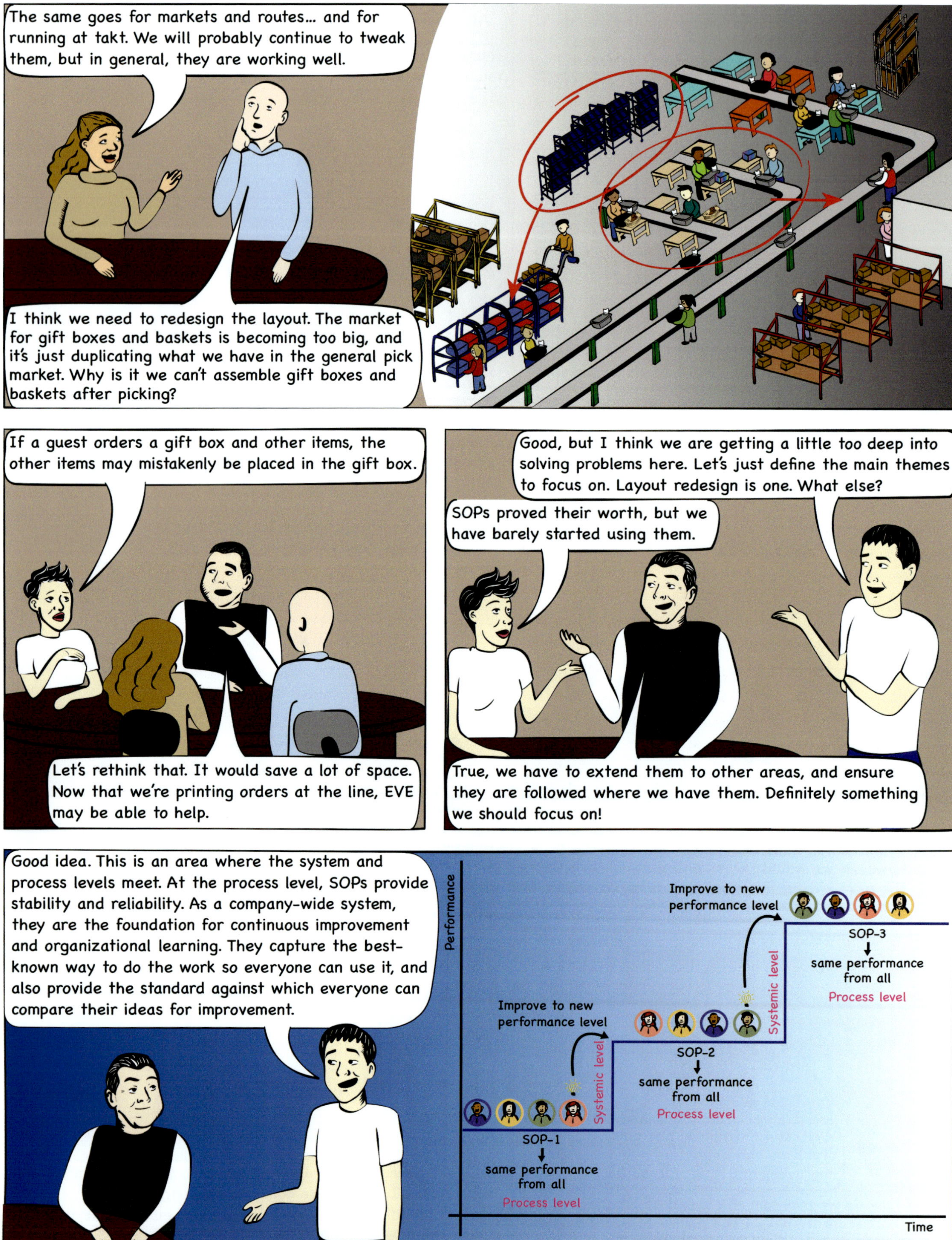
The same goes for markets and routes... and for running at takt. We will probably continue to tweak them, but in general, they are working well.
I think we need to redesign the layout. The market for gift boxes and baskets is becoming too big, and it's just duplicating what we have in the general pick market. Why is it we can't assemble gift boxes and baskets after picking?
If a guest orders a gift box and other items, the other items may mistakenly be placed in the gift box.
Let's rethink that. It would save a lot of space. Now that we're printing orders at the line, EVE may be able to help.
Good, but I think we are getting a little too deep into solving problems here. Let's just define the main themes to focus on. Layout redesign is one. What else?
SOPs proved their worth, but we have barely started using them.
True, we have to extend them to other areas, and ensure they are followed where we have them. Definitely something we should focus on!
Good idea. This is an area where the system and process levels meet. At the process level, SOPs provide stability and reliability. As a company-wide system, they are the foundation for continuous improvement and organizational learning. They capture the best-known way to do the work so everyone can use it, and also provide the standard against which everyone can compare their ideas for improvement.
Performance
Time
SOP-1
same performance from all
Process level
Improve to new performance level
Systemic level
SOP-2
same performance from all
Process level
Improve to new performance level
Systemic level
SOP-3
same performance from all
Process level

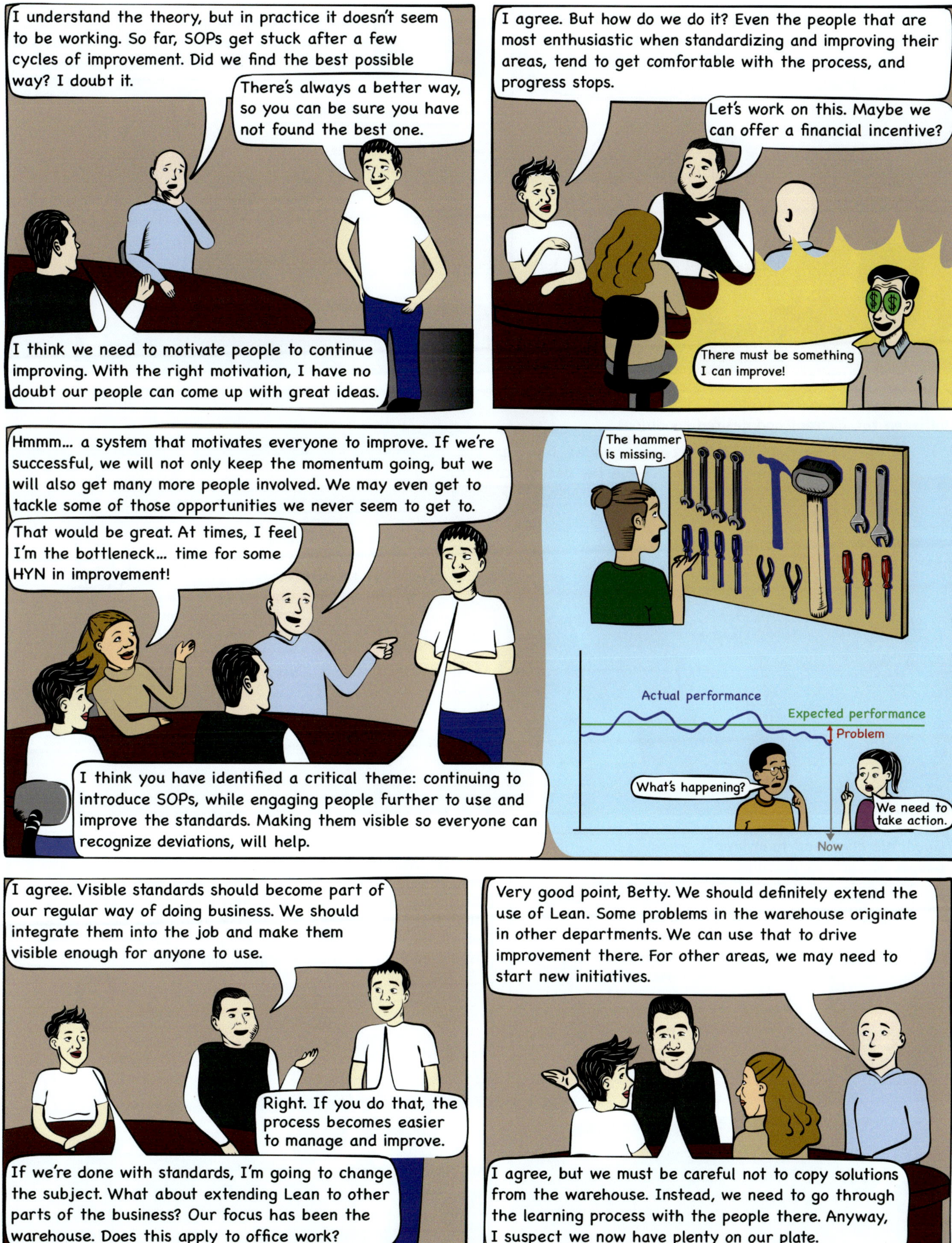
I understand the theory, but in practice it doesn't seem to be working. So far, SOPs get stuck after a few cycles of improvement. Did we find the best possible way? I doubt it.
There's always a better way, so you can be sure you have not found the best one.
I think we need to motivate people to continue improving. With the right motivation, I have no doubt our people can come up with great ideas.
I agree. But how do we do it? Even the people that are most enthusiastic when standardizing and improving their areas, tend to get comfortable with the process, and progress stops.
Let's work on this. Maybe we can offer a financial incentive?
There must be something I can improve!
Hmmm... a system that motivates everyone to improve. If we're successful, we will not only keep the momentum going, but we will also get many more people involved. We may even get to tackle some of those opportunities we never seem to get to.
That would be great. At times, I feel I'm the bottleneck... time for some HYN in improvement!
I think you have identified a critical theme: continuing to introduce SOPs, while engaging people further to use and improve the standards. Making them visible so everyone can recognize deviations, will help.
The hammer is missing.
Actual performance
Expected performance
Problem
What's happening?
We need to take action.
Now
I agree. Visible standards should become part of our regular way of doing business. We should integrate them into the job and make them visible enough for anyone to use.
Right. If you do that, the process becomes easier to manage and improve.
If we're done with standards, I'm going to change the subject. What about extending Lean to other parts of the business? Our focus has been the warehouse. Does this apply to office work?
Very good point, Betty. We should definitely extend the use of Lean. Some problems in the warehouse originate in other departments. We can use that to drive improvement there. For other areas, we may need to start new initiatives.
I agree, but we must be careful not to copy solutions from the warehouse. Instead, we need to go through the learning process with the people there. Anyway, I suspect we now have plenty on our plate.

I agree, but let's make sure we got this right. We'll continue our Lean journey by using problems to pull improvements, so first, everyone needs to be able to see those problems.
Right. We'll continue striving to improve flow, and we'll make standards visible so we can see deviations from the performance we expect.
Pull improvements by solving problems
→ Make problems visible
-Strive to improve flow
-Make standards visible
We need to define the problems clearly as a gap between the current and desired conditions.
We then need to propose changes, try them out, and refine them until we achieve the desired condition.
Pull improvements by solving problems
→ Make problems visible
-Strive to improve flow
-Make standards visible
→ Define problem = gap between desired and current conditions
→ Develop and try out possible solutions
→ Refine solution – we never get it right the first time
Good. We also need to involve people as early as possible.
→ Engage people early!!
Wow! Great work! I want to take this opportunity to thank you all. Working with you has been a pleasure and a remarkable experience. You know, I joke that I got my Doctorate degree because I spent long enough at U of M that they just wanted me out. The truth is, I got it because of all the hard work you and people at Motawi have done. In my book, it's a shared degree, and you're all Doctors.

Part III

The Power of Scientific Thinking

All improvement systems are not made equal

We're now going to jump ahead. It's not that we made no progress. Over the next few years, we changed the layout multiple times, added extensive functionality to EVE to support team members, and extended SOPs to all processes in the warehouse as well as many in the office. We also extended Lean to other areas in the business. For example, we standardized the order-taking process and revamped how we hire people. Senior management continued to drive most of the progress in our Lean journey. For this final section, we want to focus on the next level of a true Lean transformation: engaging the work force in continuous improvement. Without it, you will never reach the full potential of Lean, and progress may even stagnate.

Just before Eduardo left for Brussels in July 2007, we made our first attempt to create a structured continuous improvement process based on PDCA—Plan, Do, Check, Act—and 5-why's. It utterly failed! We then had the idea to pay for experiments, and proposed a system expressly designed to bypass top management and motivate the wider ZMO community. Let's take a look at how that worked out. It's now mid-April 2009.

That would increase focus on our priorities. Interesting...
Exactly! Now, we are thinking of tying the reward to running experiments that could improve an SOP. In the end, people would get paid whether they manage to improve or not.
We want to encourage the crew to experiment, but we do not want to penalize them if their idea does not work as planned. More experiments should result in more improvements.
Hmm... guess not.
Yes!
Did it work?
Reward
Reward
I get that, but how does the process work? If someone has an idea, they run an experiment and then come get their reward?
Well, we need a bit more structure, both to support people so they learn from the experiment, and to ensure we reward them fairly.
First, there are some pre-requisites. People need to attend the 'How to Teach' and 'How to Plan and Conduct an Experiment' classes. We'll track those in the Zingerman's training passports.
1. Attend classes
2. Apply for grant → area and SOP
Then, they need to apply for the grant by explaining to one of the counselors... initially me... which area they want to work on and which SOP they will try to improve.
Once the grant is approved, the applicant has to plan their experiment and then present the SOP and plan to the counselors.
Sounds like we will need some paperwork to track all this.
1. Attend classes
2. Apply for grant → area and SOP
3. Plan experiment
4. Present SOP and experiment plan
Good point. The 'How to Plan and Conduct an Experiment' class includes training on how to use an A3 to present a proposal and results.
An A3? I do not remember talking about that.

You may be wondering how it went. Terribly! Few people got involved. We thought that maybe it was not enough money, or the process was too cumbersome, or that we expected them to do the work on their own time. The truth is we never found out exactly why, but it was clear the experiment failed. So we continued with top-driven improvements, trying to involve people early. Unfortunately, they mostly wanted to follow our lead, not propose and drive improvements on their own.

That was October 2012. Eduardo left Toyota in early December and came to visit during our Christmas peak. Since then, we have been working with him regularly. But let's go back to our story. So far, we had failed twice at engaging our associates in continuous improvement, and now Eduardo brought from Toyota our third attempt, which we started early in 2013. Let's see how that went...

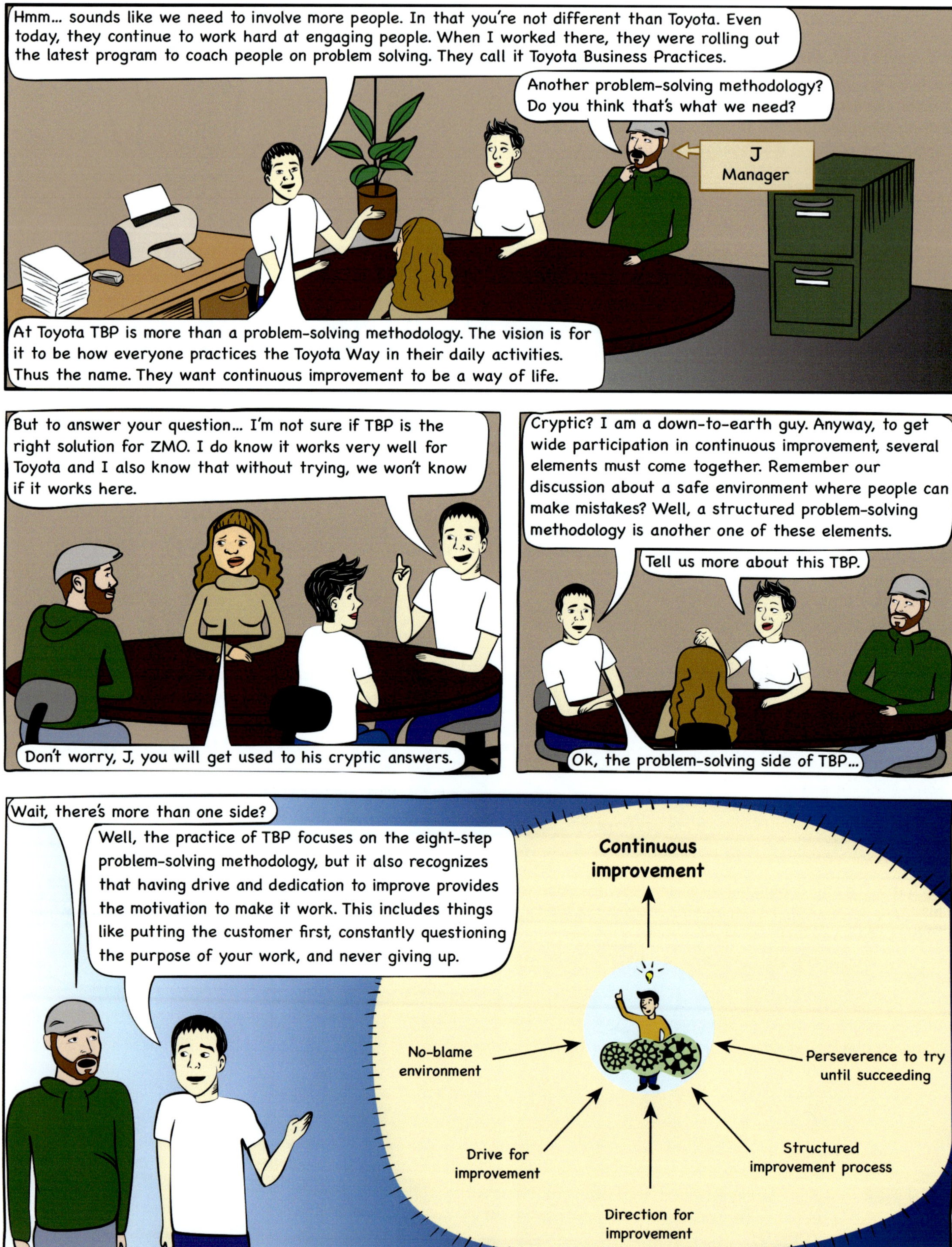
Hmm... sounds like we need to involve more people. In that you're not different than Toyota. Even today, they continue to work hard at engaging people. When I worked there, they were rolling out the latest program to coach people on problem solving. They call it Toyota Business Practices.
Another problem-solving methodology? Do you think that's what we need?
J
Manager
At Toyota TBP is more than a problem-solving methodology. The vision is for it to be how everyone practices the Toyota Way in their daily activities. Thus the name. They want continuous improvement to be a way of life.
But to answer your question... I'm not sure if TBP is the right solution for ZMO. I do know it works very well for Toyota and I also know that without trying, we won't know if it works here.
Don't worry, J, you will get used to his cryptic answers.
Cryptic? I am a down-to-earth guy. Anyway, to get wide participation in continuous improvement, several elements must come together. Remember our discussion about a safe environment where people can make mistakes? Well, a structured problem-solving methodology is another one of these elements.
Tell us more about this TBP.
Ok, the problem-solving side of TBP...
Wait, there's more than one side?
Well, the practice of TBP focuses on the eight-step problem-solving methodology, but it also recognizes that having drive and dedication to improve provides the motivation to make it work. This includes things like putting the customer first, constantly questioning the purpose of your work, and never giving up.
Continuous improvement
No-blame environment
Perseverence to try until succeeding
Drive for improvement
Structured improvement process
Direction for improvement

Yes, a desire to improve seems like the key element to me.
Right. But not knowing how, may be a reason people don't try. Besides, without a structured process, people may try, find themselves lost, and give up. Let's hear about these eight steps.
Ok. I will try to explain but will not go into all the details. The best way to learn this is by doing, so we will go into more depth when we try it.
Sounds like a plan.
Good. The first step is to clarify the problem. As you know, a problem is the gap between the ideal and the actual condition. Clarifying the problem requires you to clearly define both. For example, the ideal for continuous improvement might be having all team members engaged daily in improvement, and we are currently at... what? 10% engagement?
1. Clarify the problem
Ideal condition
Gap = Problem
Current condition
You may be overestimating where we are, but let's go with that.
The second step is to break down the problem. You take that big gap, break it into smaller, more concrete problems, and prioritize them to maximize your impact.
1. Clarify the problem
2. Break down the problem
Ideal condition
Gap = Problem
Prioritized sub problem
Current condition

What do you mean by smaller problems? I thought the gap was the problem we need to solve.
The gap to the ideal state is typically too big as a starting point. There are many issues we'll need to tackle to solve it, so we break the big problem into smaller sub problems and select the most promising one. For example, a subproblem we could start with is the crew's lack of training in TBP.
Hmm... makes sense, when you put it that way. What's next?
To set a target for the prioritized problem we selected. A target should be challenging, measurable, and concrete... and have a deadline.
1. Clarify the problem
2. Break down the problem
3. Set a target
Target
= Problem
Let me try... If our prioritized problem is lack of training, maybe a target could be for half the crew to do one TBP project by the end of the year. How's that?
Great. You can use it to measure progress and evaluate overall results at the end of the year... both needed in a good target.
That would be challenging, but I see what you mean. What's next?
Ok... the next step is to find the root cause of the problem. Focusing on the prioritized problem, we're going to ask 'why' multiple times, going deeper, until we find the root cause. Without it, it will be hard to solve the problem for good.
1. Clarify the problem
3. Set a target
4. Analyze the root cause
Target
Gap = Problem
Got it, but we have struggled with this. We usually end up with too many causes.
And it's hard to know when to stop...
We'll have to practice. In general, we want to start with a wide range of possible causes and then confirm or discard each through direct analysis of the facts at the process, before moving on to the next level.
Prioritized problem
Cause
Cause
Cause
Cause
Cause
Cause
Cause
Cause
Cause
Cause
Cause
Cause
Cause
Cause
Cause
Cause
Cause

Step five is to develop countermeasures.
1. Clarify the problem
2. Break down the problem
3. Set a target
4. Analyze the root cause
5. Develop countermeasures
Ideal condition
Target
Gap = Problem
Finally we get to solve the problem.
Countermeasure 1
Countermeasure 2
Countermeasure 3
Countermeasure 4
Cause
Plan
1
2
3
This includes developing a wide range of possible countermeasures, selecting the one you predict will contribute the most value, building consensus around it, and developing an implementation plan.
Seems complicated...
TBP is very thorough. As we practice, we will learn to size the approach to the magnitude of the problem we're trying to solve.
This is implementation, right?
It is. Rapid implementation, following the plan, without giving up until we reach the target.
I'm looking forward to that!
Good. Step six is to see countermeasures through.
1. Clarify the problem
2. Break down the problem
3. Set a target
4. Analyze the root cause
5. Develop countermeasures
6. See countermeasures through
Target
Target
Current condition
Perseverance

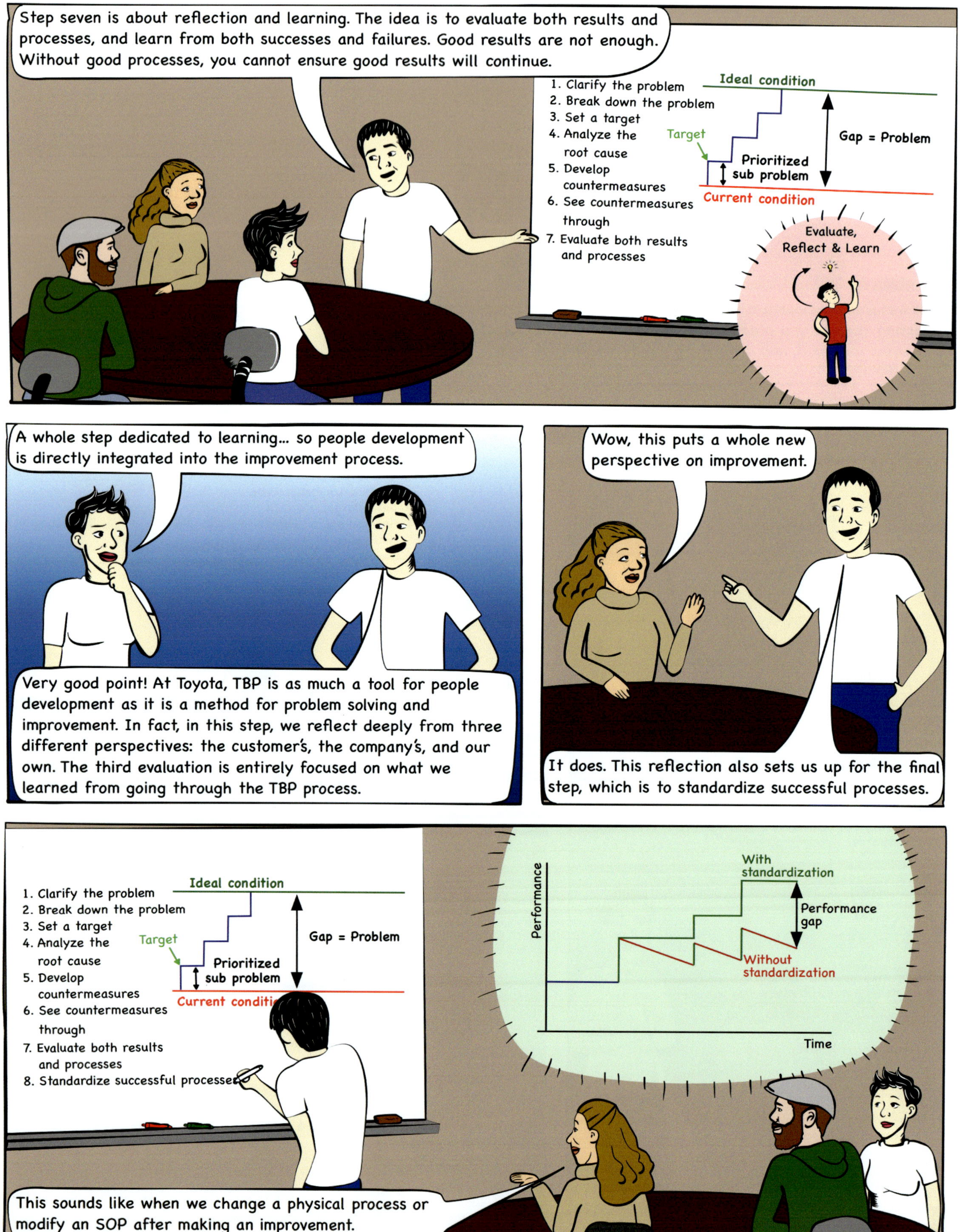
Step seven is about reflection and learning. The idea is to evaluate both results and processes, and learn from both successes and failures. Good results are not enough. Without good processes, you cannot ensure good results will continue.
1. Clarify the problem
2. Break down the problem
3. Set a target
4. Analyze the root cause
5. Develop countermeasures
6. See countermeasures through
7. Evaluate both results and processes
Ideal condition
Target
Prioritized sub problem
Gap = Problem
Current condition
Evaluate, Reflect & Learn
A whole step dedicated to learning... so people development is directly integrated into the improvement process.
Very good point! At Toyota, TBP is as much a tool for people development as it is a method for problem solving and improvement. In fact, in this step, we reflect deeply from three different perspectives: the customer's, the company's, and our own. The third evaluation is entirely focused on what we learned from going through the TBP process.
Wow, this puts a whole new perspective on improvement.
It does. This reflection also sets us up for the final step, which is to standardize successful processes.
1. Clarify the problem
2. Break down the problem
3. Set a target
4. Analyze the root cause
5. Develop countermeasures
6. See countermeasures through
7. Evaluate both results and processes
8. Standardize successful processes
Ideal condition
Target
Prioritized sub problem
Gap = Problem
Performance
With standardization
Performance gap
Without standardization
Time
This sounds like when we change a physical process or modify an SOP after making an improvement.

You may be wondering how this went. Worse than terribly! We spent about three months in weekly video conferences with Eduardo trying to use it. We tackled a couple of problems, but only with the management team, and in the second one we did not even make it past the root cause analysis. It felt complex and cumbersome, taking too much time and effort to get to the same result we would have reached with our much less structured observation and discussion approach. It did not fit our action-oriented people and culture. Back to square one... now what?

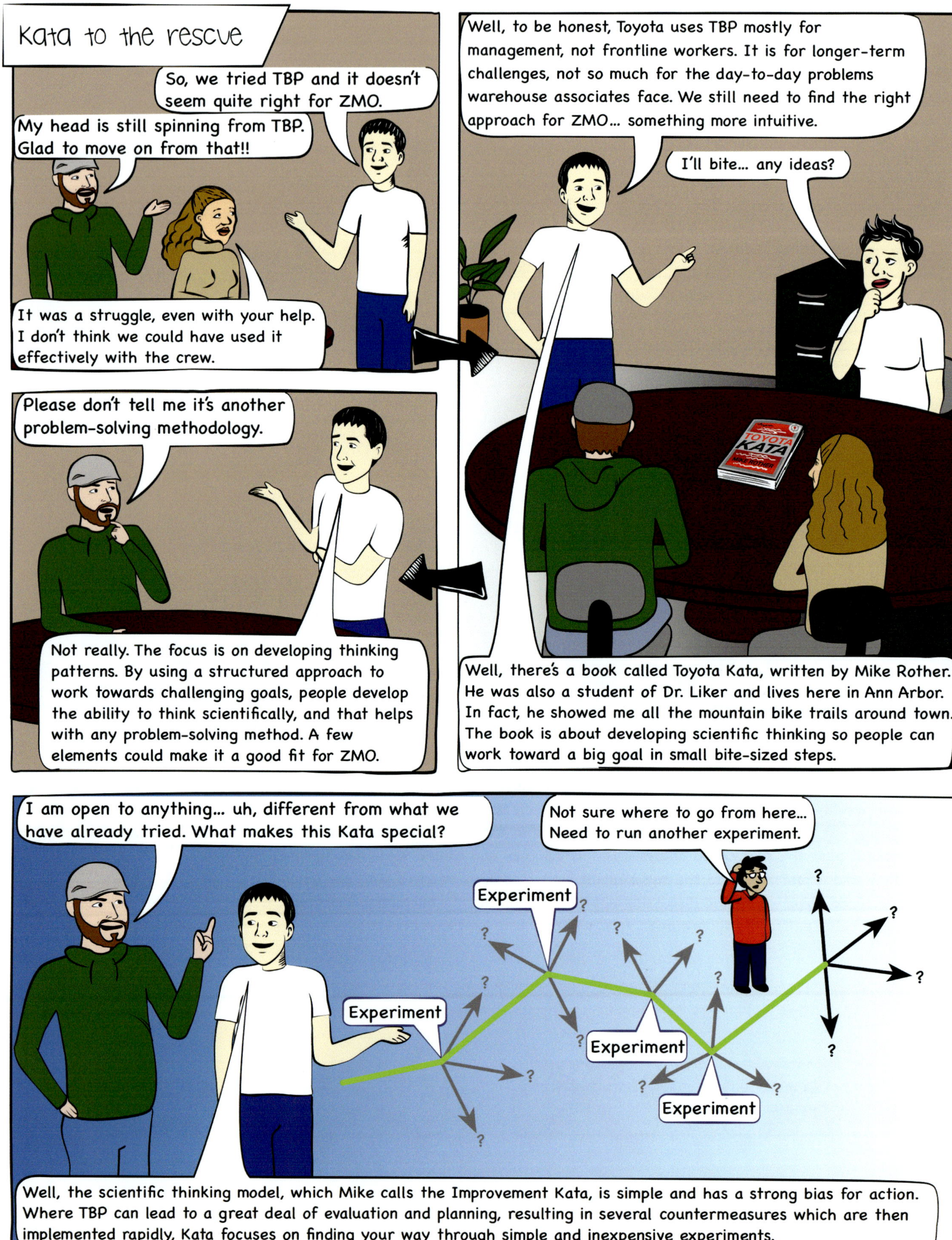
Kata to the rescue
So, we tried TBP and it doesn't seem quite right for ZMO.
My head is still spinning from TBP. Glad to move on from that!!
It was a struggle, even with your help. I don't think we could have used it effectively with the crew.
Well, to be honest, Toyota uses TBP mostly for management, not frontline workers. It is for longer-term challenges, not so much for the day-to-day problems warehouse associates face. We still need to find the right approach for ZMO... something more intuitive.
I'll bite... any ideas?
TOYOTA KATA
Well, there's a book called Toyota Kata, written by Mike Rother. He was also a student of Dr. Liker and lives here in Ann Arbor. In fact, he showed me all the mountain bike trails around town. The book is about developing scientific thinking so people can work toward a big goal in small bite-sized steps.
Please don't tell me it's another problem-solving methodology.
Not really. The focus is on developing thinking patterns. By using a structured approach to work towards challenging goals, people develop the ability to think scientifically, and that helps with any problem-solving method. A few elements could make it a good fit for ZMO.
I am open to anything... uh, different from what we have already tried. What makes this Kata special?
Not sure where to go from here... Need to run another experiment.
Experiment
Experiment
Experiment
Experiment
Well, the scientific thinking model, which Mike calls the Improvement Kata, is simple and has a strong bias for action. Where TBP can lead to a great deal of evaluation and planning, resulting in several countermeasures which are then implemented rapidly, Kata focuses on finding your way through simple and inexpensive experiments.

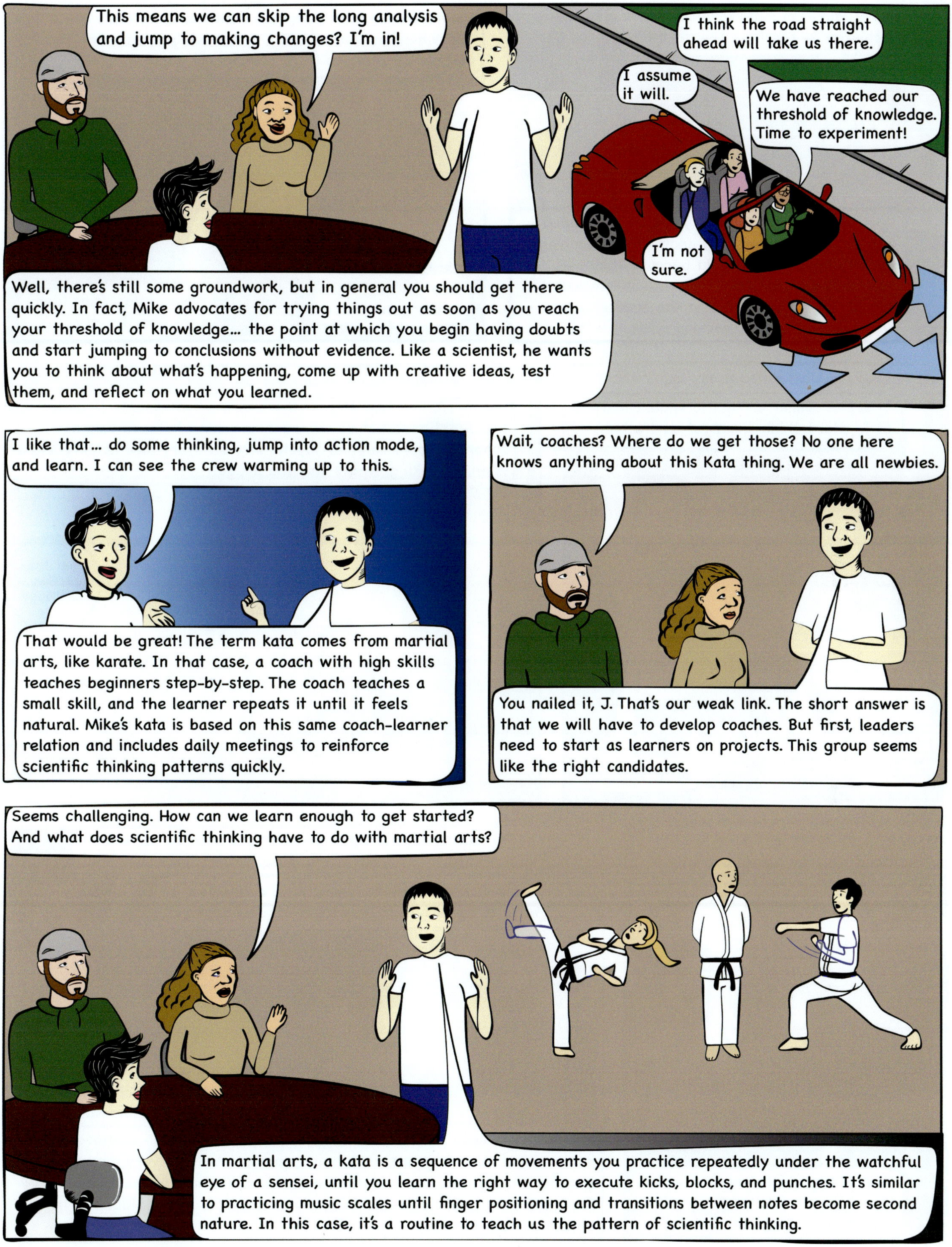
This means we can skip the long analysis and jump to making changes? I'm in!
I assume it will.
I think the road straight ahead will take us there.
We have reached our threshold of knowledge. Time to experiment!
I'm not sure.
Well, there's still some groundwork, but in general you should get there quickly. In fact, Mike advocates for trying things out as soon as you reach your threshold of knowledge… the point at which you begin having doubts and start jumping to conclusions without evidence. Like a scientist, he wants you to think about what's happening, come up with creative ideas, test them, and reflect on what you learned.
I like that… do some thinking, jump into action mode, and learn. I can see the crew warming up to this.
That would be great! The term kata comes from martial arts, like karate. In that case, a coach with high skills teaches beginners step-by-step. The coach teaches a small skill, and the learner repeats it until it feels natural. Mike's kata is based on this same coach-learner relation and includes daily meetings to reinforce scientific thinking patterns quickly.
Wait, coaches? Where do we get those? No one here knows anything about this Kata thing. We are all newbies.
You nailed it, J. That's our weak link. The short answer is that we will have to develop coaches. But first, leaders need to start as learners on projects. This group seems like the right candidates.
Seems challenging. How can we learn enough to get started? And what does scientific thinking have to do with martial arts?
In martial arts, a kata is a sequence of movements you practice repeatedly under the watchful eye of a sensei, until you learn the right way to execute kicks, blocks, and punches. It's similar to practicing music scales until finger positioning and transitions between notes become second nature. In this case, it's a routine to teach us the pattern of scientific thinking.

So Toyota Kata is a sequence of activities to teach us how to think?
How to think scientifically, yes. Mike developed a kata for improvement and another for coaching. He calls them starter kata because they help us learn the fundamentals. Mike is less interested in theoretical learning than in the mindset… the way we think about reaching goals.
Before we go much deeper… I learned a lot more about TBP when we started using it. Can we go there directly? Can we use Kata to learn how to use Kata?
Kata for Kata?
Now you're twisting my brain.
Hmm… interesting idea. Let's give it a try.
But how do we start without any experience?
It seems similar enough to what I learned at Toyota. I think I can get us started.
Ok, where do we begin?
With the end.
Now you're really trying to confuse us.
Not at all. The first step in the Improvement Kata is to understand the direction. What do we want to achieve? Okada-san, my Japanese coordinator at Toyota, started every new activity, big or small, by asking: what's the end image?
IMPROVEMENT KATA
1
Set the Direction or Challenge
I'm a bit slow, so it took a while to understand what he meant and why it was so important. What he wanted was to define what we needed to achieve… to create a clear image of what success would look like.
Hmm… in a weird way that, makes sense. Sounds like what we call 'visioning' at Zingerman's.
You're moving fast, J! What you just did took me about a year to figure out. I guess I'm done, you can take over now.
I said it kind of makes sense, but I don't know what to do with it, so you're not off the hook yet.
Fair point. We'll figure it out soon. Now, what does success look like with respect to using Kata?
For years, we have been trying to get wide participation in continuous improvement, so everyone makes their processes better every day, and ZMO benefits through the accumulation of many small steps. As management, we focus on the big picture and frequently miss opportunities hidden in the details of each process.

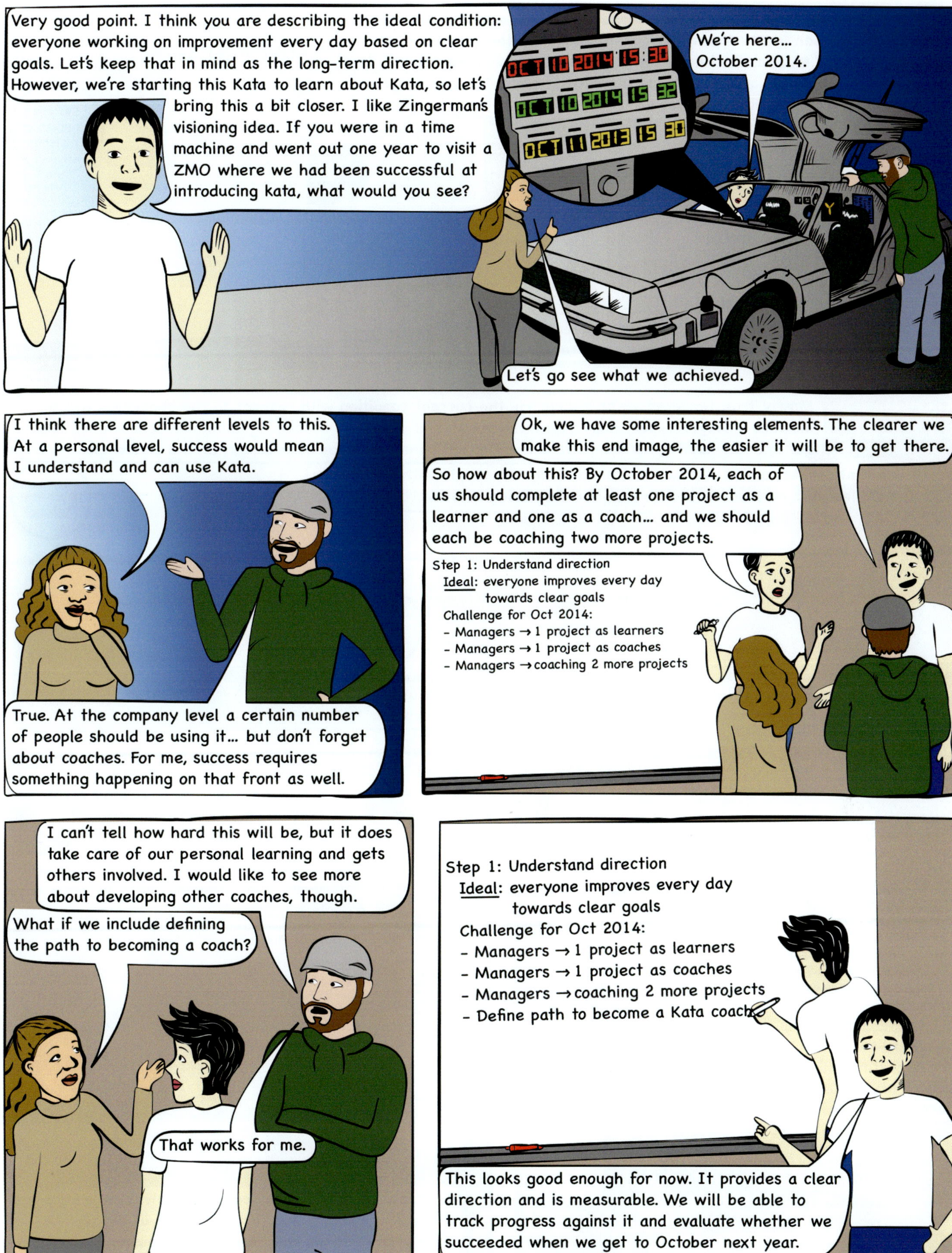
Very good point. I think you are describing the ideal condition: everyone working on improvement every day based on clear goals. Let's keep that in mind as the long-term direction. However, we're starting this Kata to learn about Kata, so let's bring this a bit closer. I like Zingerman's visioning idea. If you were in a time machine and went out one year to visit a ZMO where we had been successful at introducing kata, what would you see?
OCT 10 2014 15:30
OCT 10 2014 15 32
OCT 11 2013 15 30
We're here... October 2014.
Let's go see what we achieved.
I think there are different levels to this. At a personal level, success would mean I understand and can use Kata.
True. At the company level a certain number of people should be using it... but don't forget about coaches. For me, success requires something happening on that front as well.
Ok, we have some interesting elements. The clearer we make this end image, the easier it will be to get there.
So how about this? By October 2014, each of us should complete at least one project as a learner and one as a coach... and we should each be coaching two more projects.
Step 1: Understand direction
Ideal: everyone improves every day towards clear goals
Challenge for Oct 2014:
- Managers → 1 project as learners
- Managers → 1 project as coaches
- Managers → coaching 2 more projects
I can't tell how hard this will be, but it does take care of our personal learning and gets others involved. I would like to see more about developing other coaches, though.
What if we include defining the path to becoming a coach?
That works for me.
Step 1: Understand direction
Ideal: everyone improves every day towards clear goals
Challenge for Oct 2014:
- Managers → 1 project as learners
- Managers → 1 project as coaches
- Managers → coaching 2 more projects
- Define path to become a Kata coach
This looks good enough for now. It provides a clear direction and is measurable. We will be able to track progress against it and evaluate whether we succeeded when we get to October next year.

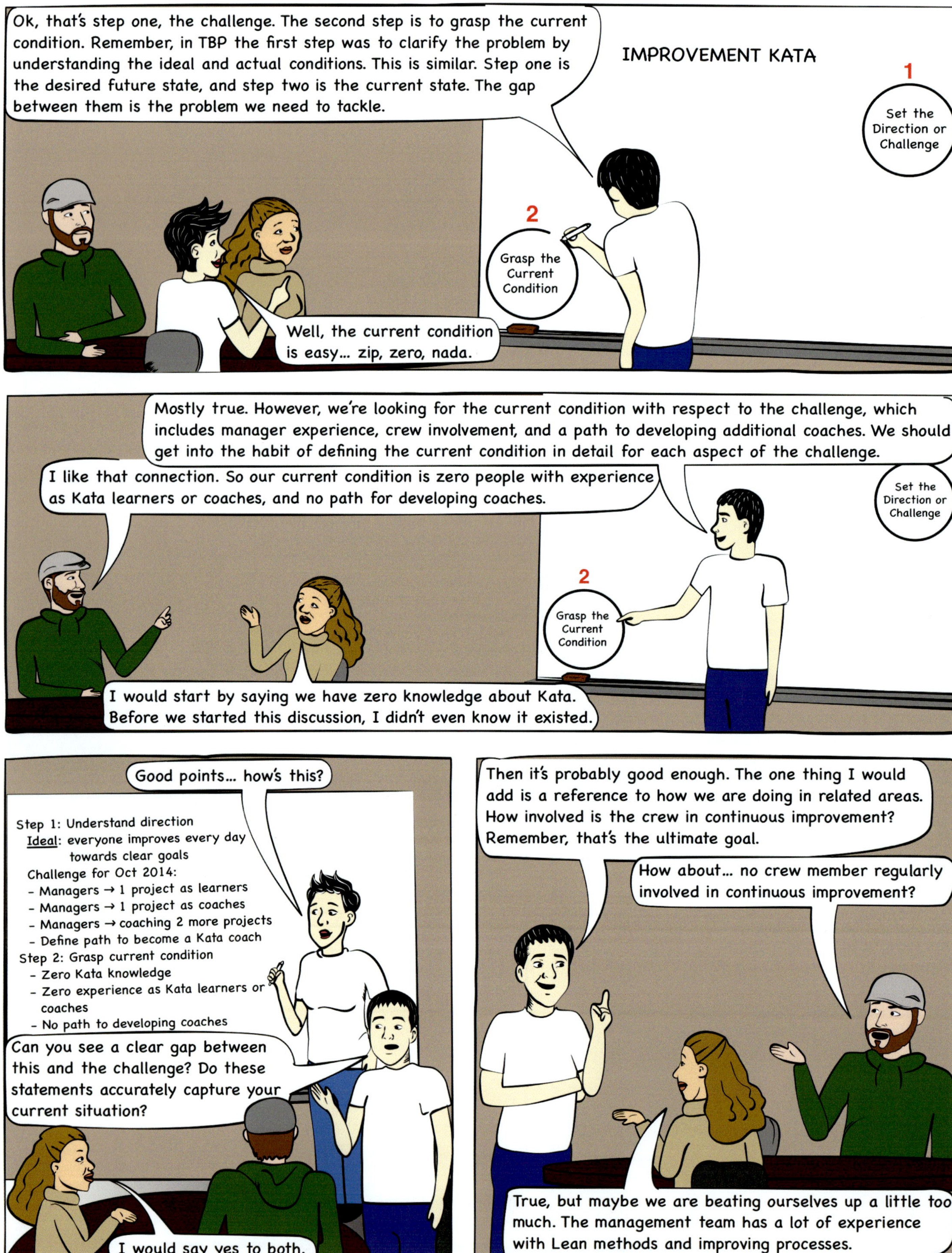
Ok, that's step one, the challenge. The second step is to grasp the current condition. Remember, in TBP the first step was to clarify the problem by understanding the ideal and actual conditions. This is similar. Step one is the desired future state, and step two is the current state. The gap between them is the problem we need to tackle.
IMPROVEMENT KATA
1
Set the Direction or Challenge
2
Grasp the Current Condition
Well, the current condition is easy... zip, zero, nada.
Mostly true. However, we're looking for the current condition with respect to the challenge, which includes manager experience, crew involvement, and a path to developing additional coaches. We should get into the habit of defining the current condition in detail for each aspect of the challenge.
I like that connection. So our current condition is zero people with experience as Kata learners or coaches, and no path for developing coaches.
Set the Direction or Challenge
2
Grasp the Current Condition
I would start by saying we have zero knowledge about Kata. Before we started this discussion, I didn't even know it existed.
Good points... how's this?
Step 1: Understand direction
Ideal: everyone improves every day towards clear goals
Challenge for Oct 2014:
- Managers → 1 project as learners
- Managers → 1 project as coaches
- Managers → coaching 2 more projects
- Define path to become a Kata coach
Step 2: Grasp current condition
- Zero Kata knowledge
- Zero experience as Kata learners or coaches
- No path to developing coaches
Can you see a clear gap between this and the challenge? Do these statements accurately capture your current situation?
I would say yes to both.
Then it's probably good enough. The one thing I would add is a reference to how we are doing in related areas. How involved is the crew in continuous improvement? Remember, that's the ultimate goal.
How about... no crew member regularly involved in continuous improvement?
True, but maybe we are beating ourselves up a little too much. The management team has a lot of experience with Lean methods and improving processes.

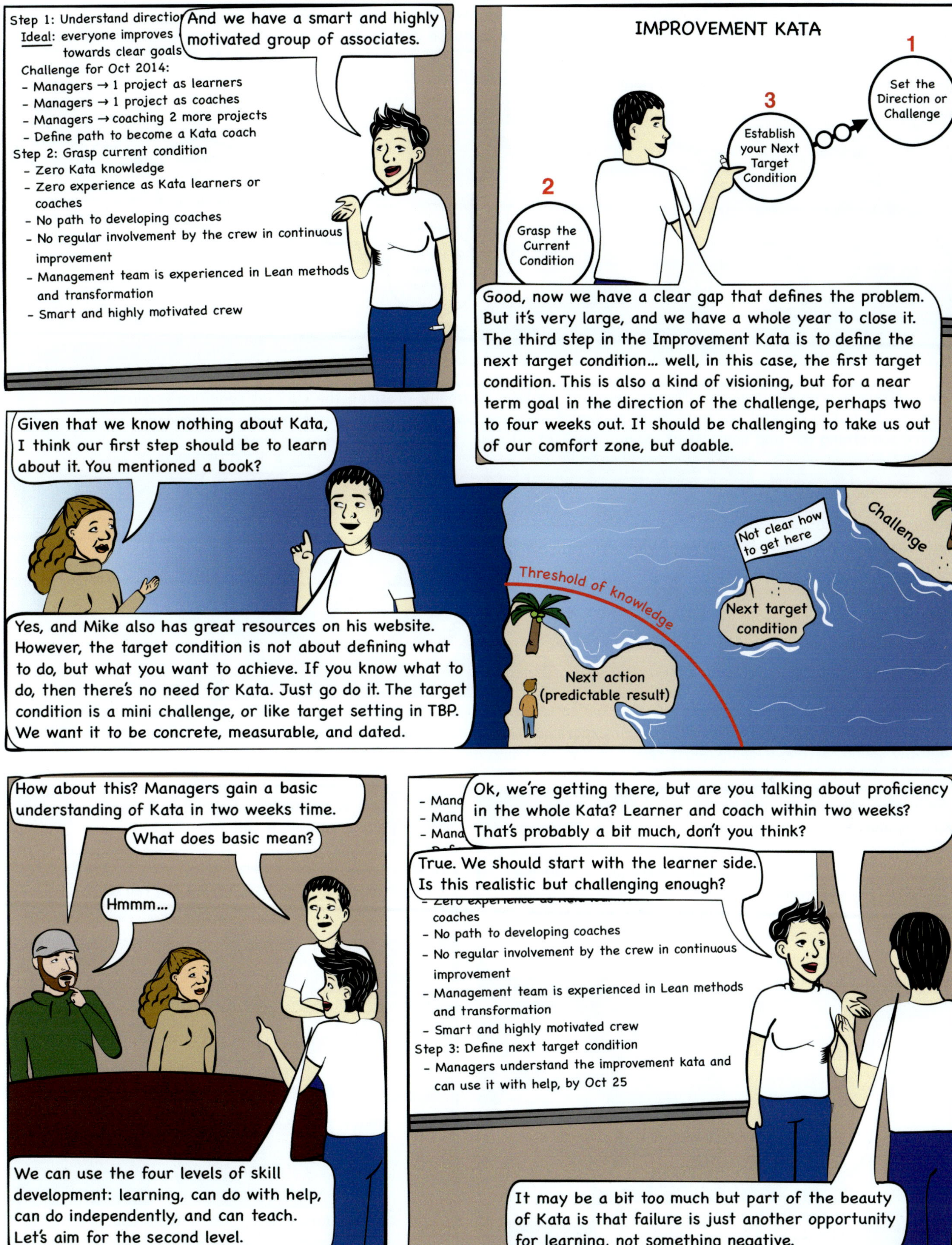

Step 1: Understand directio
Ideal: everyone improves towards clear goals
Challenge for Oct 2014:
- Managers → 1 project as learners
- Managers → 1 project as coaches
- Managers → coaching 2 more projects
- Define path to become a Kata coach
Step 2: Grasp current condition
- Zero Kata knowledge
- Zero experience as Kata learners or coaches
- No path to developing coaches
- No regular involvement by the crew in continuous improvement
- Management team is experienced in Lean methods and transformation
- Smart and highly motivated crew
And we have a smart and highly motivated group of associates.
IMPROVEMENT KATA
1
Set the Direction or Challenge
3
Establish your Next Target Condition
2
Grasp the Current Condition
Good, now we have a clear gap that defines the problem. But it's very large, and we have a whole year to close it. The third step in the Improvement Kata is to define the next target condition... well, in this case, the first target condition. This is also a kind of visioning, but for a near term goal in the direction of the challenge, perhaps two to four weeks out. It should be challenging to take us out of our comfort zone, but doable.
Given that we know nothing about Kata, I think our first step should be to learn about it. You mentioned a book?
Yes, and Mike also has great resources on his website. However, the target condition is not about defining what to do, but what you want to achieve. If you know what to do, then there's no need for Kata. Just go do it. The target condition is a mini challenge, or like target setting in TBP. We want it to be concrete, measurable, and dated.
Challenge
Not clear how to get here
Threshold of knowledge
Next target condition
Next action (predictable result)
How about this? Managers gain a basic understanding of Kata in two weeks time.
What does basic mean?
Hmmm...
We can use the four levels of skill development: learning, can do with help, can do independently, and can teach. Let's aim for the second level.
Ok, we're getting there, but are you talking about proficiency in the whole Kata? Learner and coach within two weeks? That's probably a bit much, don't you think?
True. We should start with the learner side. Is this realistic but challenging enough?
coaches
- No path to developing coaches
- No regular involvement by the crew in continuous improvement
- Management team is experienced in Lean methods and transformation
- Smart and highly motivated crew
Step 3: Define next target condition
- Managers understand the improvement kata and can use it with help, by Oct 25
It may be a bit too much but part of the beauty of Kata is that failure is just another opportunity for learning, not something negative.

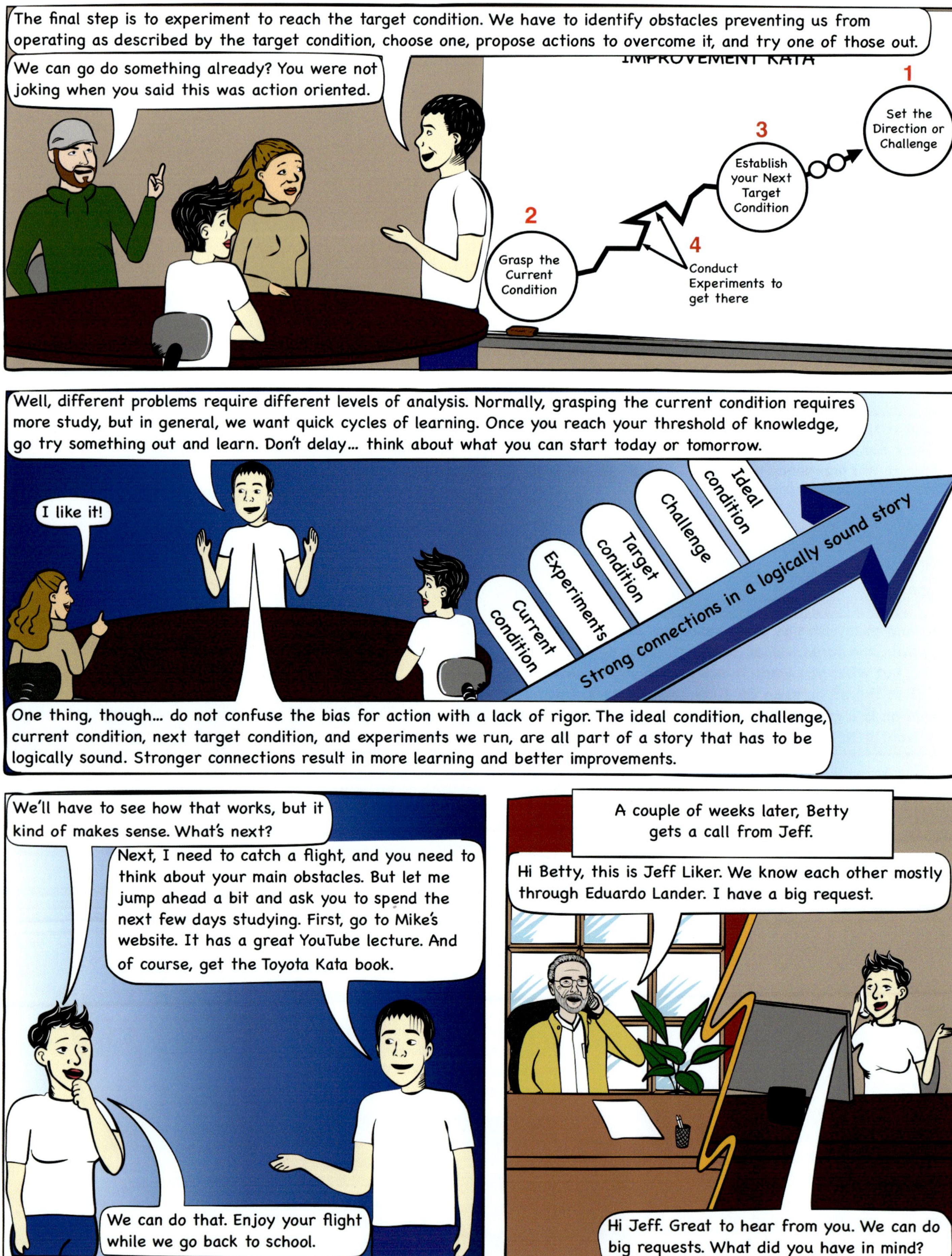
The final step is to experiment to reach the target condition. We have to identify obstacles preventing us from operating as described by the target condition, choose one, propose actions to overcome it, and try one of those out.
We can go do something already? You were not joking when you said this was action oriented.
1
Set the Direction or Challenge
3
Establish your Next Target Condition
2
Grasp the Current Condition
4
Conduct Experiments to get there
Well, different problems require different levels of analysis. Normally, grasping the current condition requires more study, but in general, we want quick cycles of learning. Once you reach your threshold of knowledge, go try something out and learn. Don't delay... think about what you can start today or tomorrow.
I like it!
Ideal condition
Challenge
Target condition
Experiments
Current condition
Strong connections in a logically sound story
One thing, though... do not confuse the bias for action with a lack of rigor. The ideal condition, challenge, current condition, next target condition, and experiments we run, are all part of a story that has to be logically sound. Stronger connections result in more learning and better improvements.
We'll have to see how that works, but it kind of makes sense. What's next?
Next, I need to catch a flight, and you need to think about your main obstacles. But let me jump ahead a bit and ask you to spend the next few days studying. First, go to Mike's website. It has a great YouTube lecture. And of course, get the Toyota Kata book.
We can do that. Enjoy your flight while we go back to school.
A couple of weeks later, Betty gets a call from Jeff.
Hi Betty, this is Jeff Liker. We know each other mostly through Eduardo Lander. I have a big request.
Hi Jeff. Great to hear from you. We can do big requests. What did you have in mind?

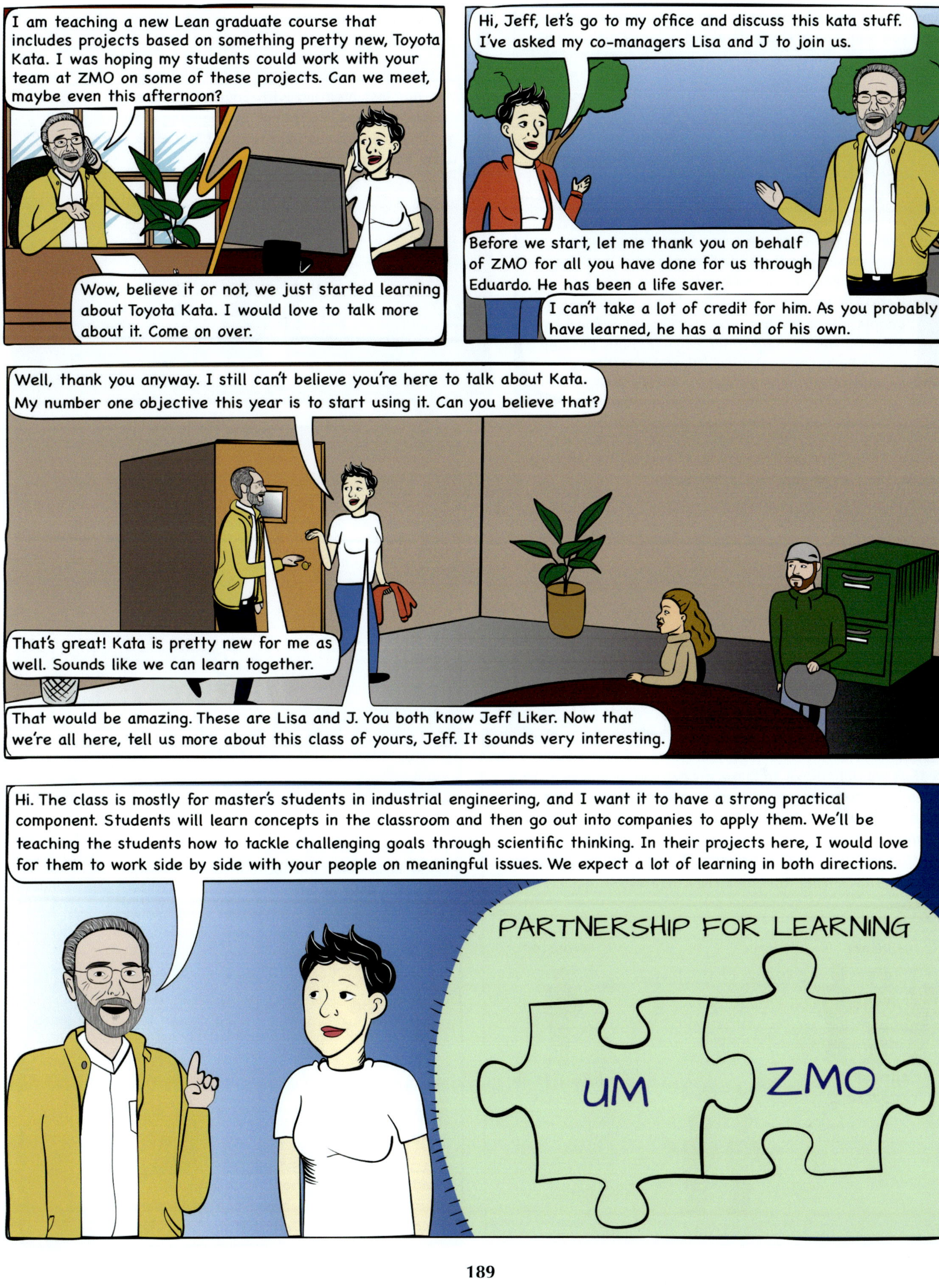
I am teaching a new Lean graduate course that includes projects based on something pretty new, Toyota Kata. I was hoping my students could work with your team at ZMO on some of these projects. Can we meet, maybe even this afternoon?
Wow, believe it or not, we just started learning about Toyota Kata. I would love to talk more about it. Come on over.
Hi, Jeff, let's go to my office and discuss this kata stuff. I've asked my co-managers Lisa and J to join us.
Before we start, let me thank you on behalf of ZMO for all you have done for us through Eduardo. He has been a life saver.
I can't take a lot of credit for him. As you probably have learned, he has a mind of his own.
Well, thank you anyway. I still can't believe you're here to talk about Kata. My number one objective this year is to start using it. Can you believe that?
That's great! Kata is pretty new for me as well. Sounds like we can learn together.
That would be amazing. These are Lisa and J. You both know Jeff Liker. Now that we're all here, tell us more about this class of yours, Jeff. It sounds very interesting.
Hi. The class is mostly for master's students in industrial engineering, and I want it to have a strong practical component. Students will learn concepts in the classroom and then go out into companies to apply them. We'll be teaching the students how to tackle challenging goals through scientific thinking. In their projects here, I would love for them to work side by side with your people on meaningful issues. We expect a lot of learning in both directions.
PARTNERSHIP FOR LEARNING
UM
ZMO

Sounds too good to be true. Can you tell us more about how you will teach students about scientific thinking?
Well, in the class we cover Lean principles so they can apply them in their projects, but the main thread of the course is based on Toyota Kata. It's similar to what Toyota uses to develop people internally but was specifically defined by Mike Rother to help other organizations develop scientific thinking skills, without having to be immersed in a culture where it's the norm.
This is an incredible coincidence.
Isn't it? I was telling Jeff we just started learning about Kata.
Yes, our last meeting with Eduardo focused on defininig our next attempt at engaging a wider group in continuous improvement. We even started using Kata to learn about Kata.
What do you mean?
Well, we defined a challenge, our current condition, and the first target condition. We're now identifying obstacles so we can start our first experiment.
That's great. It seems my timing is impeccable, or at least really lucky.
Jeff, going back to your class... how do you envision this working? We and the students will all be learning. Who's the learner and who's the coach?
I don't have all the answers, but the good thing about Kata is that we don't have to know everything in advance. This class is an experiment. We will learn and improve it for next year. My image is that small groups of say, three students team up with a few of your people to learn together, step-by-step working on real projects. I want the students to start in the learner role, but they may evolve quickly into coaches.
Students
Manager
Learner & coach
Learner & coach
ZMO crew
Learner
If a lot of learning happens in the classroom, could ZMO team members involved attend the class at U of M?
I had not thought about that. It would ensure everyone has a common understanding of Kata. Good idea! Don't tell my boss though.

Starting on the second week of January, we had eight teams of students roaming around the warehouse. Each team was paired with a couple of frontline crew members and supported by a manager. They met regularly and scheduled experiments as needed, but the students also dropped in at any time just to observe the process. And our associates took a graduate course at UM! They were intimidated at first, but ended up loving the experience.

Results? Amazing! Well beyond expectations. It's true the first year was a bit hectic. Nobody had any real experience with Kata, so the students and crew tried to learn together as they ran the projects. The difference between teams was huge in both the approach and results. Some jumped right in to make changes without understanding the current condition or how they would measure success, while others analyzed the issues to death and beyond. And evolving to become a coach was much harder than expected. However, for participants and ZMO in general, it was a transformative experience that resulted in huge engagement in improvement efforts. There was a newfound enthusiasm to try ideas out and experiment.

It was almost like flipping a switch. We went from almost no involvement to electrifying participation in a matter of months. As Betty put it... before Kata, people preferred getting a tooth pulled to participating in improvement activities. After running a few Kata projects though, we had to turn people away because we did not have the resources to support so many projects simultaneously.

Release the kata

Over the next few years, the partnership with the University of Michigan continued to bring students to ZMO during the winter term. As the managers and crew gained practice with Kata, they provided a better learning experience for students. The managers have become highly skilled coaches, allowing the students to focus on the learner role. The students bring new ideas and help our crew analyze and display data. Attending a class at UM continues to be a big draw, so we never have problems finding people to pair up with the students.

So far we have looked at the general pattern of the Improvement Kata. Now we will go through an example of a student project on bread preparation. Please keep in mind that Kata is new to the students, so we follow Mike's starter Kata rigorously. As your understanding grows, you may develop your own way to match the needs of your organization. At ZMO, we have made some changes to the Kata routine to fit our context, but we will mention only one of them below.

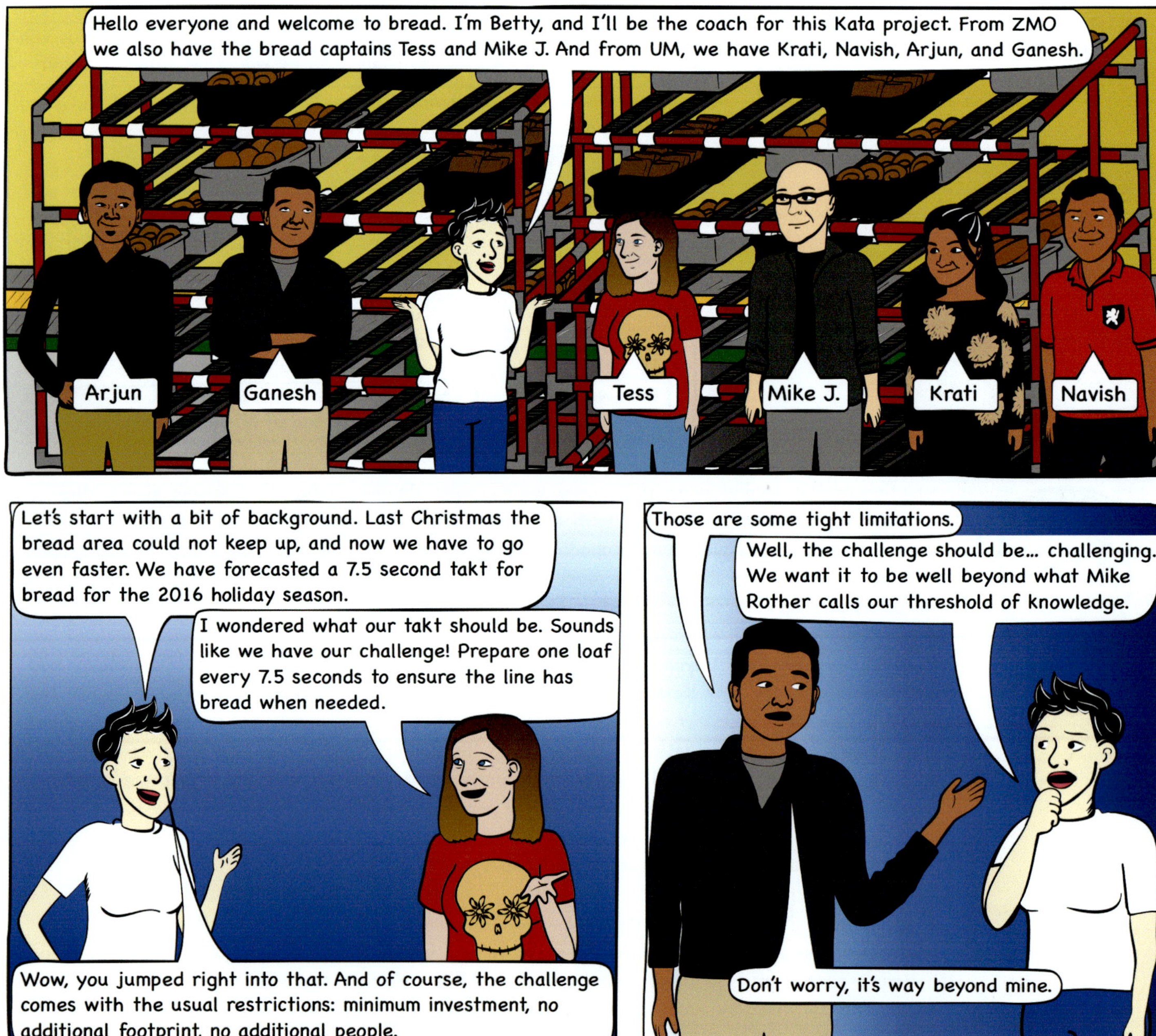

Professor Liker asked us to build a Kata storyboard and take a photo for our report. Should we use Tess' statement as the challenge?
We have an empty board we can use. And yes, Tess' statement is good. That takes care of step one.
focus process: bread
challenge:
One loaf every 7.5 s
(bread available when needed - Dec 2016)
target condition:
current condition:
pdca cycles record:
obstacles parking lot:
Any other questions? If not, I have one for you. What's the second step in the Kata?
To understand the current condition.
Exactly! Tess and Mike can probably tell us about it, but where's the fun in that? I suggest we do a general go see and observe for half an hour to grasp the situation. How does that sound?
Good idea. I work here every day and still learn a lot from observing the process.

30 minutes later
Ok, let's discuss briefly where we are. What have we learned so far?
Well, the process here consists of taking naked bread, bagging it, and putting it in totes in the market.
That's mostly the case, but sometimes the bread comes in plastic bags... and others it needs to be sliced.
The bread in plastic bags comes from the freezer. We use that when we do not have enough coming from the Bakehouse. Slicing is a special request from customers.
I saw three distinct jobs. A person takes the totes from the line and prepares paper bags with labels for the breads needed, another moves the bread to where it will be bagged, and two people bag it.
That's right. The first one is the Dispatch, and besides what you mentioned, they use the kanban returning from the line to ask EVE whether more bread is needed.

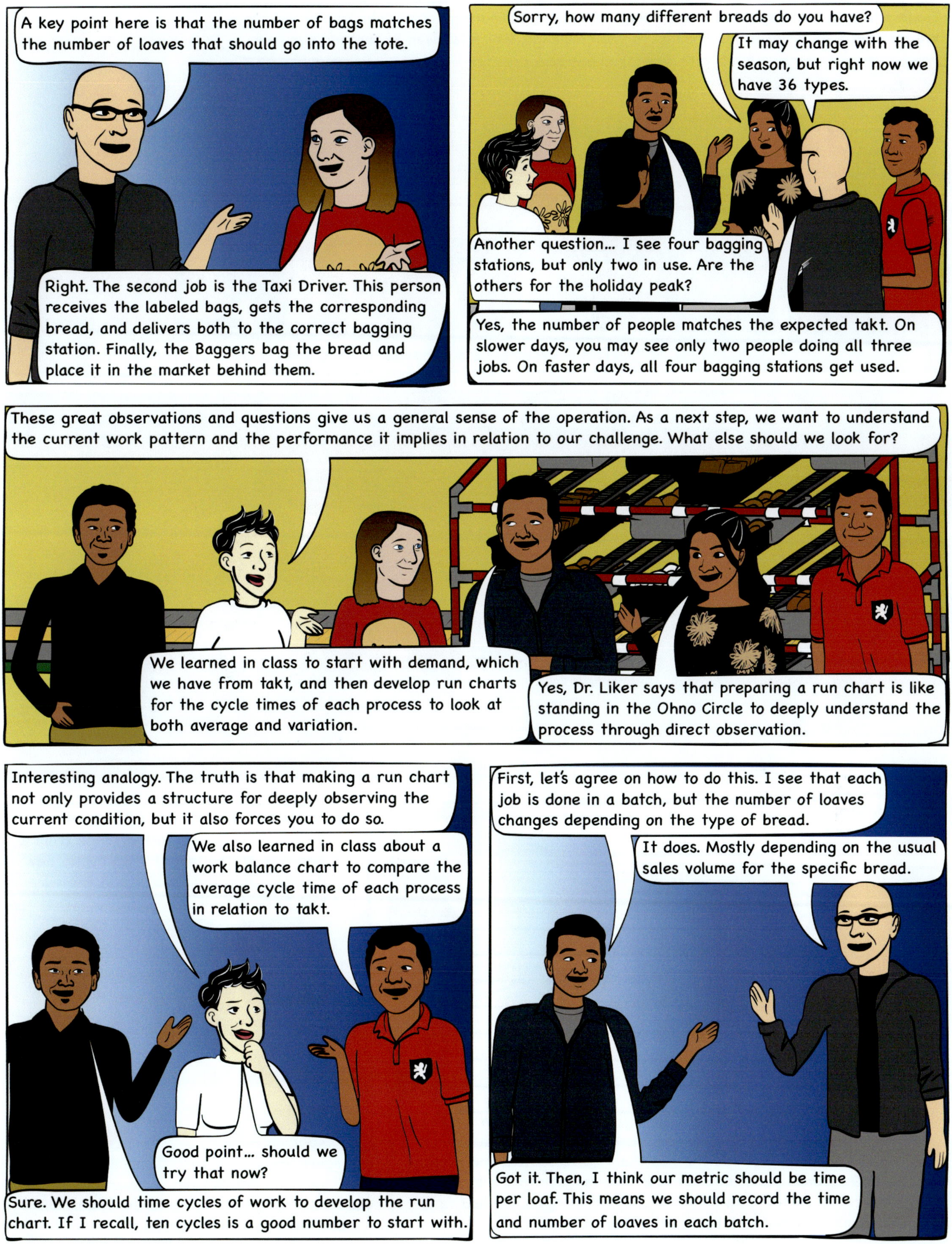
A key point here is that the number of bags matches the number of loaves that should go into the tote.
Right. The second job is the Taxi Driver. This person receives the labeled bags, gets the corresponding bread, and delivers both to the correct bagging station. Finally, the Baggers bag the bread and place it in the market behind them.
Sorry, how many different breads do you have?
It may change with the season, but right now we have 36 types.
Another question... I see four bagging stations, but only two in use. Are the others for the holiday peak?
Yes, the number of people matches the expected takt. On slower days, you may see only two people doing all three jobs. On faster days, all four bagging stations get used.
These great observations and questions give us a general sense of the operation. As a next step, we want to understand the current work pattern and the performance it implies in relation to our challenge. What else should we look for?
We learned in class to start with demand, which we have from takt, and then develop run charts for the cycle times of each process to look at both average and variation.
Yes, Dr. Liker says that preparing a run chart is like standing in the Ohno Circle to deeply understand the process through direct observation.
Interesting analogy. The truth is that making a run chart not only provides a structure for deeply observing the current condition, but it also forces you to do so.
We also learned in class about a work balance chart to compare the average cycle time of each process in relation to takt.
Good point... should we try that now?
Sure. We should time cycles of work to develop the run chart. If I recall, ten cycles is a good number to start with.
First, let's agree on how to do this. I see that each job is done in a batch, but the number of loaves changes depending on the type of bread.
It does. Mostly depending on the usual sales volume for the specific bread.
Got it. Then, I think our metric should be time per loaf. This means we should record the time and number of loaves in each batch.

That's a very good insight. We need a common way of comparing across jobs and bread types. We also need to compare our findings to the challenge, which is given in seconds per loaf.
This is exciting! Let's get some timings and create these run charts.
30 min later
Let's get back together. How did it go? Do we have data already?
Dispatcher
Time per loaf [seconds]
14
12
10
8
6
4
1 2 3 4 5 6 7 8 9 10
I think we can. Here's the run chart for Dispatch. The average is 9 seconds per loaf, but cycle time ranges from 6 to 14 seconds. In the case of 14 seconds, the Dispatcher had to change the roll of labels in the label printer.
Mine is much faster. I have 3.5 seconds per loaf for the Taxi Driver, with a range from 2 to 5 seconds. In the longest two cycles new bread coming into the area was in the way and had to be moved.
Baggers are the slowest. Combining Navish's timings and mine, we get an average of 37.2 seconds, ranging from 28 to 54. The slowest times were for frozen bread.

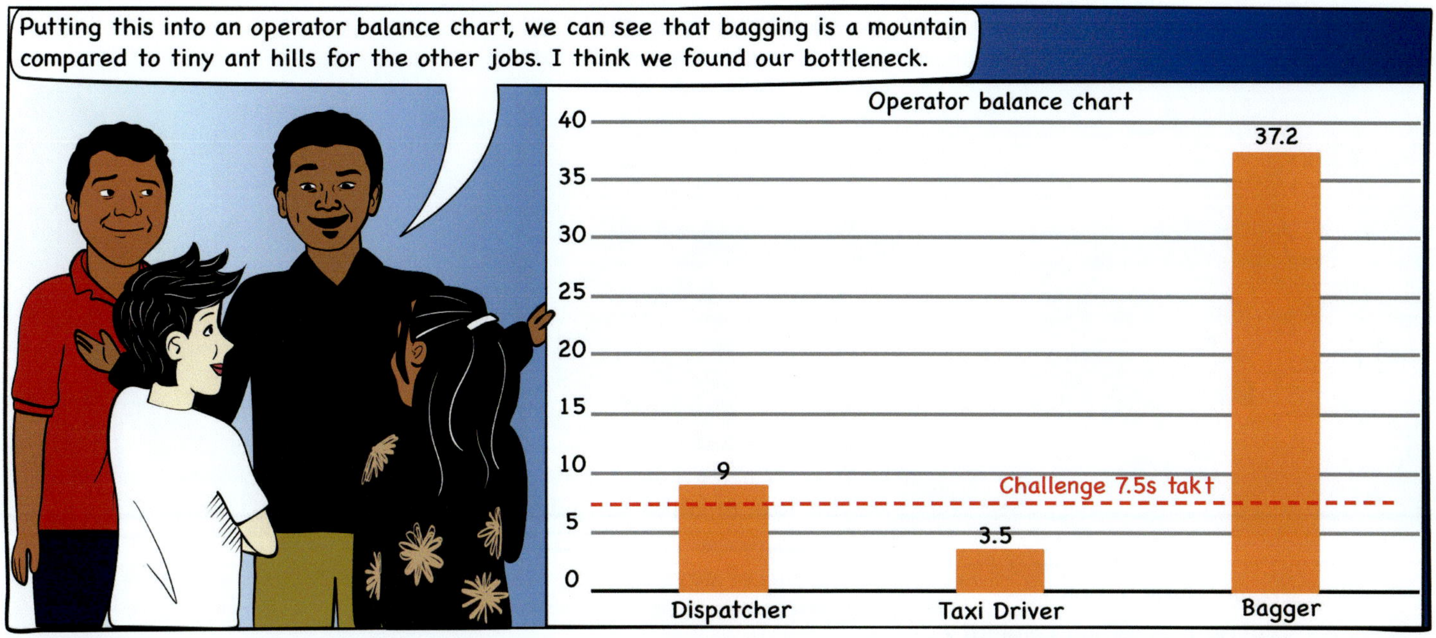
Putting this into an operator balance chart, we can see that bagging is a mountain compared to tiny ant hills for the other jobs. I think we found our bottleneck.
Operator balance chart
40
35
30
25
20
15
10
5
0
9
3.5
37.2
Challenge 7.5s takt
Dispatcher
Taxi Driver
Bagger

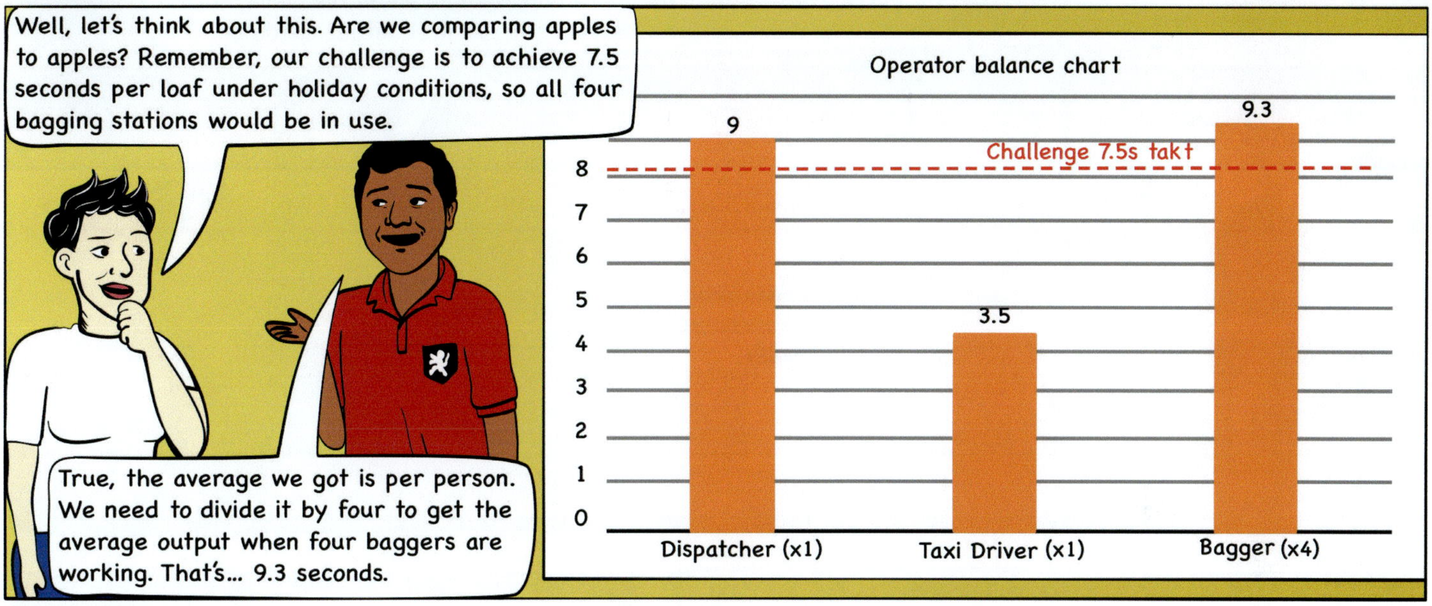
Well, let's think about this. Are we comparing apples to apples? Remember, our challenge is to achieve 7.5 seconds per loaf under holiday conditions, so all four bagging stations would be in use.
Operator balance chart
8
7
6
5
4
3
2
1
0
9
3.5
9.3
Challenge 7.5s takt
Dispatcher (x1)
Taxi Driver (x1)
Bagger (x4)
True, the average we got is per person. We need to divide it by four to get the average output when four baggers are working. That's... 9.3 seconds.

Thank you! That looks like a much more manageable gap.
Great work! Can someone summarize what we learned?
Bagging is the bottleneck, and we need to improve it from 9.3 to 7.5 seconds per loaf. At some point, the Dispatch job will have to be improved as well, since it's also over takt.

Very good. Now we need to update the board with all that information.
Don't worry, we'll take care of that. Maybe Tess or Mike can help us.
A couple of days later...
Hello, team. How's our current condition coming?
Hi, Betty. We updated the board and want to show you some work we did. We think we are ready to set our first target condition.
focus process: bread
target condition:
current condition:
36 types of bread
challenge:
PDCA cycles record:
obstacles parking lot:
As you can see, we included charts for the data we collected last time we worked with you, and...
Wait, wait. You seem to have made a lot of progress. We may be ready for the first coaching cycle. Shall we try it?
We're ready! Let's do it.
Ok. What's your challenge?

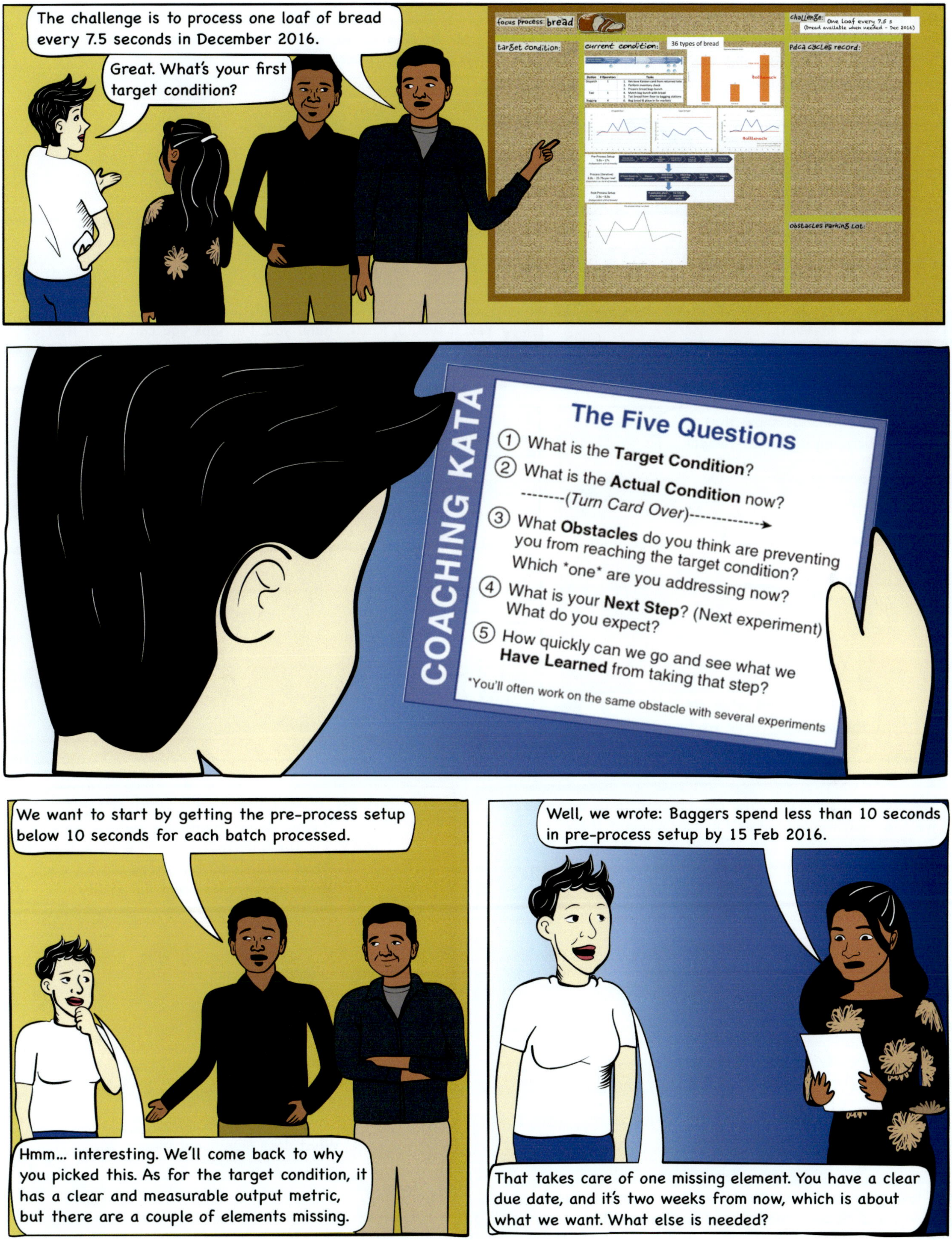
The challenge is to process one loaf of bread every 7.5 seconds in December 2016.
Great. What's your first target condition?
focus process: bread
challenge: One loaf every 7.5 s (bread available when needed - Dec 2016)
target condition:
current condition:
36 types of bread
pdca cycles record:
obstacles parking lot:
COACHING KATA
The Five Questions
① What is the Target Condition?
② What is the Actual Condition now?
--------(Turn Card Over)------------→
③ What Obstacles do you think are preventing you from reaching the target condition? Which *one* are you addressing now?
④ What is your Next Step? (Next experiment) What do you expect?
⑤ How quickly can we go and see what we Have Learned from taking that step?
*You'll often work on the same obstacle with several experiments
We want to start by getting the pre-process setup below 10 seconds for each batch processed.
Hmm... interesting. We'll come back to why you picked this. As for the target condition, it has a clear and measurable output metric, but there are a couple of elements missing.
Well, we wrote: Baggers spend less than 10 seconds in pre-process setup by 15 Feb 2016.
That takes care of one missing element. You have a clear due date, and it's two weeks from now, which is about what we want. What else is needed?

Oh, yes... Professor Liker emphasized that the target condition includes the desired outcome, in this case 10 seconds, and also the desired process condition. He mentioned that this is like taking a time machine to see how the process will look in two weeks.
Now that you mention it, we did discuss that. To consistently get to 10 seconds, we need a clear and repeatable process for the pre-process setup. Would that do it?
focus process: bread
target condition:
Target condition #1
current condition:
36 types of bread
Yes, it would, Krati. Thank you. Perhaps you can clean that up and update the board later. Now, I am curious. Why did you choose to focus on the pre-process setup?
Our timings show that bagging is the bottleneck...
Which matches what we see during the holidays. When we bring people in to help, they usually go to bagging.
In addition, we can break the baggers' activities into three blocks: pre-process setup, bagging process, and post-process setup.
That's the block diagram we have on the board.
You are on a roll! Keep going.
We chose to start with the pre-process setup because we see clear opportunities for improvement there.
I love your reasoning. There's a clear logic to your story, and it's well documented on the board.
Let's move on. What's the actual condition now?
Well, as we mentioned before, bagging is the bottleneck and the work they do can be divided into three blocks, each one having significant variability.
What does significant mean?

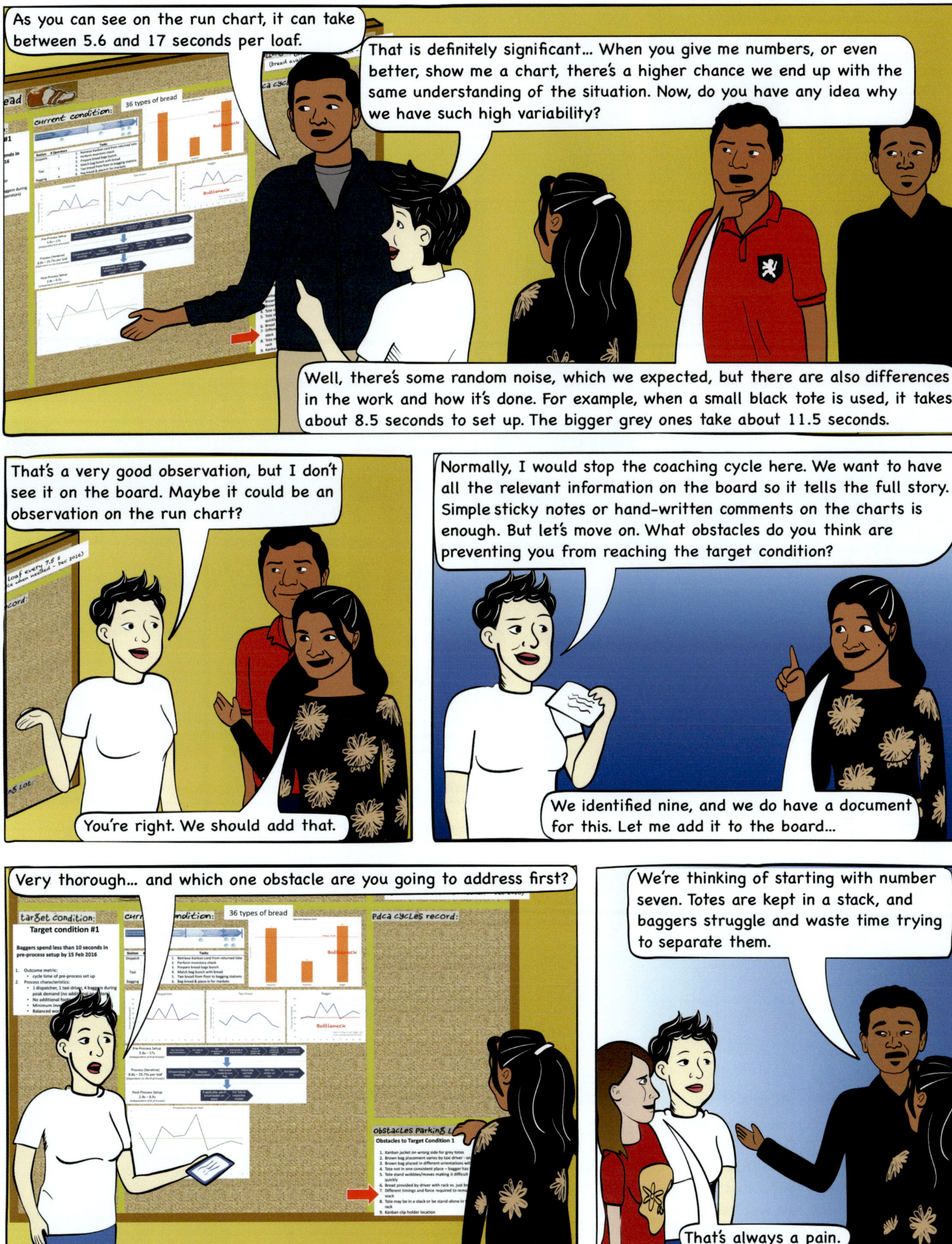
As you can see on the run chart, it can take between 5.6 and 17 seconds per loaf.
That is definitely significant… When you give me numbers, or even better, show me a chart, there's a higher chance we end up with the same understanding of the situation. Now, do you have any idea why we have such high variability?
Well, there's some random noise, which we expected, but there are also differences in the work and how it's done. For example, when a small black tote is used, it takes about 8.5 seconds to set up. The bigger grey ones take about 11.5 seconds.
That's a very good observation, but I don't see it on the board. Maybe it could be an observation on the run chart?
You're right. We should add that.
Normally, I would stop the coaching cycle here. We want to have all the relevant information on the board so it tells the full story. Simple sticky notes or hand-written comments on the charts is enough. But let's move on. What obstacles do you think are preventing you from reaching the target condition?
We identified nine, and we do have a document for this. Let me add it to the board…
Very thorough… and which one obstacle are you going to address first?
We're thinking of starting with number seven. Totes are kept in a stack, and baggers struggle and waste time trying to separate them.
That's always a pain.

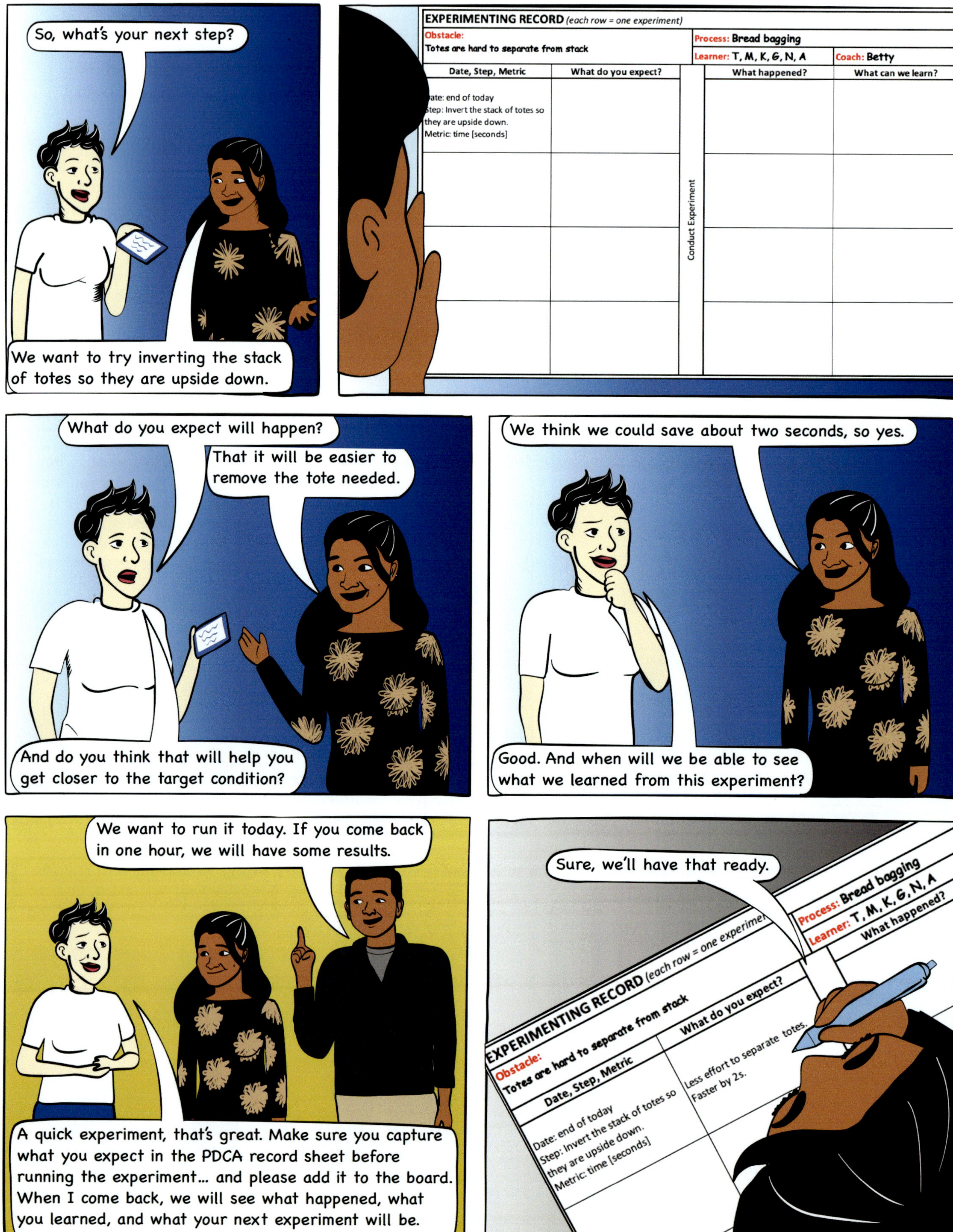
So, what's your next step?
We want to try inverting the stack of totes so they are upside down.
EXPERIMENTING RECORD (each row = one experiment)
Obstacle: Totes are hard to separate from stack
Process: Bread bagging
Learner: T, M, K, G, N, A
Coach: Betty
Date, Step, Metric
What do you expect?
Conduct Experiment
What happened?
What can we learn?
ate: end of today
tep: Invert the stack of totes so they are upside down.
Metric: time [seconds]
What do you expect will happen?
That it will be easier to remove the tote needed.
And do you think that will help you get closer to the target condition?
We think we could save about two seconds, so yes.
Good. And when will we be able to see what we learned from this experiment?
We want to run it today. If you come back in one hour, we will have some results.
A quick experiment, that's great. Make sure you capture what you expect in the PDCA record sheet before running the experiment... and please add it to the board. When I come back, we will see what happened, what you learned, and what your next experiment will be.
Sure, we'll have that ready.
EXPERIMENTING RECORD (each row = one experime
Obstacle: Totes are hard to separate from stack
Process: Bread bagging
Learner: T, M, K, G, N, A
Date, Step, Metric
What do you expect?
What happened?
Date: end of today
Step: Invert the stack of totes so they are upside down.
Metric: time [seconds]
Less effort to separate totes.
Faster by 2s.

About an hour later...
I'm back. Are you ready for the next coaching cycle?
Of course!
Let's do it, then. What's your challenge?
To process one loaf of bread every 7.5 seconds in December 2016.
Good... what's your target condition?
For baggers to spend less than 10 seconds in pre-process setup while following a clear and repeatable process by 15 Feb 2016.
And what's the actual condition now?
There are three jobs in bread. Bagging is the bottleneck. Besides the actual bagging, they also have setup work for each batch. There's significant... ehh... there's variability in each step, as noted on the block diagram.
That's a very good summary... Can you tell me where we are with respect to the target condition?
Yes. The pre-process setup takes between 5.8 and 17 seconds as you can see on the run chart at the bottom of the board.
Cool. Let's go to the back of the card and find out what you did... What did you plan as your last step?
Reflect on the Last Step Taken
Because you don't actually know what the result of a step will be!
Have the learner state the obstacle being worked on
1) What did you plan as your Last Step?
2) What did you Expect?
3) What Actually Happened?
4) What did you Learn?
Return to question 3
We planned to invert the stack of totes baggers pull from.
Ok, what did you expect?
To make it easier for baggers to separate the totes and save about two seconds from their pre-process setup.

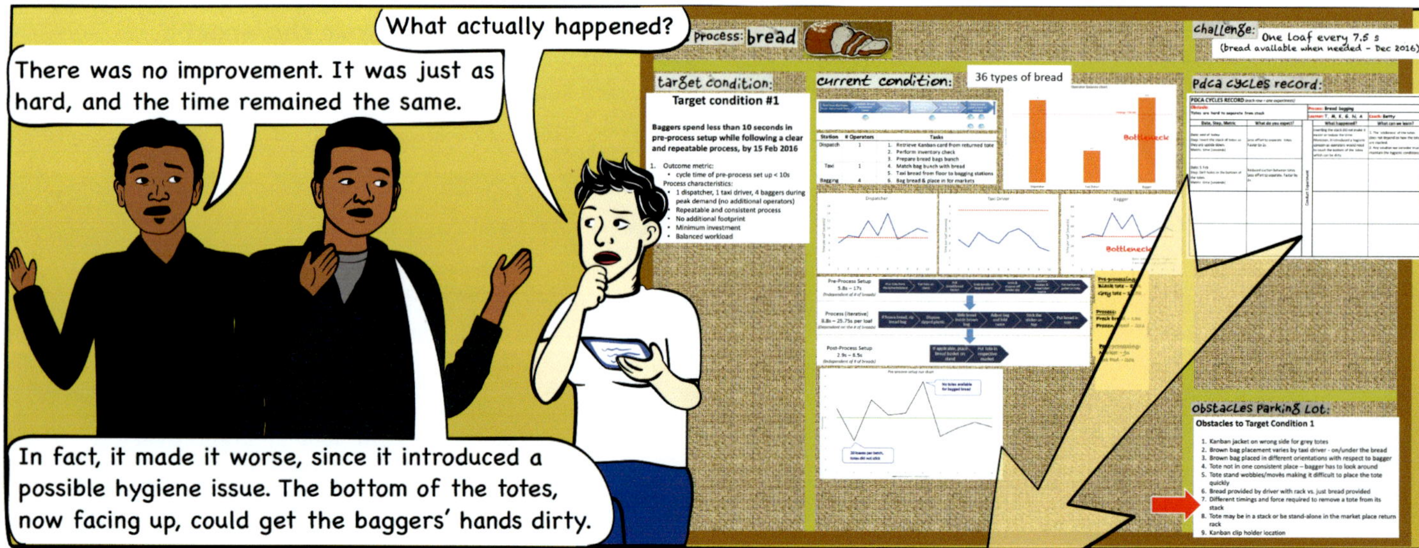

EXPERIMENTING RECORD *(each row = one experiment)*

Obstacle: Totes are hard to separate from stack			**Process:** Bread bagging	
			Learner: T, M, K, G, N, A	**Coach:** Betty
Date, Step, Metric	**What do you expect?**		**What happened?**	**What can we learn?**
Date: end of today Step: Invert the stack of totes so they are upside down. Metric: time [seconds]	Less effort to separate totes. Faster by 2s.		Inverting the stack did not make it easier or reduce the time. Moreover, it introduced a hygiene concern as operators would need to touch the bottom of the totes which can be dirty.	1. The 'stickiness' of the totes does not depend on how the totes are stacked. 2. Any solution we consider must maintain the hygienic conditions.
Date: 5 Feb Step: Drill holes in the bottom of the totes. Metric: time [seconds]	Reduced suction between totes. Less effort to separate. Faster by 2s.	Experiment		

You just answered my next question... which one you're focusing on. So, what's your next step?
We think it's hard to separate the totes because suction is generated between them as you try to pull them apart. So, we want to drill holes through the bottom of the totes.
Hmm... drill holes. Do you need to do it to all totes?
For the test, we were thinking of doing five. If it works, we'll have to do the rest.
Good thinking. We want quick experiments where possible negative effects are limited. Drilling only a few totes takes care of both. What do you expect will happen?
We expect air to enter easily between the totes and eliminate the suction effect. This will make it easier to separate the totes and speed the process by about two seconds.
Clear. How quickly can we see what we learned from this step?
We're thinking this coming Friday... the fifth. I'll come in the morning to help Tess drill the holes, and we can do the test after that.
It should not take too long. Could we do our coaching cycle at noon, before the line starts?
Noon it is. Thank you all, great work today!
This Kata process is harder than it looks, but it's starting to make sense.
Friday morning...

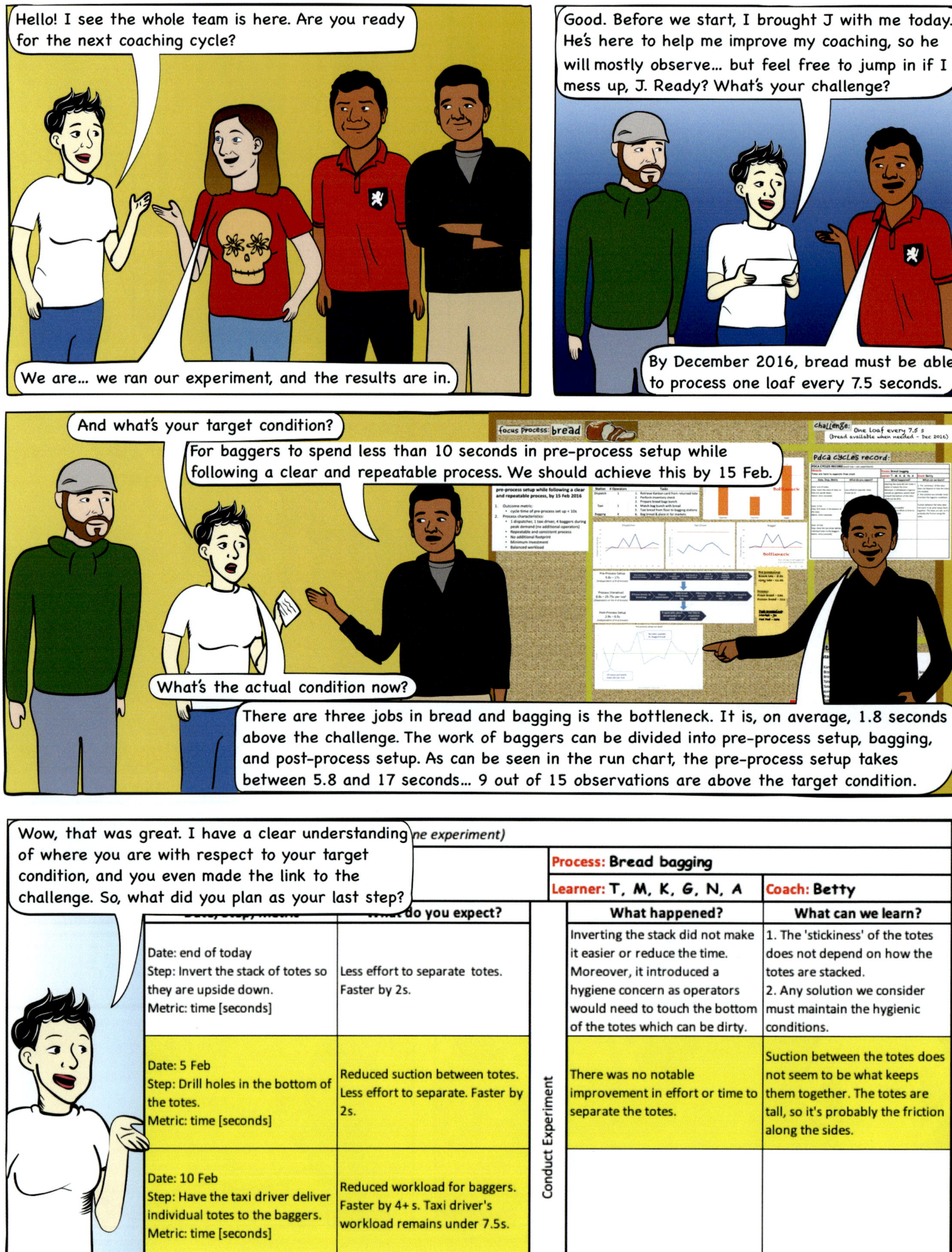

Date, Step, Metric	What do you expect?		What happened?	What can we learn?
Date: end of today Step: Invert the stack of totes so they are upside down. Metric: time [seconds]	Less effort to separate totes. Faster by 2s.	Conduct Experiment	Inverting the stack did not make it easier or reduce the time. Moreover, it introduced a hygiene concern as operators would need to touch the bottom of the totes which can be dirty.	1. The 'stickiness' of the totes does not depend on how the totes are stacked. 2. Any solution we consider must maintain the hygienic conditions.
Date: 5 Feb Step: Drill holes in the bottom of the totes. Metric: time [seconds]	Reduced suction between totes. Less effort to separate. Faster by 2s.		There was no notable improvement in effort or time to separate the totes.	Suction between the totes does not seem to be what keeps them together. The totes are tall, so it's probably the friction along the sides.
Date: 10 Feb Step: Have the taxi driver deliver individual totes to the baggers. Metric: time [seconds]	Reduced workload for baggers. Faster by 4+ s. Taxi driver's workload remains under 7.5s.			

So, what did you expect?
We planned to drill holes into the bottom of the totes.
To reduce the suction between totes, making them easier to separate. This should reduce the pre-processing setup by about two seconds.
And what actually happened?
The improvement was marginal and not consistent. Maybe half a second sometimes.
Ok. What did you learn?
It seems suction is not the main reason totes stick to each other. These totes are tall. Maybe the friction between the walls is a more important factor.
Hmm... so what obstacles do you think are preventing you now from reaching the target condition?
Same as before—it's hard to separate the totes.
Which one are you addressing now?
No changes there...
And what's your next step?
We want to give this work to the taxi driver.
Isn't that great? We can remove this large chunk of work from the bottleneck entirely.
Sounds like a great experiment. Can you walk me through the process? How would this work?
We want to build rollers under the bagging stations. We should be able to fit three totes. The taxi driver just has to bring another one every time they see an open space.
Sounds like that could work. Have you considered the effect on the taxi driver?

This will add to their workload, but they currently have considerable downtime, so we think it will be fine. Confirming this will be part of the experiment, of course.
Good thinking. So, what do you expect will happen?
We expect to eliminate about four seconds from the baggers' pre-setup time.
We also expect the taxi driver will not get overloaded.
Ok... how quickly can we see what we learned from this step?
This one will take a bit of time. At least a week.
We need to build the rollers under the station. I think the earliest we can run an experiment is next Wednesday or Thursday.
I understand there's work to do, but that seems like a long time. Is there any way we could test this faster, preferably without spending too much time and resources modifying the station?
Besides, the due date for the target condition is getting close. If this does not work, you won't have much time to try something else.
If we have pipe or rollers of the right size, we could fix them to the station's structure using tie-wraps. That would be faster.
So, when would this be ready?
Sorry, Betty, hold that thought. What are you trying to test? What do you want to learn from this experiment?
We want to confirm the baggers will save time, and the taxi driver won't be overloaded.
Thanks for that, J. I think I see where you're going. Ganesh, what do you think is needed to confirm the baggers will save time?
Quick and simple PDCA cycles
We need just ensure they have a tote available when they need it... is that what you mean?
Yes, and for the taxi driver?

Let me interrupt here. We just went through a series of coaching cycles, with each one building on the learnings from the previous one. This continued through the rest of the semester. I want to highlight a few key points:

1. You can distinguish two loops in Kata. A larger one, defined by the 4 steps of the Improvement Kata, and the shorter PDCA cycles of each experiment: plan the next step, define what to expect, run the experiment, examine the results, and reflect.
2. These two loops define the pattern of scientific thinking we want people to learn. As coaches, we need to help learners develop clear connections within and between loops. For example, at ZMO, we found it useful to start coaching cycles by asking about the challenge, to bring the learners to the larger loop before they plunge into the PDCA cycle.
3. The Kata story board reinforces a scientific thinking pattern and helps make visible the invisible thinking of the learner, so the coach can give fitting feedback. The learner updates it before each coaching cycle to tell a compelling and logically sound story linking all elements of both Kata loops.
4. Coaching in Kata is not about telling people what to do; it's about guiding them through questions so they figure things out by themselves. The questions on the card are headings, and the coach often has to add clarifying questions to recognize where the learner is in their understanding of Kata and challenge them to think deeply about their assumptions, logic being followed, and understanding of the process being improved. But the learner needs to remain in control, which creates much higher engagement and ownership.

Let's go back to our story now... In case you're wondering, the experiment worked beautifully. We ended up installing rollers under all bread stations.

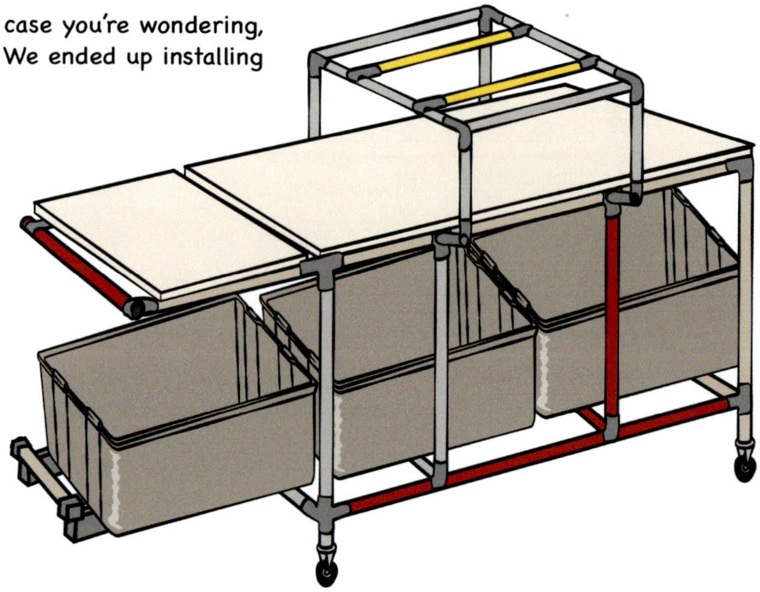

Thanks to the quick mocked-up experiment, the team had time to tackle another obstacle. This allowed them to achieve the target condition by the due date. Rapid experimentation increases the rate of improvement and learning, and frequent repetition is the most effective way to build the habit of thinking scientifically.

At the end of the semester, each team made a presentation. Jeff Liker and Mike Rother attended and provided feedback. It was a great finale to a very productive semester for developing the students, our people, and ZMO in general. Let's take a quick look as the bread team closes their presentation.

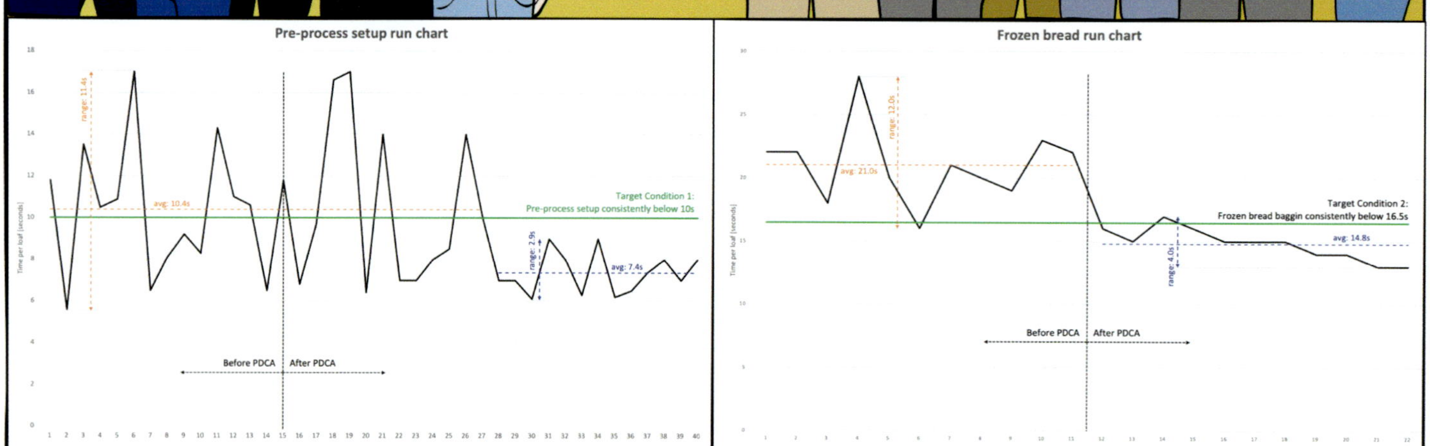

This operator balance chart shows the progress made with respect to the challenge of 7.5 seconds per loaf. We reduced the time for baggers by 1.1 seconds, which represents 61% of the gap. We're still 0.7 seconds shy from the challenge, so Tess and Mike will continue working on it, with Betty and J coaching them.
Operator balance chart
Challenge: 7.5s takt
9
9
3.5
6.5
9.3
8.2
Dispatcher
Taxi Driver
Bagger
Before
After

As we worked through this project, that strange 'Kata' word started to mean something important. We learned the power of the repetitive pattern. It was remarkable how the whole team quickly got used to this structured approach, impressive how much we learned through simple experiments, and incredible how much we improved by taking many small steps.
Finally, we want to thank Professor Liker for teaching us and setting up this great experience. We also want to thank Tess and Mike for working with us and allowing us to experiment in their area. And thank you Betty and J for coaching us, and the rest of ZMO for hosting us. As we have learned here... we appreciate you all!
Many thanks to you and all the other students here for all the ideas and hard work. Thanks also to Jeff for bringing this amazing learning experience to us. It's been three years, and it gets better every time. And thanks to Mike for coming today and giving us such valuable feedback.
No, thank you. When I wrote Toyota Kata this is the kind of thing I dreamed of.

RELEASE
THE
KATA

Part IV

Lessons from a 15-Year Journey

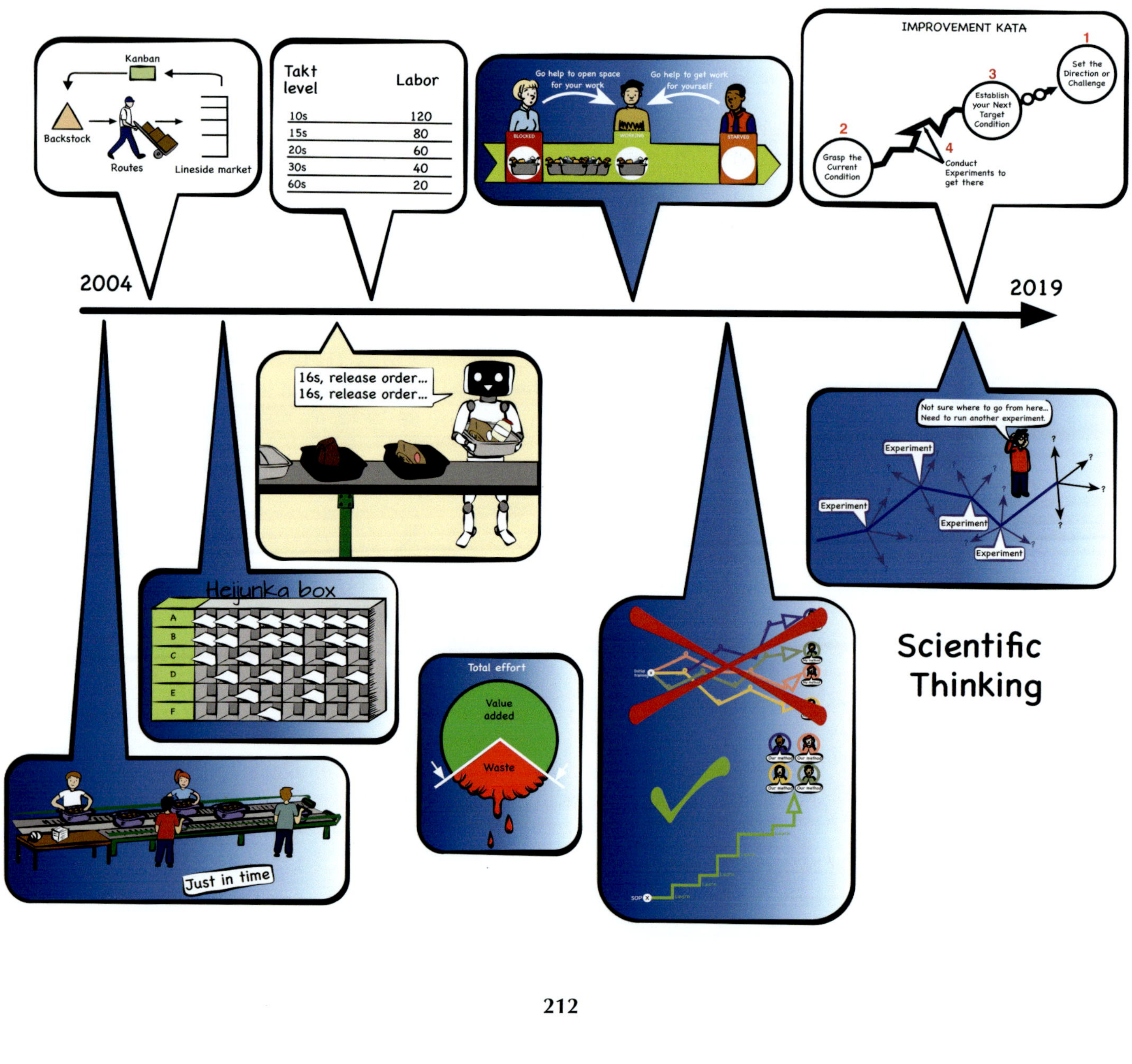

Lessons learned

In late 2019, we held a 15-year reflection meeting to celebrate our successes, identify key learnings, and think about next steps. Let's look in on it. Joining the usual group was Toni, the third ZMO partner whom you met at the beginning of the book, and Professor Liker.

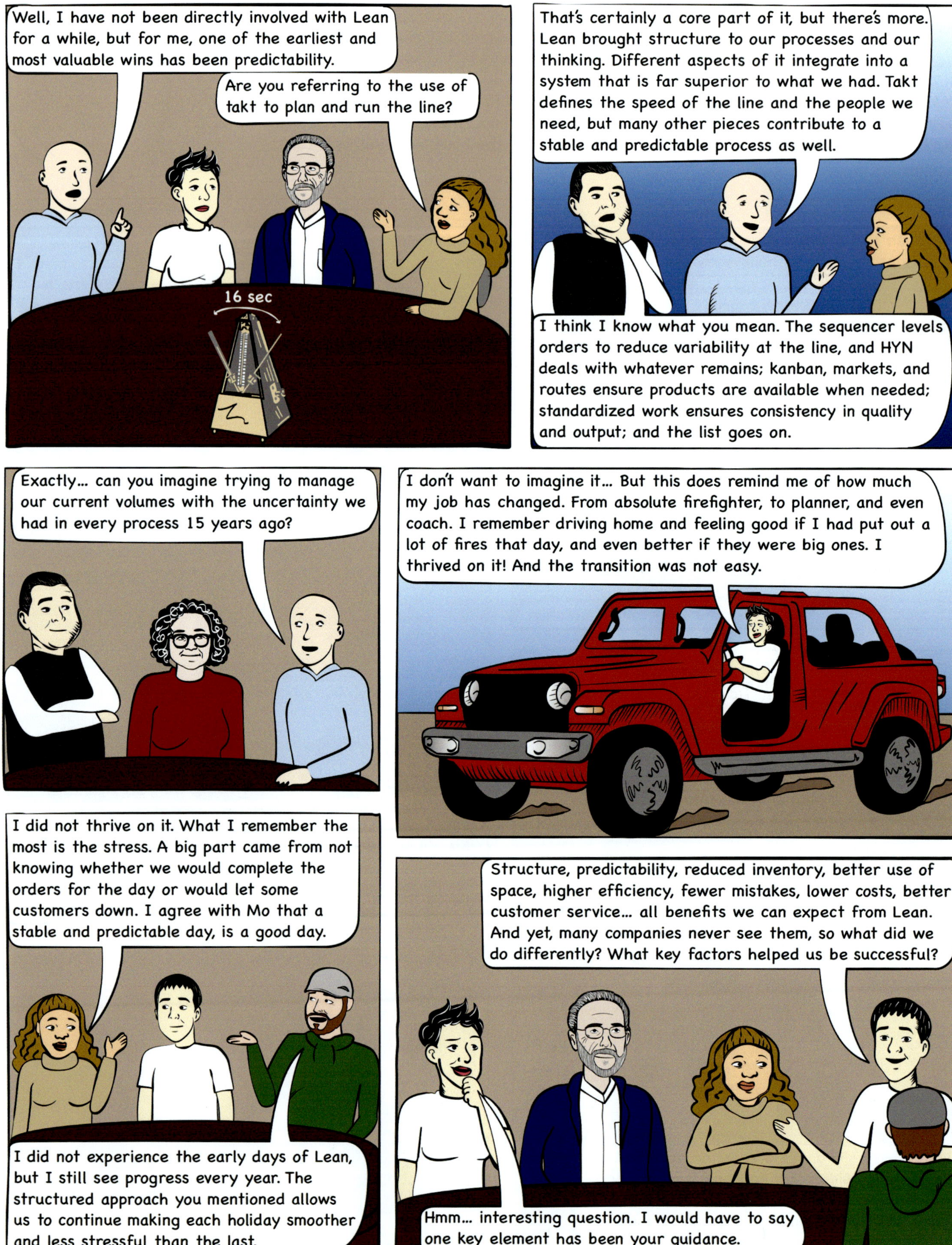
Well, I have not been directly involved with Lean for a while, but for me, one of the earliest and most valuable wins has been predictability.
Are you referring to the use of takt to plan and run the line?
16 sec
That's certainly a core part of it, but there's more. Lean brought structure to our processes and our thinking. Different aspects of it integrate into a system that is far superior to what we had. Takt defines the speed of the line and the people we need, but many other pieces contribute to a stable and predictable process as well.
I think I know what you mean. The sequencer levels orders to reduce variability at the line, and HYN deals with whatever remains; kanban, markets, and routes ensure products are available when needed; standardized work ensures consistency in quality and output; and the list goes on.
Exactly... can you imagine trying to manage our current volumes with the uncertainty we had in every process 15 years ago?
I don't want to imagine it... But this does remind me of how much my job has changed. From absolute firefighter, to planner, and even coach. I remember driving home and feeling good if I had put out a lot of fires that day, and even better if they were big ones. I thrived on it! And the transition was not easy.
I did not thrive on it. What I remember the most is the stress. A big part came from not knowing whether we would complete the orders for the day or would let some customers down. I agree with Mo that a stable and predictable day, is a good day.
I did not experience the early days of Lean, but I still see progress every year. The structured approach you mentioned allows us to continue making each holiday smoother and less stressful than the last.
Structure, predictability, reduced inventory, better use of space, higher efficiency, fewer mistakes, lower costs, better customer service... all benefits we can expect from Lean. And yet, many companies never see them, so what did we do differently? What key factors helped us be successful?
Hmm... interesting question. I would have to say one key element has been your guidance.

Thank you for that, Betty. However, I've had different degrees of success with different clients, so there are certainly other elements at play here.
I agree with Betty, though. The sensei role is critical, but it needs to focus on internal development of people, not on telling them what to do. Eduardo followed the Toyota way of guiding through questions.
That's a good point, Jeff. When I was directly involved, I never felt we were given a solution to implement blindly. We were always solving problems together, and that's how our Lean system evolved.
Development
People
Processes
Time
I like that word... Lean evolution at ZMO has never been about implementing pre-packaged solutions. Instead, it has been about finding our way by developing a Lean mindset as we improve the process by solving problems. Yes, that's it. It's been about the parallel development of people and processes.
That is similar to Toyota's saying about building people before building cars.
I'm not sure we do it beforehand, but we certainly build the people as we build the process.
And that's even more true since the introduction of Kata. Or at least, Kata extended what this group was already experiencing, to the rest of the crew.
Developing people through problem solving is standard at Toyota, and it is what Kata tries to introduce in other organizations. It's good to hear that has worked as we expected.
Let me take you back to this idea of evolving Lean by solving problems. As you may know, I came to UM to learn how to implement Lean. One of my early realizations was that although pull is a core idea in Lean, trying to implement it often seemed to be based on pushing solutions onto organizations.
BOSS

True. Early on, many efforts copied a tool from Toyota, say 5S or cells, and tried to implement it across the board. This often led to short-term success that was not sustained.
Exactly. So, I thought that perhaps we should use Lean ideas when developing Lean systems. What would it look like to pull improvements as needed, instead of pushing solutions onto people who may not need them or may not realize they do?
Go on... I'm beginning to feel like a lab rat in an experiment that I didn't quite know was going on.
Remember, we were a case study in Eduardo's thesis, so we were probably part of many experiments we don't know about.
Experimenting on people? I would never do that! Anyway, later on, I realized this pull approach is probably what Toyota used to develop TPS and the Toyota Way. After all, their focus has always been on solving the problems they face.
There's no doubt that Toyota learned from many others, like Ford and Deming. But even today, they do not copy solutions. They learn and make adjustments until the tool or approach fits the specific problem they are trying to solve.
That's been my assumption. So, the hypothesis here is that if people understand the problem and direction, they are more likely to get engaged and support the changes to help make them successful. What do you think?
IMPROVEMENTS
DESIRED CONDITION
Gap = Problem
CURRENT CONDITION
I think you're probably right. Your pull approach also ties well with this parallel development of people and processes Tom mentioned. With Kata we now involve people from the start.
We have also seen it reduces people's natural resistance to change. If people recognize the problem and are involved in developing the countermeasure to try, they will get behind it.
I think that's particularly true when the change makes the person's job easier and better.
Now it makes perfect sense why you insist on surfacing problems by trying to improve flow, striving toward the ideal, or comparing what's happening against standards. How many times have you told us to push the line until it breaks to show what we need to work on? If we see problems, we can solve them by pulling the improvements needed.

This approach has brought us a long way, but it's been a long, hard journey. People didn't always jump on the wagon the first time... or the second.
The road is always rocky, and it takes years. Which brings me to another critical factor: continuity of leadership. I know very few companies led by the same people for over 15 years. Continuity of leadership helps provide continuity of purpose.
I guess you're right. Having the same leadership team ensures we provide a consistent direction and approach the rest of the organization can rely on.
For good or bad... the crew knows there's no waiting for things to blow over. The details may change, but the general direction usually remains. I bet many other companies would have gone looking for the next silver bullet a long time ago.
Companies tend to jump from one transformation to the next as CEOs rotate through, with each one wanting to make their mark. Your case is different. Besides providing continuity, you are also committed leaders that keep fighting through obstacles in your way.
That's certainly true. If not, we would have stopped a long time ago! We're not very good at getting it right the first time.
You can say that again. We are constantly tweaking the process. Take the sequencer. After 15 years, four major redesigns, and countless adjustments, we're rewriting it entirely.
Good points. I should be taking notes. Constancy of purpose and perseverance are certainly critical factors. The first provides long-term focus, while the second ensures you keep trying to get closer to the ideal condition.
But let me shift gears a bit. What about culture? I remember Tom saying the culture side would be easy.
Ha... was I mistaken! The foundation was there, but it took a lot of work... and still does. Some of the culture we talked about was not really there in practice.
I learned culture is built every day through our joint activities. Depth and stability of culture require repeated interactions, and that takes time and effort.

From what I've seen, I would say ZMO's culture provided a strong foundation for the evolution of Lean. Profit sharing, free lunch, a fun environment, living wage, developing team members as leaders, respect for people... I believe have all been key to your success.
I think that's true. I believe Lean and our people-centered culture, based on Servant Leadership, support each other in a virtuous circle of greatness. However, even with such a good alignment, it has not been easy.
LEAN
SERVANT LEADERSHIP
Can you elaborate about this virtuous circle?
Sure. Let me give you an example. Servant leadership is about helping individuals succeed. Standard operating procedures support this by defining how to do and evaluate your job. In our people-centered culture, SOPs are accepted and even expected, because people see them as an aid to better manage and improve their processes and to help them become more autonomous, not a way for management to control them.
It's curious that you bring that up. In a people-focused culture, even extensive rules and procedures become enablers of improvement, instead of controls. It's called an enabling bureaucracy.
Hmm... I've always had a negative perception of bureaucracy... maybe it's not all bad.
I think trust is at the core of what you're saying, Tom. Our people-centered culture promotes trust. That makes it easier to introduce Lean ideas... which in turn help our people be more successful... which is the core purpose of our people-centered culture.
We're all in the same boat, so we better trust each other, no?
People-centered culture
Trust
Lean
Success
Seems logical, but it's not what happens in many organizations. It's difficult to build the mutual trust needed without a strong people orientation.
Absolutely. I think visual systems are another example of this virtuous circle. The crew uses them, since they trust the information provided and the problems highlighted are there to help them succeed, not for management to identify their shortcomings.
This is in line with Toyota's perspective on respect for people as one of the two pillars of the Toyota Way. We can give credit to Ari and Paul, who built the Zingerman's community on respect for people. I think one aspect of visual systems where you have perhaps struggled a bit more, is the fact-based exposure of problems as opportunities.
Problem
Opportunity

We have come a long way on that, but we still have situations where people do not like to visualize the facts and get defensive about possible problems in their area.
Failure is the opportunity to begin again, only more intelligently. -Henry Ford
True, but please consider that outside these walls, having problems and failing are considered bad. That's what we learned growing up. Even practicing a different approach here every day, it's hard to let go of all that baggage.
It's still frustrating at times, which is one of the reasons I like Kata so much. Its scientific thinking approach is based on facts... not assumptions, not opinions. And everyone expects it, so they do not get defensive. After using it for a while, people become energized about evaluating progress and exposing obstacles instead of hiding them.
I have not been involved with Kata much, but there's no doubt it has been a success. Can someone explain why this is?
With Kata, anyone can learn to think scientifically. The only requirement is a commitment to learn by actual practice! It is not just a theoretical exercise.
For me, Kata has made real the idea of developing people as we improve the process by solving problems. It provides a structured approach that, through repetition, develops the pattern of scientific thinking. Once you get it, it becomes part of how you think, and continuous improvement becomes a reality beyond the formal Kata project.
There's no end to people's creativity when the culture and systems allow them to develop.
Very true. I'm frequently surprised by the ideas our people have. But I want to point out that we did not start there. When we introduced Kata, we were looking for a way to engage the crew. It took a while for us to realize we were all learning scientific thinking, and that would be the true power of Kata.
Good point, but let's talk about this engagement you were looking for, which I think is one of the most interesting aspects of Kata. Perhaps it's the structured process, the easy to understand steps, its action orientation toward quick experimentation, or being able to see progress toward the challenge... whatever it is, Kata brought a level of engagement and ownership that only the leaders had before.

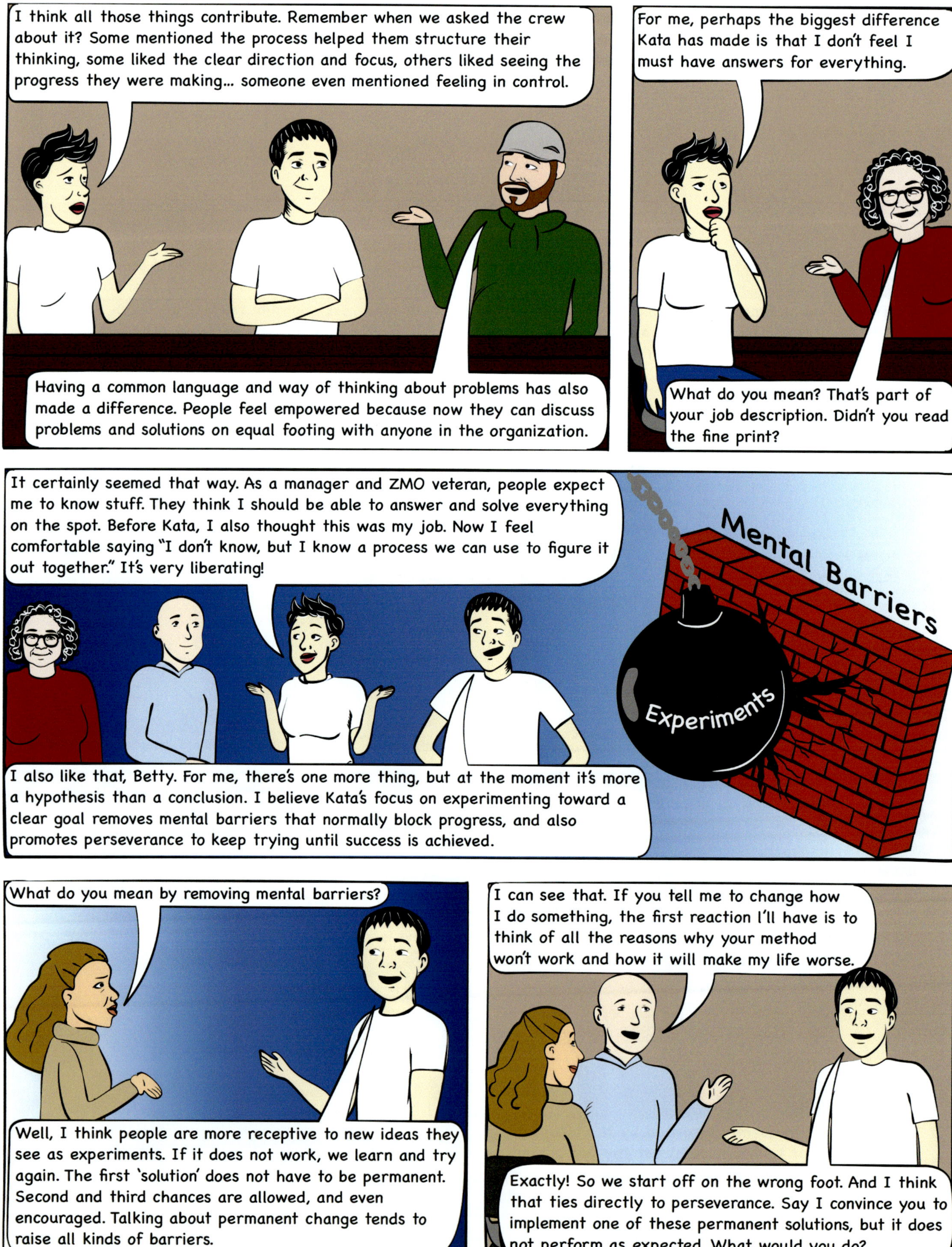
I think all those things contribute. Remember when we asked the crew about it? Some mentioned the process helped them structure their thinking, some liked the clear direction and focus, others liked seeing the progress they were making... someone even mentioned feeling in control.
Having a common language and way of thinking about problems has also made a difference. People feel empowered because now they can discuss problems and solutions on equal footing with anyone in the organization.
For me, perhaps the biggest difference Kata has made is that I don't feel I must have answers for everything.
What do you mean? That's part of your job description. Didn't you read the fine print?
It certainly seemed that way. As a manager and ZMO veteran, people expect me to know stuff. They think I should be able to answer and solve everything on the spot. Before Kata, I also thought this was my job. Now I feel comfortable saying "I don't know, but I know a process we can use to figure it out together." It's very liberating!
Mental Barriers
Experiments
I also like that, Betty. For me, there's one more thing, but at the moment it's more a hypothesis than a conclusion. I believe Kata's focus on experimenting toward a clear goal removes mental barriers that normally block progress, and also promotes perseverance to keep trying until success is achieved.
What do you mean by removing mental barriers?
Well, I think people are more receptive to new ideas they see as experiments. If it does not work, we learn and try again. The first 'solution' does not have to be permanent. Second and third chances are allowed, and even encouraged. Talking about permanent change tends to raise all kinds of barriers.
I can see that. If you tell me to change how I do something, the first reaction I'll have is to think of all the reasons why your method won't work and how it will make my life worse.
Exactly! So we start off on the wrong foot. And I think that ties directly to perseverance. Say I convince you to implement one of these permanent solutions, but it does not perform as expected. What would you do?

I would probably revert to my old process and ignore your suggestions in the future.
Sure, I would too. Now, what if we try the exact same change, but instead I tell you we're going to run an experiment, learn from it, and based on that, figure out what to do next... what would you do if the idea fails?
I would feel more in control and would be more comfortable trying something else.
There you go... and we get perseverance to see improvements through. We often think perseverance is a fixed personality trait you have to hire for. But maybe it can grow from using Kata. I think this is a key strength of scientific thinking, and of Kata in particular. Just focusing on running experiments instead of implementing solutions makes a huge difference.
Hmm... perhaps you're onto something here.
I think there's one more thing. A hidden benefit of all this activity is your team's energy and capability to adapt to change, even a crisis.
As I mentioned, it's only a hypothesis, but I'm seeing this kind of response in other companies I work with.
We have some sort of crisis every Christmas... And you're right, we adapt so much better now. I think it's a combination of Lean's structure and visualization of issues, and Kata's scientific thinking. The crew can see the problems and has a common way of tackling them together.
I'm glad to hear that. We invest significant amounts of labor hours on Kata, so it's good to know we are getting additional benefits beyond what we can quantify directly.

These are all important observations. Lean has been a success. Kata has been a success. Now what? Where do we go from here?
You say that as if we reached the end of the journey for both. I don't think we're done just because we have seen some success.
ZMO
No, I know this is a way of life that never ends. I'm just wondering if there's a next step.
I would say we continue with the same approach. Solve problems to pull improvements and develop people. The focus will depend on the specific issues we're facing, no?
Well, I think Kata may be able to help here. Remember step one—define the direction. Wouldn't it be better to pull improvements as we move in the direction of a challenge?
1
Set the Direction or Challenge
2
Grasp the Current Condition
3
Establish your Next Target Condition
4
Conduct Experiments to get there
Good point! Kata starts with a clear direction, but how do we identify the critical challenges that will define it? We may have to go beyond Kata for this. Toyota has a planning process to develop a long-term vision and an annual plan at all levels. It's this Hoshin Kanri, or policy deployment, we have talked about. Maybe it is time to think beyond individual Kata projects and shoot for true widespread continuous improvement.
But we have been talking about all the involvement we have gotten by using Kata. Is that not enough?
VISION
HOSHIN KANRI
Break down problems
Individual contribution
Vertical alignment
Horizontal alignment
Company Hoshin
Department Hoshin
Individual Hoshin
ACT
PLAN
CHECK
DO

I think Eduardo means that Kata increased participation and engagement greatly, but we're still far from the ideal of everyone improving their processes every day, together, toward a common vision. For the most part, our improvement activity continues to be project based. Run a Kata here or run a Kata there.
I agree with the idea of going beyond isolated projects. Remember that the Kata are really practice routines. Mike calls them starter Kata... a jump start to scientific thinking. As we begin to naturally think that way, we should mature to a system of clear challenges and goals people strive toward.

Right, and I think ZMO is strongest at a middle level, where improvement is based on projects focused on specific processes. This includes the Kata activity as well as the efforts we make as we strive to improve flow. We're weaker at both a higher level of bigger, longer, top-driven projects that tie directly to the long-term vision, and at a lower level where everyone makes small improvements to their processes every day.
Long-term projects
Specific process Kata projects
Everyday small improvements
For the top side, we have already had a few discussions and agreed to experiment with Hoshin Kanri at the warehouse next year.

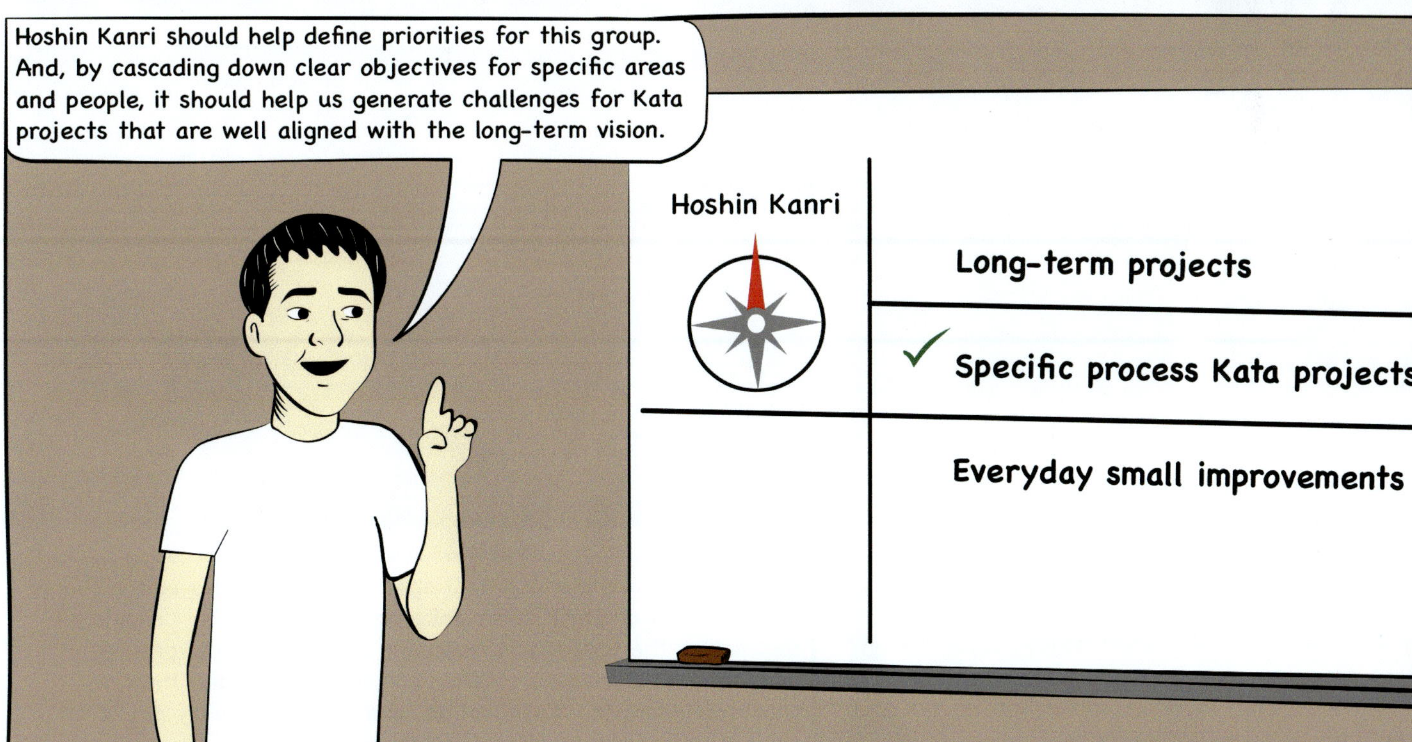
Hoshin Kanri should help define priorities for this group. And, by cascading down clear objectives for specific areas and people, it should help us generate challenges for Kata projects that are well aligned with the long-term vision.
Hoshin Kanri
Long-term projects
Specific process Kata projects
Everyday small improvements

But what drives the bottom level?
Well, I think Kata plays a role there as well, but perhaps not with structured projects. What we need is for people to apply the scientific thinking they learn from Kata, to their everyday experience.
The theory sounds good, but how do we do this in practice?
I don't have all the answers, but I think an element we're missing is a clear direction. Toyota uses the idea of producing one-by-one, in sequence, on demand, with zero waste as a guiding force. If we define a True North that is simple and enduring, we can give people a direction that they can use as the starting point to apply the scientific thinking they have learned.
Hoshin Kanri
True North
Long-term projects
Specific process Kata projects
Everyday small improvements
But won't we get more of a scattershot approach this way? One of the advantages of Kata is focus. Won't we lose some of that?
Well, the True North should help align efforts with our general direction, and Hoshin Kanri provides clear goals. Besides, I don't think scattershot improvement is inherently bad... and in fact, it may be needed for true widespread continuous improvement. A good blend of intentional improvement toward clear goals, and just solving small issues people face every day, may prove to be the right mix. The problem is not a scattershot approach but who is involved in it.
What do you mean?
Well, anyone in this group that spends time on improvement should focus on critical ZMO issues. Take capacity. Your effort should be focused on the bottleneck. However, captains should work constantly on increasing efficiency in their areas, and the crew should be improving their stations and processes every day, even if they are nowhere near the bottleneck.

I had not thought about it in that way. So everyone should be improving, but their focus depends on their area of influence.
Right. A captain improving a non-bottleneck area is not lacking focus. On the contrary, it's a lost opportunity if they are not doing it. The chance the bread captain will drive improvements at the bottleneck in check are slim to none. So why not have them improve their area? Perhaps they will stay ahead of demand growth and never become the bottleneck.
Let me see if I got this right. Hoshin Kanri helps the leadership team focus on critical issues and helps define challenges for Kata projects. Those Kata projects drive needed improvements and develop scientific thinking. But we also want a lot of other improvements in the direction of this True North, even if they do not directly relate to the defined challenges. For this, the crew uses the scientific thinking they learn through Kata.
Perfect. But this is an experiment, so now we have to try it out and see what we learn.
Am I hearing another meta-experiment with us as guinea pigs?
At least this one I know about!
We're all together in this one. At least around here I will be a well-fed guinea pig.
Good! We have learned a lot today and we even have a direction to continue evolving. Anything else?
Just one more thing... here's to the next 15 years of experiments and surprises!

For Product Safety Concerns and Information please contact our EU representative GPSR@taylorandfrancis.com Taylor & Francis Verlag GmbH, Kaufingerstraße 24, 80331 München, Germany

Batch number: 10733489

Printed by Printforce, the Netherlands